Inside the Robot Kingdom

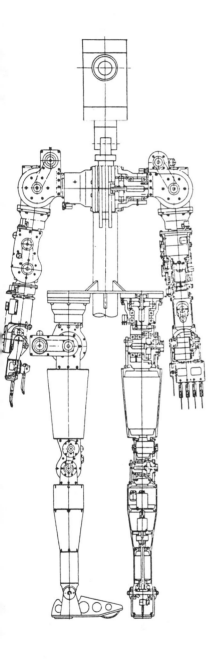

INSIDE THE ROBOT KINGDOM

Japan, Mechatronics, and the Coming Robotopia

Frederik L. Schodt

KODANSHA INTERNATIONAL LTD.
Tokyo and New York

*To my parents, who encouraged me
to see the world in different ways*

Note: All Japanese personal names appear in Western order,
that is, given name first and family name last. Macrons have
been omitted on Japanese words. All translations by the
author unless otherwise noted.

Book design by Eric Jungerman.

Composition by Harrington-Young, Albany, California.

Distributed in the United States by Kodansha International/
USA Ltd., through Harper & Row, Publishers, Inc., 10 East
53rd Street, New York, New York 10022. Published by
Kodansha International Ltd., 2-2 Otowa 1-chome, Bunkyo-
ku, Tokyo 112 and Kodansha International/USA Ltd., 10 East
53rd Street, New York, New York 10022.

Library of Congress Cataloging-in-Publication Data

Schodt, Frederik L., 1950–
    Inside the robot kingdom.
    Bibliography: p.
    Includes index.
1. Robotics—Japan. I. Title.
TJ211.S39 1988   338'.06   87-81686
ISBN 0-87011-854-4 (U.S.)
ISBN 4-7700-1354-x (Japan)

Contents

Preface

Most books about robots fit into one of three categories: science fiction, technical, or romantic speculation. This book fits into none of them. It is about robots and Japan, and in the larger sense, about technology and culture. Like most people, until recently my image of robots confused science fiction and real life. I have always been fascinated, however, by the way robots in all forms—in fantasy and industry—are so celebrated in Japan. Around the end of 1984, while touring some factories in the United States, and seeing so few industrial robots at work, I began to realize that "robots"—in all their various forms—can really be seen as a symbol of a larger relationship between people and technology. To understand why America was having trouble with robotization and other steps on the road to the twenty-first century, and why Japan seemed to be more successful, it would be necessary to look beyond the machine. This led to my interviewing people with all kinds of different connections with robots in both nations, touring factories, attending international conferences, and reading hundreds of books, magazines, and journals and, especially, the daily industrial newspapers of Japan.

Japan and robots is a complex and treacherous subject to venture into. This book is a bit like a helicopter tour of it. The pilot—the author—is not a technologist, and is fascinated by certain areas but not by others. In a somewhat idiosyncratic journey, therefore, the helicopter sweeps quickly over vast plains, hovers briefly over some areas, and occasionally alights for a close-up inspection and to solicit local opinions. In the process, many questions will be raised, and only some will be answered. That is the intention.

I would like to thank the following for granting me personal interviews over the course of my research from 1985 to 1987.

Academia and government: Shigeo Hirose, Masahiro Mori, Yoji Umetani (Tokyo Institute of Technology); Shinnichi Yuta (University of Tsukuba); Hiroyuki Yoshikawa (University of Tokyo); Ichiro Kato, Yukio Hasegawa (Waseda University); Susumu Tachi, Eiji Nakano (Mechanical Engineering Laboratory); Yoshiaki Shirai (Electrotechnical Laboratory); Soichi Kumekawa, Noboru Sugimoto (Research Institute of Industrial Safety, Ministry of Labor); Hiroaki Ando (Advanced Robot Technology Research Association); Takumi Kojima (Research Institute of Japan Small Business Corporation); Tetsuo Yokoyama, Seiji Furihata (Tokyo Metropolitan Industrial Technology Center); Naoyuki Kameyama (National Institute of Employment and Vocational Research); Kenneth J. Waldron (Ohio State University); Yutaka Kanayama (Center for Robotic Systems, University of California, Santa Barbara); Bernard Roth (Stanford University).

Industry/labor organizations: Akihisa Terasaki (Federation of Japan Automobile Workers' Unions); Kanji Yonemoto (Japan Industrial Robot Association); Eric Mittelstadt (Robotic Industries Association); Tatsuoki Masui (JAROL); Tadao Tamura, Toyokatsu Sato (International Robotics and Factory Automation Center).

Private industry: Gensuke Okada, Naohide Kumagai (Kawasaki Heavy Industries Ltd.); Seiuemon Inaba (Fanuc Ltd.); Takuya Kato (Kato Seiki, Inc.); Kenichi Natsume, Tsugio Nakamoto, Jun-ichi Chiba (Kyodo Printing Co., Ltd.); Nobuyuki Fujita, Noriyuki Tanaka, Hiroji Mizuguchi, Sumio Nagashima, Tetsuo Suzuki, Masana Minami, Yoshinori Kuno, Michael Caine (Toshiba Corporation); Kosei Minami, Tsuyoshi Miura, Toshiya Yamamoto, Hirokazu Shimatake (Nissan Motor Co., Ltd.); Keigo Ushimaru, Iwato Fujii, Tatsuya Nakamine (Seibu Department Stores Ltd.); Toshi Inada, Kenro Motoda (Motoda Electronics Co., Ltd.); Sueo Matsubara (Automax/Mukta Research Institute); Yoshiyuki Nakano, Hideo Maki (Hitachi Works, Hitachi Ltd.); Kisaku Suzuki, Junichiro Nishimura (Suzumo Machinery Industry Co., Ltd.); Hajime Karatsu, Sukeji Ito (Matsushita Electric

Industrial Co., Ltd.); Kiyoshi Tawara (Yamasaki Seisakujo); Yoshiaki Maeda, Katsuhiro Kawasaki, Shigeru Tabei, Yuki Gessei (JVC–Victor Company of Japan Ltd.); Brian Carlisle (Adept Technology, Inc.); Joseph Engelberger (Transitions Research Corporation); Victor Sheinman (Automatix); Walter Weisel (Prab Robots, Inc.); Eric Mittelstadt (GMF Robotics, Inc.).

Toy industry: Hideki Konishi, Katsumasa Yabu (Namco Ltd.); Yoshiyuki Matsumoto, Yoshiro Yamasaki (Tomy Corporation); Satoru Matsumoto, Takayuki Morishima, Akira Murakami (Bandai, Inc.); Hideaki Yoke (Takara Co.); Yukio Tanaka, Tetsuro Sugawara (Fuji Bussan, Inc.); Teruhisa Kitahara ("Toys"—Tin Toy Museum); Douglas Thomson (Toy Manufacturers of America).

Fantasy industry: Takeyuki Kanda, Ryosuke Takahashi, Yoshiyuki Tomino, Eiji Yamaura (Nippon Sunrise, Inc.); Osamu Tezuka (Tezuka Productions); Go Nagai (Dynamic Pro); Kosei Ono (comic and film critic); Shunichi Mizuno (Cybot, Inc.).

Other fields: Shoji Tatsukawa (Kitasato University); Shobe-e Tamaya (*karakuri* master); Teijiro Muramatsu (University of Tokyo Honorary Professor); Kiyoshi Mori (Haniuda Iron Works/author); Itsuo Sakane (*Asahi shinbun* Department of Arts and Sciences); Satoshi Kamata (journalist).

I am grateful to all the people and organizations who helped me on this project. The following deserve special mention: editor Peter Goodman, who liked my eccentric book proposal, encouraged me during writer's angst, and advised me with skill and tact; Takumi Kojima, of the Research Institute of Japan Small Business Corporation, who was unsparing of his time and of use of his organization's library and data bases; Toshiba's Yoshinori Kuno and Shigenobu Uchikoshi; Kato Seiki's Kato family; Hitachi's Yoichi Suga; Nissan Motor's Kumiko Yamaguchi; JVC's Junko Yoshida; Yoshiyuki Tomino and Nippon Sunrise; Akihisa Shirasaki of the Japan Industrial Safety and Health Association; Kiyohide Chojima of JIRA; Hiromi Yoshimura; and Jo and Nanae Inoue. For unswerving help during trips to Japan, I thank the Narita family. For reading drafts, I am deeply indebted to my parents and my brother David, to Donald Philippi, Leonard Rifas, Candice Allgaier, Robert Takagi, Joseph Fox, and Joseph Engelberger. Finally, thanks to Taku Kuno and Chris Komater for advice and help with photograph enlargements, to Okinori Murata for liaison with Japan, to Eric Jungerman for the design of this book, and to Mimi Locke for her constant support and affection.

PART ONE

Introducing the Robot
Kingdom and the Robot

Wasubot playing with the Japan Broadcasting Association (NHK) symphony orchestra.

Wasubot performing at Expo '85.

1

The Robot Kingdom

Japanese robot technology will change the world.

ROBOTICIST
ICHIRO KATO

It was inorganic and rigid, with a body of wires, burnished black metal, and carbon-fiber-reinforced plastic; a TV camera formed its cyclops-like head. It sat bathed in light before an organ in the center of a darkened hall, waiting, while computer-controlled images on the walls showed a naked Japanese man and woman in a graceful dance. Then, after an introduction by a uniformed young woman speaking in high-pitched, formal Japanese, it scanned the sheet music before it, and—with tubular legs pumping pedals and steel fingers gliding across the keys—began to play J. S. Bach's *Air on a G String*. Thanks to a hook-up with a giant video screen outside, the organ player was faithfully accompanied by the entire NHK Symphony Orchestra and watched by a crowd of thousands that included the crown prince and princess of Japan. Later, the aging emperor made a personal visit, and was said to have been enthralled.

Wasubot, as the robot organist was called, was the star of Japan's Expo '85, a six-month-long robot circus where twenty-three million people swarmed into pavilions—dubbed "time tunnels into the twenty-first century"—to gawk at and pay homage to robots lifting barbells, robots constructing models of themselves, robots carving ice blocks, and robots painting portraits. Most of the shows were merely clever adaptations of existing industrial robots or specialized mechanical arms, and had been installed in corporate pavilions as advertisements for their makers. But Wasubot was different.

Wasubot was a humanoid, and when he played it was not a recording, but a provocative performance. Some listeners saw an enormously complex and expensive machine usurping a most emotive human activity, and felt a chill. Others

Matsushita Electric's Pana Robo, configured with a vision system to paint portraits.

saw a robot—a mechanical mirror of themselves—and heard music that moved them to tears.

Moreover, Wasubot (along with a four-legged insectoid robot and a two-legged robot that swaggered, tottered, and "walked") had the special honor of being displayed in the Japanese government pavilion. There had been resistance to robots there at first. Some members of the planning committee feared for the nation's image—Japan's industrial robots have been accused of aggravating trade friction and unemployment overseas. But in showcasing the nonindustrial Wasubot and its companions, the exhibit's producer was determined to show that "Japan is not simply using technology for economic and production purposes, and that as a race the Japanese are extremely receptive to technology." Along with other exhibits of ancient mechanical dolls, he wanted the robots to symbolize "the marvelous coexistence that Japanese have achieved with machines."[1]

Japanese people often refer to their nation as *robotto okoku*, or "the Robot Kingdom." But like Japan, and even like the

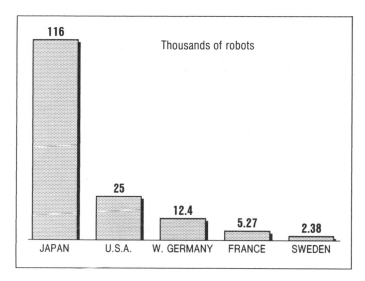

Number of industrial robots In operation in select nations at end of 1986 (excluding manual manipulators and fixed-sequence robots). Source: JIRA, August 1987.

robot itself, the "kingdom" is an exceedingly complicated entity; depending upon the viewing angle, its appearance can change radically. Outside of a cultural context, it becomes nearly incomprehensible.

Industrial robots may have been invented and developed in the United States, but in 1986 America had 25,000 of them while Japan had around 116,000, perhaps over 60 percent of the entire population of robots in the noncommunist world.[2] The Japanese media—ever mindful of their audience's obsession with knowing how Japan stacks up against other nations—have seized on these numbers as an excuse to crown their nation the "Robot Kingdom," just as they also refer to Japan as the "Comic Book Kingdom" and the "Facsimile Kingdom." There are few dissenters.

Despite great diversity, many Japanese perceive their nation as being highly homogeneous, with (officially) no minorities and an ancient shared language and history. On this semitribal level, fashions, dogma, and skewed self-images can flourish and attain almost monolithic proportions. Indeed, the idea of Japan as a Robot Kingdom has moved like a juggernaut through the public consciousness and is part of a larger, intense pride in manufacturing and technology.

On the surface, at least, Japan does not at all seem like a superpower in robotics. Most robots are out of sight in factories, and most tourists see only people—120 million of them crammed into a California-sized archipelago. And al-

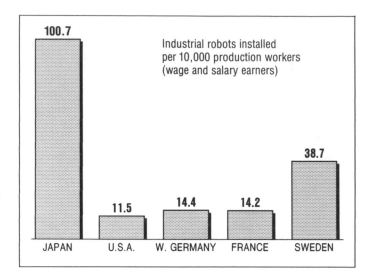

100.7

Industrial robots installed per 10,000 production workers (wage and salary earners)

38.7

11.5   14.4   14.2

JAPAN   U.S.A.   W. GERMANY   FRANCE   SWEDEN

Industrial robot density in select nations. Calculation based on estimated 1986 robot populations; 1983 OECD labor force statistics. Source: IPA, Stuttgart, 1987.

though Japan is a cornucopia of gadgets, the country, like the recent Casio calculator with built-in abacus, sometimes still seems to have one foot in the eighteenth century and the other in the twenty-first: sandwiched between rows of high-tech electronics stores are quaint little shops run by craftsmen working with methods and tools little changed from hundreds of years ago; super-efficient trains carry well-groomed commuters with the latest pocket electronic entertainment, while next to them ride wizened and stooped peasant women, their heavy packs filled with goods for market. In many department stores, young women in uniforms do nothing but greet customers getting on and off escalators or operate utterly modern and automated elevators, by hand.

Differences in the way industrial robots are defined and counted also turn international comparisons into a statistical minefield. One often-cited index of robotization is the ratio of robots to workers, and here, too, Japan is now usually shown towering above other nations. But at international conferences on robotics, much to the chagrin of Japanese attendees, speakers from Sweden until recently could delight in pointing out that *their* tiny nation—a long-overlooked manufacturing giant with only about eight million people—had the highest robot-to-worker ratio in the world. The Swedish firm ASEA, moreover, with nearly 10 percent of the entire world market, is one of the world's largest and most technologically innovative robot manufacturers, one of the few foreign robot makers with a strong presence in Japan.[3]

Technological sophistication is certainly not what sets Japan's robots apart either. Many Japanese robots are of U.S. design and use American software. Even the robots at Expo '85, while presented as state-of-the-art, failed to impress many foreign experts. But what about the nonindustrial Wasubot, which read music, moved its ten fingers faster than the best human pianist, and incorporated advanced sensors and new materials in its body? As one roboticist said, Wasubot was certainly a sophisticated application of existing technologies, and very interesting, but it was also highly impractical and, at a cost of over a million dollars, terribly extravagant. In 1987 American Joseph Engelberger, regarded as the founding father of the industrial robot, and a great admirer of Japan, could still state flatly that "our technology and Europe's is still superior to theirs."[4]

Yet as another American robotics pioneer, Victor Sheinman, has pointed out, "the most advanced technology is not necessarily the best solution. The Japanese are simply better at applying the technology." No other nation has put so many robots to work in so many industries as Japan, or with so much success.[5]

Robots at Work

Few ordinary people have actually seen industrial robots at work, but if they have it was probably in an auto plant. At Nissan Motor Company, for example, over two thousand industrial robots perform welding, painting, sealing, and assembly. Inside the cavernous Auto Body Assembly Plant No. 1 of Nissan's Tochigi factory, the welding has been nearly 97 percent automated. Everything seems to be moving in all directions at once. On the floor, a buzzer sounds a warning as conveyors shoot an unpainted car chassis to each station of the operation, where it is automatically positioned between huge American-designed spot-welding robots, looking like buzzards ready to feast on their prey. Ceiling transport systems automatically lower unpainted metal panels to the floor at specified points, whereupon the hydraulic robots swing into place, clamp their beaklike "hands" on the metal surfaces, and with a series of bangs and sparks fuse them together. Each car has over three thousand welds on it, and humans are involved only in those too structurally awkward for robots.

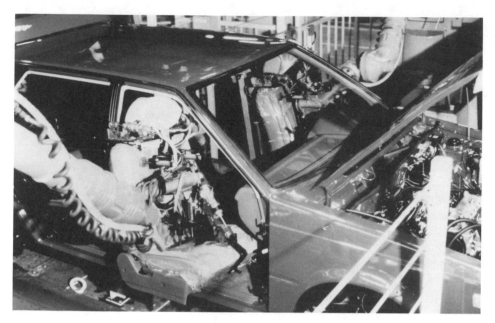

An industrial robot installs car seats at Nissan Motor's Zama factory.

Again, at Nissan's Zama plant, graceful and slim electric-powered robots are used in over 10 percent of the difficult final assembly of the car, installing window glass, front seats, tires, rear lights, rear doors, headlights, the gas cap, window cleaning fluid, and other items. One robot equipped with sensors inspects the painted finish of the cars for quality. Zama has become a virtual shrine to robots; according to plant officials, each year over a hundred thousand people visit, most of them elementary students on field trips.

The use of robots at Nissan is not unique. Similar scenes can be found at other auto plants in Japan and around the world. Nissan was not the first auto maker to use robots; American firms were. Nor does Nissan have the most robots in use; General Motors has far more. But Nissan and other Japanese auto makers are world models because of their early, aggressive, and *successful* use of robots.

In most of the world, the bulk of industrial robots are still stuck in auto factories, doing welding. But not in Japan. Most new Japanese robots—over 40 percent—are now put to work in electronics assembly, where they help feed hungry consumers in a hundred nations a steady diet of video cassette recorders, calculators, television sets, and other gadgetry. In these industries, robots are often configured in long rows along an assembly line, with each robot performing a spe-

At a Seiko Epson factory, forty-seven Accusembler robots, with vision systems and automatic parts feeders, assemble watch faces.

cialized operation. Small, light, and electrically powered, they are mostly horizontal in their movements, and almost entirely of Japanese design. If the larger robots in auto plants look like huge buzzards in the way they swoop and weave, these are nimble sparrows, hunting and pecking, picking up components from supply shoots, inserting them into holes on printed circuit boards, soldering, tightening screws, drilling holes, or feeding parts to more specialized machinery. The assembly lines are supplied by computer-controlled robot carts, or Automated Guided Vehicles (AGV), which bring parts as needed from automated warehouses, following magnetic tape or wires buried in the floor, like dogs tracking a scent.

In most of the world, industrial robots are the property of huge corporations. But again, not in Japan. The most heavily publicized factories in Japan are the giant, ultramodern "lights out" plants nearly devoid of people, where machines work around the clock and in the dark of night. Far less well known, but just as important, are the Japanese small businesses that use robots. These manufacturers by government definition have less than three hundred people, and include neighborhood "mom and pop" operations with only three or four employees and a robot. In 1985 they purchased over 20 percent of all robots shipped (in yen terms), and in nonfer-

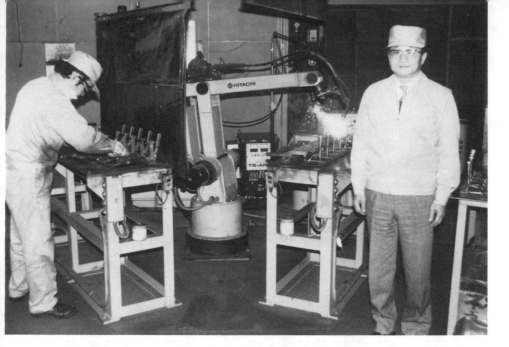

Yamasaki Seisakujo: a proud president, a busy worker, and a rented Hitachi Process robot.

Komatsu Ltd.'s giant, eight-legged, undersea, rubble-leveling robot, displayed on shore.

rous metals and wood products industries their share was 62 and 71 percent, respectively.[6]

At Yamasaki Seisakujo, a sub-subcontractor for Tokyo Electric Power Company, thirty employees make bolts, screws, and clamps for high-tension power lines. Unlike the immaculately clean and brightly lit factories of large electronics corporations, the buildings at Yamasaki are tired and gloomy and house press machines, stampers, and grinders manned by employees feeding them parts, repetitive work that a larger company might care to automate. But for the last five years the company has proudly rented a Hitachi Process

Robot for $900 a month and used it to weld the metal steps that attach to high-tension pylons. The robot stands between two tables; while it welds parts together on one, a worker positions more parts for the robot on the other. The company was the first in its field to use a robot, and subsequently has been widely imitated by other small contractors.

Robots can be found in nearly every industry in Japan today. In the machining industry they often act simply as servants to other automation, feeding parts to computerized machine tools when needed, removing them when processed; in plastics manufacturing they pull formed parts out of high-speed injection molding machines; in die-casting they pull metal parts out of metal molds; and in any industry with an assembly line, they often simply transfer products from one line to another. They do this work the world over, but in Japan they do it in far more companies and industries. Robots today help build pianos, polish trumpets, paint toilet bowls, and assemble printed circuit boards, bicycles, fountain pens, lipstick cases, and houses. In many cases, using visual and tactile sensors, robots even inspect the quality of the work. There are few major Japanese manufactured products that have not been touched by an industrial robot at some stage of their evolution.

But a robot can be far more than a slave to industry. As technology advances around the world, mobile robots are gingerly emerging from laboratories to serve in a variety of nonindustrial roles: as underwater explorers, as spy planes, as sentries, and even as extraterrestrial explorers. The undisputed leader in nonindustrial robotics has been the United States, as symbolized by one of the most advanced mobile robots thus far—the little Voyager spacecraft rocketing toward the outer reaches of the solar system. Japan, however, with little fanfare, has increasingly been using advanced mobile robots in very down-to-earth applications. On the bottom of Tokyo Bay, a giant eight-legged robot—perhaps the world's largest—currently levels the seabed for underwater construction sites.

In Japan, the "robot," industrial or otherwise, has also become a symbol of a commitment to advanced technology. One of the most striking examples of this can be found, not in a factory or a laboratory, but a department store. Industrial robots are far too expensive and complicated to sell as con-

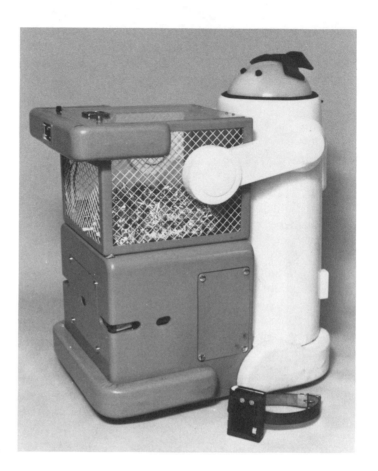

Roporter, a Seibu Department Store "robot," follows patrons and holds up to 65 pounds of purchases.

sumer goods, but Seibu Department Store's branch in Tokyo's Ikebukuro district for several years displayed (and claimed to sell) one such model on its electronics floor. The robot has since been displaced by video equipment, but Seibu now holds seminars on robotics and takes orders for vision-equipped robots and robot carts (AGV) configured as miniature factory automation systems for educational purposes.

At Seibu's Tsukuba branch, near the site of Expo '85, the company has gone a step beyond selling—it actually uses robotics technology. Inventory is stored in a three-dimensional automatic warehouse, and retrieved and shuttled around at night to staging areas on each sales floor by AGVs. In the grocery section, what the store calls a "ham slicer robot" slices meat as requested by customers and confirms selections with a synthesized female voice. And on several floors are stationed cute little mobile "robots," called Roporters, that follow any customer equipped with a special sonar wand. The robots carry baskets to hold the purchases of lazy shoppers.

Seibu spent over ¥1 billion, nearly $6.5 million, on the robotized store to create, as a pamphlet says, a "humanlike heart and mechatronic stage." In principle it was to further efficiency, reduce labor costs, and free people for better service. But the real reason was publicity. "Department stores have been somewhat left out of the high-tech age," says Tatsuya Nakamine, a Seibu public relations representative. "Entering it is a challenge for us. Besides, if our industry doesn't pursue these technologies, we'll have a hard time of it in the twenty-first century."[7] Yet as one worker grudgingly admits, "sometimes the robot carts do get in the way."

More Than Machines

The idea of a "Robot Kingdom" is partly the result of a collective infatuation with advanced technology, an infatuation propped up by Japan's government and corporations and sustained at a fever pitch by the exhortations of its powerful print, broadcast, and advertising media. Any advanced techology, whether it be superconductors, computers, or biotechnology, can become a pseudoreligion in Japan. But robots have a distinct advantage. Because of their history, and the many shapes they can assume in fantasy and industry, robots are easier to popularize and cloak with an aura of accessibility. Robots are popular in other nations, too, but only Japan has so successfully linked ancient automata, comic book and animation characters, toys, industrial robots, and research robots into one giant romanticized entity in the public mind.

For young children, interest is planted early by the world's largest selection of robot comics, toys, and animation films. Robot character masks are sold at temple fairs; robot rides regale children at amusement parks and on the tops of department stores; mechanical "robot-friends" stamp passbooks at science museums; and at school sporting events, the theme song from an animated robot TV series known abroad as *Astro Boy* is ritually played.

For adults, this playful spirit is continued. The cartoon character Astro Boy advertises securities and high-tech products in the media: The "sexy robot" girls drawn by artist

Shunichi Mizuno invents sophisticated and erotic servo-controlled robots for exhibitions and displays.

Hajime Sorayama and the weirdly erotic humanoid entertainment robots of inventor Shunichi Mizuno titillate the imagination. Remote-control "robots"—more conversation piece than convenience—serve customers in restaurants and coffee shops. Seibu leases a radio-controlled "RoboRobo" for parties and weddings, the perfect touch for the thirty- to forty-thousand-dollar matrimonial extravaganzas staged today with laser shows and smoke effects. "People think of today as the robot age," says Seibu's Nakamine, "and that's why they like robots."[8]

For those with a more serious bent, there are mountains of information available on real robots. Bookstores carry works on industrial robots and robotics ranging from technical manuals to those for the general reader that cover robot mechanics, the impact of robotics on society in the future, and new directions in technology. General-interest periodicals, in addition to running occasional articles on robotics, showcase ads for industrial robots with exaggerated proclamations of how "infinitely close to human" they are or how the manufacturer is making a valuable contribution to human happiness and prosperity. On television, one manufacturer advertises its industrial robots during prime-time viewing hours. Advertising in these forms may not result in sales of robots, but it symbolizes a commitment to the technology and its development.

The quarterly *Robotist*.

For the specialist, there are magazines of the type found in Europe and America, issued by the Japan Industrial Robot Association (JIRA) and the Robotics Society of Japan (RSJ). One unique magazine is called *Robotist*. This quarterly is pitched at a unified "community" of people in manufacturing, robotics research, entertainment, and toys—in short anyone of any age interested in robots of any form or size. *Robotist* articles range from interviews with children and office secretaries on their dreams for future robots, to forecasts by the chief of planning at one of the national labs, to a regular column by a senior manager at robot manufacturer Kawasaki Heavy Industries, who reminisces about his erotic escapades in the course of his career in robotics.

For those who want their information in a hurry, there are the industrial newspapers unique to Japan, published on a daily—not weekly or monthly—basis. Two of the biggest, the *Nikkan kogyo shinbun* (*Daily Industrial News*) with a circulation of 544,000 and the *Nikkei sangyo shinbun* with 200,000, offer articles on new robots developed at home and abroad, discussions of new applications, or comments from users nearly every day. The papers are available throughout Japan, and their readership is by no means limited to a technological or corporate elite but includes people simply curious about manufacturing and the direction of technology. In a tightly knit society such as Japan, these media have an inestimable power to glamorize and influence attitudes to robots and technology in general.

And then there are the industrial robot fairs. In September of 1985 the 15th International Symposium on Industrial Robots (ISIR) was held in Tokyo, and it was accompanied, as usual, by an exposition at Harumi pier, east of the city. In front of the huge halls, a billboard-sized painting of the ultimate cliché in industrial robot art, a metal hand reaching out to touch a carbon-based life form (a butterfly, in this case), announced the robots inside.

In concept this show was nearly identical to those held annually in the United States. But the Japanese version differed dramatically in several important ways. It was sponsored not only by the Japan Industrial Robot Association but also by the *Daily Industrial News*. Inside the jam-packed halls, the latest hydraulic, electric, and vision-equipped direct-drive robots solved puzzles, assembled electronic circuitry, and pretended to weld and paint car bodies, while manufacturers' representatives hyped their merits. With each booth separated by only a few yards, and with each representative amplified, the din of competing explanations merged in the center of the cavernous hall into a garbled, high-pitched roar.

The robotics industry worldwide is dominated by men, and utterly so in Japan, but at Japanese exhibitions nearly all the announcing is done by professional young women called "companions." These are not seasoned engineers or sales managers, as in the United States, but young women with good memories hired to recite otherwise boring specifications—part of a seemingly inexhaustible supply of alluring females who cloak the very masculine, hard world of Japanese technology with a soft, innocent overlay in media ads and industry fairs. Megumi Endo, twenty years old, primly uniformed and working at the Seiko booth that year, had carefully memorized and rehearsed a ten-minute presentation she could deliver with impeccable grace and precision, using all the right formalities while keeping her voice pitched appropriately high. Since she had no real understanding of what she was saying, however, technical questions were referred to male company employees who always lurk nearby—the next day Megumi might be hawking toothpaste at a health show.

There was something for everyone at Harumi. Most of the robots were the one-armed industrial variety, but part of the exhibit featured some of the highly unorthodox research being conducted in Japanese laboratories on mobile robots. A prototype of an insectlike, wall-climbing robot, called a MELSPIDER, and MELDOG—a robot replacement for a "seeing-eye" dog—represented the government labs. Chiba Walker, a bipedal robot walking machine, represented Chiba University and the large faction of Japanese scientists earnestly pursuing humanoid robots.

In advanced nations outside of Japan, serious attempts to build humanoids in robotics are rare and are regarded as highly eccentric; trying to build them with current levels of technology for actual use in industry is considered next to madness. Nonetheless, across the aisle from the Seiko industrial robots was a display of a prototype bipedal "factory" robot being developed by Motoda Electronics and a group of

MELDOG, a prototype "seeing eye dog" robot, was created at the national Mechanical Engineering Laboratory (MEL) in 1985. It uses sensors to navigate and guide the blind.

university professors. Called the BORN System, it looked like the lower torso of a truncated mechanical man. A sign, in English for foreigners, stated: "Purpose: To search the way of evolution of the Industrial Biped Robot through practice. . . . The robot 'The BORN' has just begun to walk. It is our eager desire to evolve them step by step literally." For much of the exhibition it was broken, and an embarrassed uniformed "companion" passed the time handing out brochures.

In yet another area of the fair was a selection of the latest products from Tomy Corporation, "personal robot" toys that zoomed around in circles on a table top, holding newspapers and drinks on trays to the delight of ogling crowds of

The 17th ISIR conference was held in Chicago in 1987, and the exhibition attached to it highlighted the different approach to robotics in Japan and America. The Tokyo show and the Chicago show both lasted similar intervals and had similar admission costs. In the United States, however, as was customary, no one under sixteen was allowed, and attendees were almost entirely men in the robotics industry; visitors numbered only 12,398. At the Tokyo show, however, 223,351 people attended, nearly forty times more than in America, relative to population.[9] And, according to those

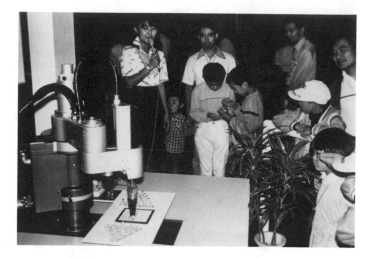

Children vainly try to solve a puzzle faster than a vision-equipped Sony SRX-2CH industrial robot at the 1985 International Industrial Robot Exhibition.

manning the gates in Tokyo, as many as one-quarter of them were children, dragging their parents to see the robots. In Japan, technology is supposed to belong to everyone.

Why have robots flourished so dramatically in Japan? When asking people in Japan, answers range from religion, to economics, to engineering skills, to thinly veiled assertions of racial superiority, and even to the influence of comic books. There is no single answer, just as there is no single Robot Kingdom. But throughout the broad spectrum of the Robot Kingdom, there does exist a continuum. The march of history is also the march of technology, and the robot, in all forms, is one of the ultimate metaphors for the relationship between man and technology.

Technology itself is becoming less and less culture specific. Cars, computers, and airplanes are made and designed with the same basic tools and formulas around the world, and increasingly look the same. Nor does any particular culture have a monopoly on technology. But the application of technology, the way in which it is approached, and the direction in which it is pushed can be profoundly influenced by a people's collective expectations, their history, and their culture. In Japan, the Robot Kingdom is part myth, part reality, and part state of mind. The robot itself is a crystallization of a mechanical dream.

What Is a Robot?

What is a robot? A machine that does work in place of man? Mechanization of human labor? Zen riddles of this sort will satisfy few. . . . Everyone has his own image of what a robot is. They are all right, and all wrong.

ROBOTICS ENGINEER
SHOTARO OZAKI

The word "robot" came from a 1920 play titled *R.U.R.*, or "Rossum's Universal Robots," written by Karel Capek. Capek, a Czech, had coined the word from *robota*, the Czech noun for "work," which is derived from a root for "slave" or "servant." His play had a rather simple plot that fed on old fears in Western civilization: men mass produce artificial slaves, or robots, to take over their work and later to wage war as well; the robots, of high intelligence, decide not to kill each other, and instead slaughter their masters, the humans. Written after World War I, when the world had discovered the negative side of the assembly line, *R.U.R.* was tremendously popular. "Robot" was easy to pronounce, had a rather nice ring to it, and was adopted by the mass media of the day.

Today's broad usage and the dark origins of the word are reflected in the 1986 *Webster's Ninth New Collegiate Dictionary* definition. A robot is said to be

1. **a:** a machine that looks like a human being and performs various complex acts (as walking or talking) of a human being; also: a similar but fictional machine whose lack of capacity for human emotions is often emphasized **b:** an efficient, insensitive, often brutalized person

2: an automatic apparatus or device that performs functions ordinarily ascribed to human beings or operates with what appears to be almost human intelligence

3: a mechanism guided by automatic controls.[1]

In 1924, one year after *R.U.R.* was staged in English in the West, it was performed at Tokyo's Tsukiji Theater in Japanese, with the title *Jinzo ningen*, or "Artificial Man." This became the de facto Japanese term for robot, until the nation fell into step with the rest of the world over a decade later and

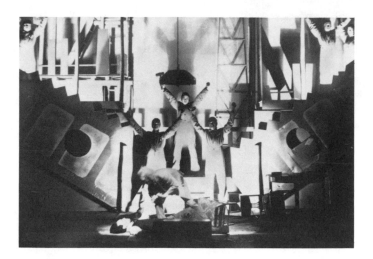

began using the word *robotto*. Unlike *jinzo ningen*, which is written with Chinese ideograms, *robotto* is short, punchy, and written with a phonetic script used for foreign words. The 1983 *Kojien* dictionary defines *robotto* as

> **1.** an artificial, automatic doll, made of complex, precision mechanisms; [*jinzo ningen*] an artificial man, an automaton

> **2.** generally, machinery or devices capable of automatically performing designated operations or work [as in a robotic measuring device, or industrial robot]

> **3.** a person who acts under someone else's control; a person with status, but no ability; a puppet.[2]

Metal men have starred in hundreds of novels, plays, and films since *R.U.R.*, often with distressingly similar plots, but in Capek's original script "robots" were flesh-and-blood creations grown from an organic soup; they only became mechanical in later stage productions. Today there are fantasy robots in science fiction, industrial robots in factories, and autonomous robots in laboratories, but to most people around the world a robot in some way approximates the physical movements or shape of a human (or animal), yet is a machine.

The Birth of the Industrial Robot

When the first robot finally arrived in industry, it hardly looked like a metal man. It was only a metal arm, and it began as a patent application for a device called—not "robot"—but "Programmed Article Transfer," filed in 1954 by a self-taught American inventor, George C. Devol, Jr.

Science fiction robots were the last thing on Devol's mind. His goal was to create what he called "unimation," or "universal automation." Almost all manufacturing requires the handling and manipulation of objects, but until the end of World War II, the mechanization of this process had depended on men operating the machines that did the work (such as cranes) or on "hard automation," which then used cams and limit switches to control repetitive operations in specialized tasks. The former was flexible, but labor intensive and costly. The latter worked fine for single tasks that rarely changed, as in automatic bottling plants, but needed huge volume to justify and was extremely expensive to alter. Devol's idea was a form of flexible automation, a transfer apparatus or manipulator that could do many things, such as pick cartons off a series of pallets and then put them on a conveyor belt to be transferred into a truck—a simple operation usually performed by hand that was, he wrote, "a waste of manpower that is here corrected."[3]

The Programmed Article Transfer was made possible by advances in feedback and servomechanism technology during World War II. As MIT mathematician-genius Norbert Wiener articulated it in 1948, in his theory of cybernetics, or control and communication, feedback is used by both animals and automatic machines when "behavior is scanned for

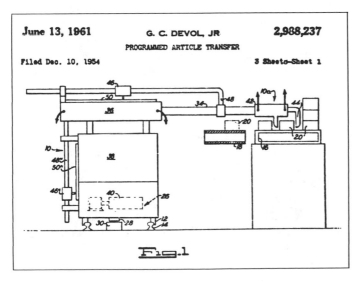

A side view of the Programmed Article Transfer in George Devol's original patent application. A telescoping arm (34) with a gripper attached (10a) picks up a carton (20) and places it on a conveyor (18). The control unit (26) and program drum (40) are in the body of the robot.

Joseph Engelberger and George Devol enjoy a drink served by a Unimate robot in the early days.

its result, and . . . the success or failure of this result modifies future behavior."[4] In humans, when an arm is extended, nerve cells in the joints sense and send the brain information on its position. This information is then processed, and the position of the arm corrected. In the mechanical world, one of the simplest and most common types of feedback device and servomechanism is the household thermostat, a sliver of metal that bends according to temperature and thus turns on or off a heater to regulate the temperature of a room. With both the arm and the thermostat, information "sensed" is used to drive the difference between actual and desired positions to zero. Manmade servomechanisms became vastly more sophisticated with the introduction of electro-mechanical technology, which used electricity to transmit feedback information from sensors and to actuate and control mechanical devices. The result has been self-propelled missiles and radar-controlled guns, numerically controlled machine tools, the industrial robot, and practically every self-correcting automatic mechanism we use today.

In 1954 there were a few new numerically controlled machine tools—lathes and other tools with servo controls that could be programmed to perform a variety of movements. In fact, Devol had earlier invented a memory system that magnetically recorded these movements. But such tools worked primarily "inward." That is, they ground, cut, or drilled in a circumscribed space. There were also mechanical and servo-controlled manipulators in existence—"magic hands," sometimes called robots in those days—that remote operators could use to handle dangerous radioactive materials. By combining a servo-controlled manipulator with his magnetic recording system, Devol's invention in effect created a marriage between manipulators and nascent computer technology. According to his patent application, when the arm of the transfer device was moved to a spot in space, the position could be recorded digitally on a magnetized revolving drum and then played back, rather like a tape recorder. With motors and positioning sensors as servo controls, the system could automatically compare the actual arm position with the recorded position, and correct the former until the two matched.

Devol had absolutely no luck when he first tried to sell his marvelous idea. But then, at a cocktail party in 1956, he met a young physicist and engineer named Joseph Engelberger, an early student of servo controls. A man who wears a trademark bow tie and a grin, and whose voice still cracks with the enthusiasm of a teenager, Engelberger was the perfect entrepreneurial counterpart to Devol, the inventor. For the dogged role he played in shepherding the new technology to practicality, Engelberger, even more than Devol, would become known as the "father of industrial robots."

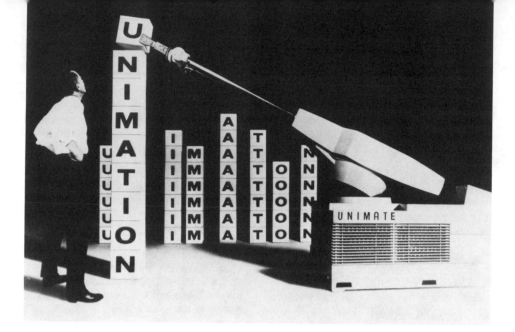

One of Unimation's first Unimates. All the control apparatus is built into the base structure.

Engelberger was fascinated by Devol's invention and saw its potential right away. As he recalls today, "Devol's real contribution was to realize that most people in factories are doing 'put and take,' and that a machine to replace them must be teachable. He knew that there were all kinds of automation devices that could go from A to B, but saw the value of one that could go to any or all points desired."[5]

After touring around twenty factories to find out what type of performance such a machine would really require, the men drew up plans, and with financial backing found by Engelberger built a prototype called the Unimate in 1959. In 1962, with Engelberger as president of Unimation Inc., the first production model was made based on Devol's patent. It weighed over 3,500 pounds and looked like a tank with a gripper on the end of its turret gun. Hydraulically driven, with a computerlike memory and digital feedback, it could pick up and transfer as much as 75 pounds and keep track of 150 sequences or moves.[6] The Unimate was taught by guiding its "hand" to the points in space desired and pushing a button to record their coordinates, which could then be played back. For the time, it was exceedingly advanced, and instead of vacuum tubes used transistors. But it deviated in one major sense from Devol's patent. The original Programmed Article Transfer was supposed to move on rails along a conveyor belt; the Unimate was stationary.

From the beginning, Engelberger was determined to call this machine a robot. He was a fan of Isaac Asimov, the science fiction writer who rails against the robot's "creaky Gothic menace" image. Engelberger also knew the value of a good name. As he frequently says, terms like "computer-aided manufacturing" are vague and hard for the average person to understand, but because of science fiction films everyone at least thinks he knows what a robot is. The name did result in tremendous media interest in Unimation and its machine, but few sales—the company didn't turn a profit until 1975. Today Engelberger is convinced he chose the right name, but it may have been part of the problem. Some people, he recalls, thought it too "poignant."

Canon's laser rotary encoders function like nerves in human limbs and measure actual position and angle, providing information that, when compared with the expected position, can be used to position the robot arm exactly.

> Everyone said, "No, don't call it a robot. That's bad. Let's call it a production terminal." Ford Motor Company insisted it was a Universal Transfer Device. "U-T-D," they called it for short. The purchasing department said, "Wanted, three U-T-Ds," and in parentheses they'd write, "Industrial Robots," so you'd know what they were talking about![7]

While the name eventually caught on, the huge gap between expectations and reality among the public invariably caused a question that still bedevils those in the industry: what is a robot?

Defining Industrial Robots

Although robotics technology has progressed by leaps and bounds since the first Unimate (and its competitors) appeared on the market, most industrial robots can still be divided into three parts: the mechanical manipulator, the power supply, and the control system. The manipulators are usually classified as cylindrical coordinate, spherical coordinate (polar), jointed arm (revolute), and rectangular coordinate (Cartesian), depending on whether their joints rotate, swivel, or slide along an axis. Their agility is measured in axes of motion, or "degrees of freedom"; compared with the human arm, which has seven, most robots have six degrees or fewer.

Every machine must have some form of power; robots today are electrical, hydraulic, or pneumatic, in that order of popularity. Control systems vary from the simple to the complex. The simplest industrial "robots" are non-servo-controlled and have their arm movements set and limited by mechanical stops or switches. Servo-controlled robots can be controlled either on a "point-to-point" basis (only the desti-

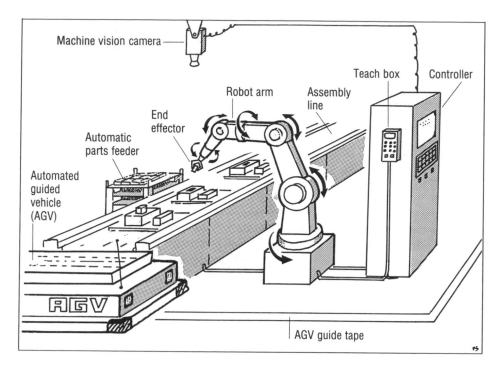

Machine vision camera

Teach box   Controller

Robot arm   Assembly
line

End
effector

Automatic
parts feeder

Automated
guided
vehicle
(AGV)

AGV

AGV guide tape

Illustration of a common industrial robot configuration, showing degrees of freedom.

nation points of the arm are specified) or on a "continuous path" basis (the entire path the robot arm traverses is memorized and controlled). Except for the non-servo variety, most robots are controlled by computers, and some are "intelligent" and can react to their environment with information from tactile or vision sensors to alter their programmed movements as required.

Humans, in their desire to anthropomorphize objects wherever possible, still label the manipulator with terms such as "forearm," "shoulder," "upper arm," "wrist," and "hand" and refer to "teaching" it. Other robot terminology is much more arcane. There are "end effectors," or hands or tools; "actuators," the "muscles" that physically move the joints; stepper motors and servomechanisms that control the force of movement; feedback sensory devices such as "encoders," "resolvers," "potentiometers," and "tachometers"; and "work envelopes," or areas in which the robot arm can operate.

Then there is the visible robot and the invisible robot. The first, the hardware, or what American roboticists call "the iron," interacts with the real world. The second, the software or programs, is coded instructions the controller uses to send electronic signals to motors, which drive the arm in the proper directions at the proper speed. By changing the programming, and changing the end effector at the end of a robot arm, the task performed can theoretically be switched from welding a car body to painting one. Like philosophers trying to decide whether a man's body or soul is more important, roboticists still take sides over the relative importance of software or hardware for robots, with Americans traditionally stressing the former, and Japanese the latter.

Aside from the above shared traits, industrial robots (or IR, as they are called) have become increasingly varied and specialized. Whereas all were once mounted on the floor, now many, called "gantry" robots, are suspended from a ceiling framework that allows them to travel brief distances in a horizontal plane; some robots travel on short rails. There are robots mounted on walls, robots that look like elephant trunks, robots that work on pendulum principles, robots with two arms, and robots that can automatically change the tools they hold. Devol's idea was for a type of "universal automation," that is, a nonspecialized manipulator. Today's robots, however, are increasingly designed and used for welding, painting, assembly, and other specialized tasks.

In 1979, sensing that the general public was utterly confused by the concept of "industrial robot," the Robot Institute of America (RIA) did an extraordinary thing. Its committees whittled a page-and-a-half description of this technological chimera down to a single sentence, defining it, in one labored breath, as

> a reprogrammable, multifunctional manipulator designed to move material, parts, tools, or specialized devices through variable programmed motions for the performance of a variety of tasks."[8]

This masterpiece of a sentence fails to corral all the nuances of a robot, but with the words "reprogrammable" and "multifunctional" it is nonetheless vastly more specific than many other definitions.

The Japan Industrial Robot Association (JIRA) has also tried to define a robot, with different results. Its Terminology Standardization Committee has compiled a draft definition suggesting that robots can be considered

Toshiba Corporation's prototype "elephant trunk" robot, articulated for hard-to-reach locations in nuclear power plants and equipped with a camera for inspection.

Devices capable of moving in a flexible manner analogous to the moving parts of living organisms, with or without intellectual functions, allowing operations in response to human commands. "Intellectual functions" refers to judgment, recognitions, adaptation, or learning, by means of sensing, memory and other capabilities.[9]

Officially, however, the JIRA has no definition. As Kanji Yonemoto, the head of JIRA, explains, "It's not because we didn't try. We had been doing standardization work for four years since 1974, and all we could do was come up with classifications. We decided that it was better to classify rather than define them."[10]

Both the JIRA and the Japan Industrial Standards (JIS) organization have done important work in classifying robots. As of 1986 they counted eight categories in order of increasing sophistication: manual manipulators, sequence-control robots, playback robots, numerically controlled (NC) robots, "intelligent" robots, sensory-controlled robots, adaptive-controlled robots, and learning-controlled robots.[11] The core concept of a robot is the same in Japan and the West, but perhaps because Japan has stressed the visible robot—the mechanical side as opposed to its computer brain and software—the JIRA has included manual manipulators and fixed-sequence robots (also called "pick and place" robots) in its definition. The former require human operators, while the latter are often not easily programmed; both are therefore not included in the RIA definition.

To the person who wonders, "So what?" the answer is that in this high-tech age, the number of robots a nation has is a symbol of its commitment to modern manufacturing and automation and can convey considerable prestige. Japan's claim to be the Robot Kingdom is based on a census of its robots, yet it has no single definition with which to count them and it classifies as robots things which other nations say are not. By JIRA count, in 1986 Japan had over 224,000 robots. When stripped of manual manipulators and fixed-sequence robots, this figure plummets to 116,000. Although the number of "disputed" devices being manufactured today is a fraction of the total (and is carefully excluded when JIRA makes international comparisons), JIRA still counts as robots thousands of automatic component insertion machines—programmable machines that insert integrated circuits into printed circuit boards; these have every quality of a robot except versatility, and therefore do not fit the American definition.

Japan's system of defining robots has had some major benefits. First, in the early years, before definitions became an issue, it enabled the mass media to make lopsided comparisons that reinforced the idea of the nation as a Robot Kingdom—a tremendous propaganda coup. Second, it brought manufacturers of low-tech robots into the larger robotics community, in effect "inviting them to the party" and encouraging them to upgrade their technologies. Many manufacturers of manipulators now make sophisticated robots, and many of the most advanced manipulators nearly equal robots in technological sophistication. "With its sophisticated servo-control system," says Kanji Yonemoto, "I don't see how people can say a high-tech manipulator used in a nuclear reactor is not a 'robot.'"[12]

Even the legalistic American definition has proved inadequate. If applied in a narrow sense, every plotter attached to a computer in the United States could be counted as a robot—it is programmable, servo controlled, and has a "manipulator" that grabs different-colored pens. And what about mobility? The American definition ignores the very future of robotics.

For the last four years, the very staid International Standards Organization (ISO) has been grappling with the problem of defining a robot, and in the process demonstrating how difficult it is for countries to agree. Nations participating have included Japan, the United States, West Germany, France, the United Kingdom, and Sweden. In 1985 Jean Chabrol, the French chairman, reported "until a recent date, the ISO working group dealing with IR suffered from an identity crisis due to the robot definition; the situation was confused because of the rigid stance of some experts, and at ISO we no longer knew what an industrial robot was or was not."[13]

The definition they may soon agree on is closer to the U.S. one, and at the same time more comprehensive. In its compressed form, it states:

> In common language, a *robot* is a machine which can be programmed to perform tasks which involve manipulative or locomotive actions under automatic control. "An *industrial manipulating robot*" is a multitask, automatically controlled, reprogrammable manipulative machine, with or without locomotion, for use in industrial applications.[14]

The Linguistic Mystique of Automation

The Japanese are sometimes accused of calling anything automatic a robot, but this is an unfair charge, since the English-speaking world also uses the word quite loosely. It is true, however, that in Japan the brand names of automatic devices often contain the word "robot" only because manufacturers know it will help sell their products. Sometimes even vending machines are referred to as robots. To place robots in their proper context in today's Japan requires knowledge of the vocabulary and mystique behind automation, both in the factory and outside it.

Japanese often use English words for things that are exotic and new, and for convenience turn them into acronyms easier to pronounce and remember. Automation-related acronyms used and abused include not only OA (office automation) and FA (factory automation), but HA (home automa-

THE ROBOT MIND OR BODY?

The physical robot, the hardware, interacts with the real world, but software and "intelligence" are increasingly important. If we humans were insensate and incapable of reasoning when trying to pick an object up off the ground, our arms would be much less accurate than those of rigid, mechanical robots. Because we can see, feel, and think, however, our limbs are among the most sophisticated tools in the world. Currently, with limited "intelligence" in the form of computers, software, and sensors that provide some form of vision or touch, some industrial robots can identify and sort parts moving randomly down an assembly line.

Says Victor Sheinman, vice-president of the U.S. robot firm Automatix and a pioneer inventor in the field, "My motto is trust in software. In the long run, software will make the promise of robotics come true, but in the short run mechanics play a significant role." Sheinman believes that software and more powerful computers will reduce the complexity of the mechanisms the robot needs; the current lack of intelligence and sophisticated sensors is one reason so much emphasis is put on mechanical accuracy today.

Eiji Nakano, chief of planning at Japan's Mechanical Engineering Laboratory, acknowledges the importance of software, but believes in hardware. "I think hardware control is basic, and that software development will depend on it. I've watched disabled people, and no matter how intelligent they are it can be extremely difficult for them to function. Intelligence alone is not enough."

---

tion), SA (store automation), BA (banking automation), LA (laboratory automation), RA (restaurant automation), and even the exotic PA (personal automation), which refers not to human robots, but to things like wristwatch computers. PA is used infrequently, but not so OA and FA. Newspapers and television daily bombard consumers with ads for the latest OA equipment, or with proclamations of a firm's commitment to FA. Sometimes OA and FA differ subtly in meaning from their English roots. Popular books on robots, for example, commonly have sections on office automation.

OA equipment in Japan refers to computers, Local Area Networks (LAN), optical character readers (OCR), optical file disks, facsimile machines (FAX), copier machines, and cheap word processors that are little more than typewriters. But for most Japanese even the last item is a tremendous automation of labor, and, in that sense, a robot. The Japanese written language is so complex that, until a few years ago, business letters were either handwritten or laboriously typed by professionals on a monstrously difficult mechanical contraption. Today's "intelligent" word processors help select which of thousands of ideograms to use and help organize the proper mix of four writing systems (ideograms, two phonetic scripts, and the Roman alphabet). In the process, they are helping Japan make the great leap from a handwriting/scribe–based society to the "Information Age," and skip the manual typewriter stage of civilization.

Marol's servo-arm "robot," a top-of-the-line power manipulator that still requires human operation.

All this OA has been made possible by ME, or micro-electronics—the science, or art, of reducing electronic circuitry to a microscopic level and providing it with "intelligence" in the form of programmed instructions. In a culture that historically has focused on the microcosm, in the form of bonsai, haiku, and—in the Chinese tradition—writing sutras on single grains of rice, this is a field in which many Japanese believe they have a unique advantage. Japan is the world's largest consumer today of cheap mass-produced semiconductors, and it uses them in everything from "intelligent" bidet-toilets to vending machines. Nearly five and a half million of the latter, about human height, line the streets of Japan; many are equipped with built-in electronic games and synthesized voices and increasingly resemble "robots."

Since ME is a superset of all automation technologies, including OA and FA, it is intrinsically linked with robotics, which relies on miniaturized circuitry for computers, sensors, motors, and servomechanisms. The effects of robots on unemployment and on society at large are therefore usually dealt with in conferences or books with ME in the title. When an English book titled *The Micro-electronics Revolution*, which discussed the effects of ME on the white-collar world, was translated and published in Japan it was given the title of *Ofisu robotto ga yatte kita*, or "Here Comes the Office Robot."

The visible robot is also a "mechanism," a word that has been abbreviated to *mecha* in Japan and imbued with special significance. *Mecha* are all things mechanical, but they have a romantic, transcendent aura—for young boys, the schematics of imaginary warrior robot mechanisms or the innards of a racing car have a powerful appeal. Among the general public, people referring to their mechanical aptitude say they are either "strong" or "weak" at *mecha*.

Using "electronics" and *mecha*, Japan has coined a new word to sum up the confusing technologies of robotics. Ironically, it is currently in the process of being adopted in the English-speaking world. This is "mechatronics," the mirror image of the English "electromechanical" and a reflection of the emphasis Japanese engineers have put on mechanisms. It is under the heading of mechatronics, or *mekatoro*, that articles on robots are always listed in industrial newspapers.

The word "mechatronics" first appeared in Japanese journals in the 1970s. Now widely used, as a concept it is an integral part of a national strategy of enhancing resource-

WHAT IS A ROBOT?

Joseph Engelberger, "Father of the Industrial Robot": "I may not be able to define one, but I know one when I see one."

Gensuke Okada, advisor to Kawasaki Heavy Industries: "A robot is a slave . . . a mechanical slave that can do very hard work for humans, as told."

Dr. Seiuemon Inaba, president of Fanuc: "That is a very difficult question."

Takayuki Morishima, robot designer at Bandai Toy Company: "A robot is something that gives boys dreams, and bravery."

Anonymous designer at a successful robot toy company supplying the American market: "It used to be fun to make robots. Now we're so busy they're just a way to make a living."

Dr. Shinnichi Yuta, robotics researcher at Tsukuba University: "A robot is a machine modeled after man or an animal, which decides what work it should do, and does it."

Dr. Susumu Tachi, director of the Robotics Department at MEL: "A robot is an artificial realization of a machine man or animal that serves man. In the future it must become, like a dog, man's best friend."

Dr. Yoshiaki Shirai, director of the Automatic Control Division at ETL: "A system that works on the outside world and processes information and can be made to work in conjunction with human goals."

Wall Welsel, president of Prab Robots and former president of the RIA: "A robot is a conglomeration or collection of pieces that in some fashion takes a shot at simulating the perfect creation, which is a human."

Shunichi Mizuno, creator of erotic humanoid robots: "A robot is a doll; it is the ultimate medium of expression."

Yoshiyuki Tomino, robot animation director: "A robot is only a tool, but just as the samurai sword contains the spirit of the samurai, a robot can also express a persona."

Sueo Matsubara, chairman of Automax, a robot manufacturer: "A robot is a tool, and also our friend."

Five children in Kanagawa Prefecture polled in the January 1986 issue of *Robotist*: (1) "A helper robot." (2) "Gundam" [an animation character]. (3) "Machines making cars." (4) "Robots like in Star Wars and Expo '85." (5) "Something interesting, that transforms."

---

poor Japan's position in the world through *gijutsu rikkoku*, or "building the state with technology." This strategy is symbolized by the 1971 Extraordinary Measures Law for Promotion of Specific Electronic and Machinery Industries and by the 1978 Extraordinary Measures Law for Promotion of Specific Machinery and Information Industries. As Susumu Tachi, head of robotics at the national Mechanical Engineering Laboratory (MEL), explains in his book *Mekatoronikusu no hanashi*, or "Speaking of Mechatronics," the goal is to fuse mechanisms, electronics, and the information industries and to create a synergism whereby "one plus one . . . can be made to equal not two, but three, and even ten."[15] Mechatronics are intelligent mechanisms, and robots are mechatronics.

Japan today is a mechatronic empire whose unrivaled flagships are robots in the form of servo-controlled computer

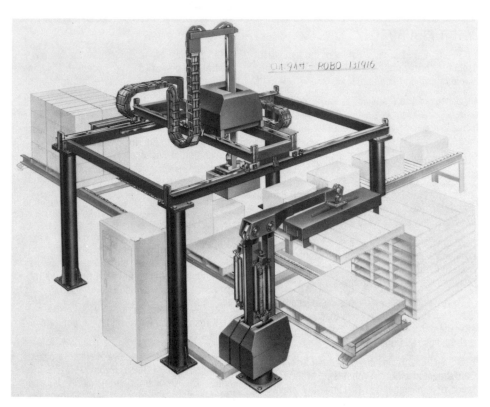

Motoda Electronic's Robotizer, a small automated palletizing system that pairs a simple robot arm and a gantry robot.

printers, compact disks, portable video equipment, and autofocus cameras. But the real strength of Japanese mechatronics is not in the goods or the "product technology," much of which comes from overseas. Instead, it is in the "process technology," in the manufacturing systems and the tools and arms that create the products at such a high quality and low price, that they are invincible in world markets.

The apex of microelectronics and mechatronics in process technology is the factorywide implementation of Devol's goal of "universal automation." Instead of churning out thousands of identical widgets with hard automation, industries throughout the world today are trying to create flexible manufacturing systems (FMS) that enable the production of small batches of several varieties of goods. But the way flexible automation is being pursued differs from nation to nation, and so do the attendant buzzwords. Manufacturers in the United States wax enthusiastic over computer-integrated manufacturing, or CIM, and hope to leap toward the "Factory of the Future," an elegant but still vague concept

The JIS code is followed by the official English translation and JIS description [with author's comments].

1110: "Operating robot": A robot having controllers, and actuators for mobility and/or manipulation, remotely controlled by a human operator. [Includes what are called mechanical or power manipulators in the United States.]

1120: "Sequence control robot": A robot that operates sequentially with preset information (sequence, conditions, and positions). "Fixed sequence robot": A sequence robot for which the preset information cannot be easily changed. "Variable sequence robot": A sequence robot for which the preset information can be easily changed. [Sometimes the above three robots are called "limited sequence robots," "pick and place robots," or "bang-bang devices"; they often rely on mechanical end stops or limit switches instead of computer control.]

1130: "Playback robot": A robot that can repeat an operation on the basis of instructions concerning sequence, condition, position, and other information imparted by moving the robot under operating control. [The original Unimate was a playback robot.]

1140: "Numerically controlled (NC) robot": A robot that can execute the operation commanded in compliance with information on, e.g., sequence, conditions, and position loaded numerically or by program, without being moved.

1150: "Intelligent robot": A robot that can determine its own actions through artificial intelligence. "Artificial intelligence" refers to such artificially created abilities as recognition, learning, abstract thinking, or environmental adaptivity.

1151: "Sensory-controlled robot": A robot whose operation is controlled by sensory information.

1152: "Adaptive-controlled robot": A robot having an adaptive control function. "Adaptive control" refers to control in which the characteristics of the control system change in response to changes in the environment in order to satisfy prescribed conditions.

1153: "Learning-controlled robot": A robot having a learning control function. "Learning control" refers to control in which an appropriate operation is executed based on operating experience.

---

wherein the computer controls and coordinates everything from design to robot movements to sales. Japanese industrialists pursue the same goals with the acronyms FA and FMS, automating incrementally. They also use a term that Western societies avoid, owing to its obvious, unpleasant implications for labor. This is *mujinka kojo*, the "unmanned factory," and it is a concept being implemented now.

The Factory As Robot

Electronics firms in Japan used to release publicity photos of their factories showing hundreds of disciplined young women in company uniforms, with white gloves and kerchiefed hair, toiling at long lines of tables, soldering, wiring, and assembling radios and other products. Today these same companies show photos and video tapes of long lines of robots and other automated machines doing the same work, without a human in sight. The humans are still there, but in smaller numbers and behind the scenes. The goal of the publicity has changed. Corporate prestige now demands commitment to the concept of the "unmanned factory"; the fewer the workers in the photos, the better. It is not yet possible to dump raw materials in one side of a factory and with no human assistance have finished products spew out the other side. But it is almost possible. Casio's calculator factory in the city of Kofu, a miniature "silicon valley" of semiconductor manufacturers, robot manufacturers, and electronic consumer good plants, is an example.

According to a company representative, Casio's success began in 1969 when it developed a calculator called AS-A, which stood for "Auto Soroban A-type"—*soroban* being the Japanese word for abacus. The AS-A incorporated the latest in microelectronics technology from the United States, at a third of the cost of anything else then on the market. The Kofu factory complex, originally built to mass produce the AS-A, now also manufactures personal computers, cash registers, and other items, but Plant No. 5 is still dedicated to calculators. In April 1985 it received the prestigious Nikkei Award for implementation of a flexible manufacturing system. Its function, says the proud representative, "is to make more calculators available to the people of the world."

Years ago, consumer products rarely changed much, and when they did, whole production lines had to be scrapped and rebuilt. This was expensive and time consuming, especially if they used "hard," or fixed, automation. Today's customers are increasingly sophisticated and demanding. Competition has increased, and product life cycles have dramatically shortened. Objects like calculators now transcend utility and are fashion. The Casio catalogue lists 160 types of calculators. Typically these have a life cycle of no more than a year and a half. The goal of the FMS system at Kofu is to manufacture as many calculators as possible in the shortest period of time, and to be able to change models easily.

As if in a Japanese home, visitors to the Casio plant all remove their shoes and don special rubber slippers on entering the spotless manufacturing area. Cleanliness is important, but so is prevention of static electricity—the mortal enemy of microelectronics. On the second floor the calculators are assembled in two production lines, with two people per line. An automated warehouse rotates its racks of parts, rather like the revolving shelves in a jewelry store, and,

Inside the Casio calculator factory at Kofu: An AGV resupplies the Casio assembly line and its robots.

A machine vision system reads the numeric display on the calculator after a robotic device has punched its key pad.

selecting one out of eight thousand boxes resembling soda pop bottle containers, disgorges it onto a waiting robot cart, or AGV. Tooting a little ditty to warn off humans, the AGV takes the parts to the lines, where seventy robots and other computerized machinery assemble and connect the VLSI (very large scale integration) chips, the LCD display, and the solar battery to a printed circuit board base—in this case a thin carbon film—and package it. Robots using vision systems also test the keypads and displays to see that they function properly, and then discharge the finished calculator at the end of the line to an AGV, which returns it to the automated warehouse.

Actual assembly of a calculator takes only 2.8 seconds. Operating day and night, Casio claims to be able to produce 1.5 million calculators per month in these facilities alone. With robots, AGV, and other computer-controlled machinery, the Casio factory is a true FMS system; over sixteen different models of calculators in a variety of different sizes can be produced in virtually any quantity desired. By simply instructing the system from the plant's computer control room (manned by Casio computers), the appropriate model changes can be made in not months, but one minute.

In 1950, before industrial robots existed, Norbert Wiener saw that feedback and servo technology would make possible not only programmable tools, but even an "automatic" factory. "The overall system," he predicted, "will correspond to the complete animal with sense organs, effectors, and proprioceptors, and not, as in the ultra-rapid computing machine, to an isolated brain, dependent for its experiences and for its effectiveness on our intervention."[16] Today's unmanned factory increasingly resembles his vision. The waving and pecking industrial robot arms—along with robot carts, artificial vision systems, artificial intelligence, numerically controlled machining tools, and automated warehouses—are only one component of the computerized whole, of the factory itself. And the "robots" are becoming harder and harder to isolate from the rest of the system. Are two robot arms that run off one computer as part of a well-engineered machining cell one robot, or two? When a robot arm is paired with a computerized jig that positions a car panel, and the jig uses more servo-controlled technology and costs more than the arm, which is the robot?

MECHATRONICS

From the Report on Policies in the Machine Industry, No. 8:

"After the war, Japan aggressively invested in plant and capital and developed technologically under the slogan 'Catch up to and Surpass the Advanced Nations of the West.' Now that Japan belongs to the community of the advanced nations, South Korea, Taiwan, and other developing nations are adopting the same strategy and will probably catch up. The only way Japan, as a trading nation, can continue to progress is to develop more advanced, value-added products—in other words, to move toward more knowledge-based industries. Mechatronics, the fusion of machinery and electronics, symbolizes these 'intelligent' products and will become a key industry supporting Japan in the future. Mechatronics is essential."

And is the robot the hardware, or is it the software?

Because the technologies for robots, sensors, vision, and AGVs have become so intertwined, and the term "robot" is so limiting, the Robot Institute of America changed its name several years ago to the Robotic Industries Association. Like "robot," "robotic" has its roots in science fiction. It was coined by Isaac Asimov in 1942, but it is now used as a conveniently blurred term that encompasses all robot-related technologies. In Japan, *robotto*, which is still the main term in use for "robot," sometimes means "robotic" as well. In both nations, the industrial robot is on the verge of becoming little more than a synonym for factory automation. In systems engineering in the factory, the individual industrial robot—the iron arm—is being swallowed.

Resolving the Robot's Identity Crisis

Traditionally there have been two distinct types of "real" robots—those in industry and those in research laboratories. Creators of the former have specialized in manipulation and precision positioning, while creators of the latter have dealt with broader issues of mobility and autonomy. Often the two have had very little in common. Starting in the 1960s, at United States universities such as MIT and Stanford, and now in laboratories around the world, scientists have been trying to make robots that can move about on their own in the real world. This has led them to study artificial intelligence, sensors (needed to react to changes in the environment), and different forms of locomotion. Also in the labs are robot-related fields of research, such as telechirs, which are "robots" operating under a form of remote control called teleoperation; exoskeletons, which surround and amplify the human skeleton; and even mechanical prostheses to replace lost arms or legs.

Since robots in laboratories are not exploited as a symbol of national manufacturing strength, definitions have not been an issue. As with industrial robots, however, the Japanese emphasis has been on hardware and mechanisms, while that of the United States has been on software and "intelligence." The difference is symbolized by the many researchers in Japan who make unusual hardware and whose background is in mechanical engineering, while their U.S. counterparts, with degrees mostly in computer science, work on artificial intelligence. As one Japanese researcher says, "To the Americans, a robot is a computer attached to a mechanism. To Japanese, a robot is a mechanism attached to a computer."

In 1981 Dr. Eiji Nakano, head of the Planning Department at Japan's Mechanical Engineering Laboratory (MEL), published a paper that divided industrial robots, like computers, into generations according to the technologies they employ. The first generation (most of the machines toiling away in factories today) is only an incremental improvement over Devol's original Programmed Article Transfer—a blind, deaf, and dumb mechanical arm, capable only of repetitive actions and possessing servomechanisms and internal sensors that help it position itself. The second generation, which emerged in the late 1970s, is capable of making limited "decisions" on the basis of information about the outside world received via visual or tactile sensors. It is used in areas such as arc welding and assembly. The third generation, which will not become practical until the 1990s, will certainly be equipped with artificial intelligence and will not need constant programming—it will be able to "make judgments" and "learn," and will be used for a wide range of assembly chores. Most significantly, it will probably be mobile.[17]

Third-generation industrial robots will be the great reconcilers between the two divergent trends of robotics in factories and laboratories. Already, the trend is evident. The 1980s has witnessed an explosion in automated guided vehicle (AGV) technology for industry. Originally these robot carts simply followed magnetic tape or wires buried in the floor to reach their destinations. Now, some of the most sophisticated models use infrared and ultrasound to navigate their surroundings, which they compare with maps of the factory layout in their computer memories. They are, in a sense, a

Shinko Electric's latest AGV: the AVH 0.5, an intelligent, autonomous robot, is equipped with sonar sensors for navigation and has a manipulator arm to load and unload items for transport to other stations in the factory.

type of autonomous robot. In Japan, the U.S., and Europe, some have also been outfitted with manipulators, or industrial robot arms. Mobile and dexterous, they look more like "real robots" and combine the twin themes of manipulation and locomotion.

In the larger sense, robot research in both industry and in universities involves understanding exactly what sort of world we live in, what really happens when we "see" or "hear" something, and how it is that we really make simple, common-sense decisions in our heads. It is the ultimate introspective art: an attempt to simulate our world and a fusion of all technologies. Someday some robots may be anthropomorphic, but probably most will not. Only one thing is clear now. At present, even when equipped with advanced sensors, artificial intelligence, and crude forms of locomotion, most robots are best at those jobs humans are worst at—dangerous, boring, repetitive, fanatically specialized jobs. Conversely, they are still incompetent at some of the simplest tasks for humans—things like picking one of a random assortment of parts out of a bin, wiggling a stiff bolt into a hole, frying an egg in the morning, or walking across a crowded street to buy a newspaper.

In trying to define current robots, we face problems shared by all emerging technologies. Is a simple photocell that detects a shopper and activates a supermarket door artificial "vision"? Do "artificial intelligence" programs really have "artificial intelligence," or are they only user friendly? The debates rage on, but with one difference for robots—the high expectations we hold for them, thanks to Karel Capek and others. To some people a robot is a metal man on the screen, or a transforming toy; to others it is an iron arm or a mobile robot; to some it is a vending machine; to some it is a space craft. Whatever robots are, and whatever they become, they will be hard to define. And it may be best not to try too hard; like children outgrowing their clothes, robots will evolve out of any definitions we give them.

Before Industrial Robots:
A State of Mind

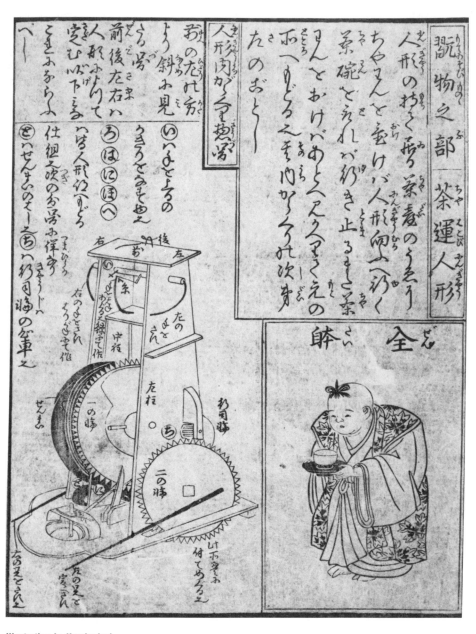

翫物之部　茶運人形

人形の持くるゝ茶盤の上へ
ちやわんを置けば人形向ふへ行く
茶碗と取ればいふ人形向ふへ行く
茶碗をとればそれが好き止るさて茶
碗をあげべあともへんくまくえの
所へもどるこゝを内からくるれ次身
たのおとし

人形肉がらゝ熱湯

一、いよとよろの
　うきろをのきて之
二、ろはにほへ
　いはゝ人形かうもどろ
　人形ふたりて
　竞むべし下ゝ
二、仕廻之次の分房に体守
二、いせきものうまち一ゝ約司海の

齢のたれ方
より斜み見
ちや男

前後左右
人形ふたりて
竞むべし下ゝ
之ことふくらふ
べ一

Illustration in *Karakurizui*.
The tea-carrying doll and
its inner mechanism.

The First
Japanese Robot

*Every tool has a
genealogy.*

NORBERT WIENER, 1950

When asked about the origins of their nation's interest in robots, many Japanese refer to a seventeenth-century mechanical doll. Its image—that of a kimono-clad boy servant carrying a cup of tea—is used today in advertisements for factory automation, and a replica of the original is on display at the National Science Museum in Tokyo. Dolls are an important part of Japanese culture and even merit a special holiday, but this one has become a national technological monument.

The tea-carrying doll is called a *karakuri* in Japanese, a "gadget" or "mechanism." It is really an automaton—a self-operating machine—and a type of robot. Fourteen inches high, when wound up and aimed properly it will "walk" toward a person while bearing a cup of tea and nodding its head. When the recipient lifts the cup from its hands to drink, the doll will stop and wait until the cup is replaced. Then it will about-face and carry the cup back to its starting point.

Automata are by no means unique to Japan or the eighteenth century. Norbert Wiener, for example, saw automata as part of a cybernetic continuum in Western civilization that stretched from the artificial men of legend to steam engines in the nineteenth century and to the computers we enjoy today. As he observed, " the ability of the artificer to produce a working simulacrum of a living organism has always intrigued people. This desire to produce and study automata has always been expressed in terms of the living technique of the age."[1]

In the beginning there were legends and magic. It is said that Daedalus, the father of Icarus, devised lifelike, mechanical moving statues. Then there were "real" automata. Hero

55

自動化の原点

ユーザーサイドに立った
高性能システムとして
いま、大きな反響を呼んでいます。

Process ＝工　程
Automation ＝自動化
Management＝管　理

株式会社
芙蓉情報センター
FUYO
●お問い合せは ─ 03(461)6384・6124

〈セミコン・ジャパン出展〉 晴海3号館3-242 12/4・木～12/6・土

COMETS-PAM

Fuyo Information Center's advertisement for a factory automation system shows the tea-carrying doll superimposed on a wafer of integrated circuits.

of Alexandria's "Treatise on Pneumatics," written in the first century A.D., described how pneumatics, counterweights, and cams could be used to construct mechanical singing birds, drinking animals, and even a type of coin vending machine. In the eighteenth century, European automata reached their zenith with the application of complex mechanisms from clock technology. Jacques de Vaucanson fascinated the entire continent with a mechanical duck that quacked, ate, and defecated. The androids of Pierre Jaquet-Droz and sons could draw, write messages, and play musical instruments and were so uncannily lifelike they are said by some to have inspired Mary Shelley to write her novel *Frankenstein*.

Compared with all this, Japan's history of automata is rather spotty. As in nearly all cultures, there are plenty of stories of magical beings in Japan; tales of mechanical dolls date back to the ninth century. But the real pinnacle of Japanese automata—the tea-carrying doll—pales in mechanical sophistication next to European automata. The Jaquet-Droz androids, for example, were engineering marvels, highly programmable, with scores of brass gears and cams. The tea-carrying doll was rather simple. Seeming to "walk," it really moved on wooden wheels under its kimono, shuffling its feet only to create a clever illusion. But it was autonomous in the sense that once it left the hands of the winder it was on its own. And rare among automata in Japan, it was equipped with a simple governor of the type used by old Japanese clocks. This controlled its speed, so that it would not dash off fully wound and slowly come to a humiliating stop. The doll was, in the classification scheme used by the JIRA today, a fixed-sequence robot. Its real sophistication and historical significance can only be understood in the context of Japan's unusual technological development.

Technology and Isolationism

Starting in the seventh century, the Japanese islands received a tremendous infusion of culture from China, the dynamic giant to the West whose civilization at that time was already over a thousand years old. Into Japan came the Buddhist religion, the Confucian social structure, a writing system, and methods of architecture, ceramics, and metallurgy. It was an aggressive period of borrowing, and Japan's refinements of what it received helped raise its primitive culture to one of great sophistication in literature, arts, and crafts. It is safe to say that when the first Europeans—three Portuguese adventurers—arrived on the Japanese island of Tanegashima in 1543, they encountered a civilization whose level of technology in many crafts and industries, such as sword making and ceramics, was superior to that of the civilization they had left behind. Major exceptions to this were the scientific advances achieved in the West during the Renaissance, and the technology of guns and clocks.

Gun manufacturing was easy and was soon mastered by Japanese craftsmen. Clocks represented a far more sophisticated technology. St. Francis Xavier, the Spanish Jesuit missionary, is said to have introduced the first mechanical timepiece into Japan in 1551 when he presented one to a local lord as part of an application to open a mission. When Japanese craftsmen saw it and other such mechanisms, their jaws must have dropped. They had absorbed basic mechanical principles and devices such as levers, pulleys, and simple springs from China, but "when [they] opened these clocks, they saw for the first time in their lives the elements of a perfectly automatic mechanism, with a wound spring, gears, cams, crankshafts, and a control device such as a governor in the form of a crown-type escapement with a balance."[2]

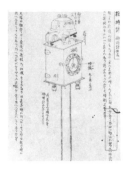

Illustration in *Karakurizui*. A seventeenth-century weight-driven Japanese wall clock, with a single-handed dial, a bell, and a single balance mounted on top. The clock had to be set once in the morning and once at night.

Thousands of Japanese-made guns, meanwhile, were employed by warlords to slaughter their enemies and, in 1590, to finally unify a land long wracked by civil war. But soon after, in 1639, the Tokugawa shogunate (the winners) proclaimed a policy of national isolation, fearing both Portuguese and Spanish encroachment and the divisiveness of Christianity. Except for a tiny amount of trade with the Dutch and the Chinese on the island of Dejima in the southern port of Nagasaki, all contact with the outside world was severed. Japanese were prohibited from leaving Japan or re-entering, on pain of death. Christianity was violently eradicated, and a rigid class system was established. In a quirk of history possible only in an island nation, over the next quarter-millennium of peace that ensued the use and manufacture of guns was essentially abandoned. Isolation would have a profound and lasting effect on the relationship of Japanese people to technology.

After 1639 the only Western clocks Japanese craftsmen saw were the few that trickled up from the limited trading allowed with the "southern barbarians" at Dejima. By and large they were forced to make their own. At first Japanese clocks were mere copies of those from the West, but because of isolation several differences soon appeared in both their design and their contribution to technological development.

On the other side of the world, in Europe, clocks quickly advanced in precision and accuracy, driven by rivalries among nations for control of the seas. Open sea navigation required comparing local time with a standard time such as Greenwich time, using either chronometers or mathematical tables of the motion of the moon. As Norbert Wiener notes,

> the advance guard of the craftsmen of the industrial revolution consisted of clockmakers, who used the new mathematics of Newton in the design of their pendulums and balance wheels, and optical instrument makers, with sextants and telescopes. . . . Both demanded accurate circles and straight lines, and graduation of these into degrees and or inches. Their tools were the lathe and the dividing engine. These machines for delicate work are the ancestors of our whole machine tool industry of the present day.[3]

Japan, however, no longer permitted travel to foreign nations, and therefore had no need for such accuracy. And although today it is the world's most time-obsessed nation, and the world's largest exporter of clocks, until 1872 it did not even tell time the same way as in the West. Instead of twenty-

EARLY ROBOT LEGENDS IN JAPAN

As in the rest of the world, the first robots in Japan were not mechanical. According to the *Senjusho*, a twelfth-century collection of stories, the famous Buddhist priest Saigyo used magic to recreate a deceased friend whom he badly missed. But the result was imperfect. Saigyo consulted with a local wizard named Moronaka, who told him he had already created several perfect human clones, some of whom, unknown to anyone, were famous political figures of the day. The thought of this was so unnerving that Saigyo abandoned his attempt.

One of the oldest references to "mechanical" automata in Japan appears in the early-twelfth-century *Konjaku monogatari-shu* ("Collection of Tales of Long Ago"). In the ninth century, it says, the local rice paddies dried up during a drought. A clever prince named Kaya created a four-foot-tall child-doll and placed it in the fields. The doll held a bowl in its hands and when water was placed in the bowl the doll would lift it and pour it over its face. This so fascinated people that they came from all over Kyoto bearing water to pour in the bowl. Thus the fields were saved.

---

four hours of equal length, the Japanese used a Chinese system that divided day and night each into six equal segments that therefore varied by season, an hour in the summer obviously considerably longer than an hour in the winter. To accommodate this mathematical nightmare, Japanese craftsmen deliberately improvised mechanisms that had to be adjusted each morning and night in a complex and difficult procedure. They did develop creative and unusual designs using the materials available to them, but in the long run they were pursuing a technological deadend. And only much later did they ever learn how to make wound steel springs (most of their clocks were powered by weights, and even sand). Because Japanese clocks were so complex and expensive, they remained largely in the hands of the rich and titled.

An eighteenth-century print of a Takeda *karakuri* show in *Dai Karakuri-ezukushi* ("The Great Picture Book of Automata"). Dolls balance on tightropes and draw Chinese characters with hands and mouth at the same time.

As in the West, many clock technicians in Japan also turned to the manufacture of *karakuri*, or automata. Omi Takeda, for example, began giving shows using automata in the bawdy entertainment district of Osaka in 1662, and his family continued the tradition for nearly a century, making "Takeda *karakuri*" famous far and wide. Records show that some of the dolls were quite sophisticated and used clock mechanisms, weights, water, and sand power. An account of a Takeda family show from around 1750 reveals it as being very much a spectacle. In between live acts, mechanical carp jumped out of the water; dolls shot darts from blow pipes at fans, simultaneously wrote characters holding one brush in the mouth and one in each hand, climbed ladders, and even urinated on stage.

Takeda also made a tea-carrying doll. The famous poet and eroticist Saikaku Ihara, in a 1675 work, has left us a

Shobe-e Tamaya's exact replica of the tea-carrying doll with a baleen spring, minus costume.

description of it. Noting that Takeda had mastered the "wisdom of the Chinese," and that the doll used a cleverly fashioned "wound spring with wheels," he states that "when given a cup of tea, and pointed toward someone, in the way it moves its eyes, mouth, and legs, and holds out its hands and bends its body, it looks just like a human."[4]

The Quest for a True Tea-Carrying Doll

Were it not for a late-eighteenth-century *karakuri* manual and a Tokyo professor, the tea-bearing doll Saikaku described might have been relegated to myth; the original has long since vanished.

The manual, called *Karakurizui*, or "Sketches of Automata," was written by Yorinao (Hanzo) Hosokawa in 1796 and still survives today because it was printed in quantity with woodblocks. It consists of a set of three bound volumes, with descriptions of how to make various types of Japanese clocks and, using some of the same technologies, nine types of automata, including a doll with a mercury mechanism that does somersaults, a wind-up doll that beats a drum and plays a flute, and the tea-carrying doll.

In several lavishly illustrated pages Hosokawa carefully described the tea doll's parts—including the propulsion gear, spring mechanism, ratchets, steering mechanism, and all-important governor—and he showed how to assemble and dress it. Although Japanese artists had never fully mastered the art of perspective, Hosokawa illustrated his book—like today's manuals—with frontal views and three-quarter views and labeled the parts with numbers and general dimensions. In keeping with the level of technology available, however, except for the metal parts in the governor mechanism, everything in his designs was of wood; the frame was of cherry, and gears used laminated oak and Japanese cedar for strength. Clocks at the time sometimes contained simple half-turn screws, but the Japanese had never mastered the art of making true ones, so Hosokawa's doll was put together with wooden pins. Late-eighteenth-century Japanese also did not know how to make wound steel springs, and fashioned them from baleen, or "whale whiskers," instead.

In the early 1960s, Shoji Tatsukawa, then lecturing on the history of Japanese science at Waseda University in Tokyo, became obsessed with Hosokawa's manual and the tea-carrying doll described therein. *Karakurizui* was remarkable, he felt, because it was a textbook at a time when most technological information was transmitted in Japan by word of mouth or as a trade secret, from father to son and from master to apprentice. "It could be said," he later wrote, "that Hosokawa was merely an ancestor of today's toy designers. But since *karakuri* at the time represented the pinnacle of precision mechanisms in Japan, a more appropriate analogy for the book—only exaggerating slightly—would be a blueprint for a computer."

While acknowledging that the pitch of the gears, the precision of the teeth, the energy of the spring, and the governor's speed were not mathematically calculated as they would have been today, Tatsukawa nevertheless considered the doll important for the way the parts were put together, and for what they did. "It had simple elements of self-control, or sequential control," he wrote, "in that it could start, stop, and proceed a fixed distance and turn, and return, and it incorporated a governor to run at a fixed speed. . . . Its use, furthermore, of a cam and spring rather than a bevel gear to solve the difficult problem of changing directions is a truly brilliant idea."[5]

Tatsukawa's fascination with the tea-carrying doll led him to scour Japan in a quest for one that fit Hosokawa's specifications. Ultimately he was unsuccessful. Despite the fact that hundreds were made during the Edo, or Tokugawa, period (1600–1867), those surviving were all in poor condition, lacked all of the original functions, or were of such recent vintage that they used European mechanisms. The next step, therefore, was to make one himself.

First, Tatsukawa presented an abstract exercise to students in the computer science and automatic control course of his university's mechanical engineering department. He asked them to design an automaton, using components similar to the tea doll, that would perform similar functions. The students were not allowed to look at the original manual. "Some people failed right away," Tatsukawa says, "confounded by the problem of making the legs move alternately. All were caught up in the problem of turning and regulating speed. Most failed because they were thinking in too complex a fashion." Then in 1967 he and six undergraduates attempted to replicate the doll exactly according to the specifications in *Karakurizui*. After two months of work and many problems getting the wooden gears to mesh properly, they

Shoji Tatsukawa in 1986, proudly showing the tea-carrying doll he and his students made in 1967.

finally succeeded, with one major compromise. Unable to obtain baleen for the spring, they used steel.[6]

Until Tatsukawa's experiment, few people had ever heard of the tea-carrying doll—in the rush to modernize, much of Japan's traditional culture had been ignored, even forgotten—but this success created a sensation. On May 17 the evening edition of the *Nihon keizai* newspaper, Japan's equivalent of the *Wall Street Journal*, headlined an article on the project with the words "Successful Recreation of a Robot from the Edo Period—A Pure Japanese Doll That Moves." The very next day, Tatsukawa and his students also appeared on a television program to demonstrate the doll. As it clattered across the table bearing its cup of tea in front of millions, its fame was assured.

———

Today, a perfect replica of the original tea-carrying doll can be purchased in Japan for around ¥3 million ($20,000). In 1969 an acquaintance of Tatsukawa's from Tokyo Metropolitan University approached Shobe-e Tamaya, an elderly craftsman in Nagoya city, and asked him to revive an old tradition and recreate the tea-carrying doll exactly. Tamaya was the

A MODERN AUTOMATA ARTIST

Shunichi Mizuno, the president of Cybot, Inc., is a modern-day automata creator in the European tradition—but in Japan. Mizuno makes what he calls "cybots," or "cybernetic robots," which are not for industry or research but for display. Appropriately, his background is in both electronics engineering and animated storefront displays. His goal is to create robots that, with emotional expressions, are as lifelike as possible. "I want to see how close I can get to a human using cybernetics," he says. The ultimate expression of humanity, he believes, is eroticism, and eroticizing the machine therefore "will be essen-tial for the coexistence of man and machine in the future." One of Mizuno's most famous robots is Marilyn Monroe, seated and playing a guitar. Ironically, Mizuno has often been frustrated in converting people to his viewpoint in Japan. Like roboticist Ichiro Kato, he believes that Japanese people favor the world of deformation and the softening of reality as seen in Japan's traditional theater and arts. As a result the Japanese public often find his dolls too realistic and unnerving. Westerners and even the Taiwanese, says Mizuno, have been far more appreciative of what he is trying to do.

perfect choice. The seventh generation in a family of doll and mask makers, his ancestors at one time had made tea-carrying dolls, and, more importantly, he was still repairing many *karakuri* with similar mechanisms.

"My ancestors," says a proud Tamaya today, "were originally doll makers, but they learned how to incorporate clock mechanisms from Tsukezaiemon Tsuda." In 1598 Tsuda had repaired a prized Western clock belonging to the warlord Ieyasu Tokugawa—later to become shogun—and, based on that experience, produced a successful copy of it, the first in Japan. For his service he was rewarded with the post of official clock maker in the Nagoya area, where he taught clocks and their mechanisms to his assistants, among whom he would divide the labor. "In those days," says Tamaya, "the best materials were used and improved upon, both in our clocks and our dolls. The hands, heads, the neck, and the mechanisms were all made by specialists. Only later, after demand for the dolls declined, did a single craftsman take charge of the whole process."[7]

Shobe-e Tamaya with a spring-driven *karakuri* doll made by his ancestors over 250 years ago and still used in religious festivals today.

Over the centuries, the art of making tea-carrying dolls was lost as wealthy patrons sought other diversions and as Takeda-style spectacles fell out of favor. But dolls with similar mechanisms survived, not as playthings for the rich but as part of the many religious festivals and fairs enjoyed by the masses. Today, in towns near Nagoya, such as Takayama in Gifu Prefecture, for example, neighborhood associations still maintain huge wheeled floats called *dashi* that twice a year are pulled through the streets by crowds of chanting men. Elaborate dolls on the floats perform for the crowds, manipu-

At a festival in Hida, Takayama, a spring-driven automaton swings through the air on a trapeze while another watches.

lated by teams of men handling a complex array of strings. Unlike Western marionettes, the strings are all contained inside the doll bodies, and the men stand not above, but below them. Many of the dolls, moreover, have extremely complicated joints and movements. A few called *hanare kara-kuri*, or "free automata," delight the audience by swinging from a series of trapezes, landing on the shoulders of other dolls, and beating drums—all without the aid of strings. These dolls are the direct descendants of eighteenth-century Takeda *karakuri*, and some use spring mechanisms nearly identical to the tea-carrying doll's.

Using his own experience, Hosokawa's *Karakurizui*, and lessons learned from Tatsukawa's experiment, Tamaya was able to craft the tea-carrying doll and others in the manual exactly, and to relearn what his family once knew. Since 1969 Tamaya has only made about ten tea dolls. These are scattered around Japan, except for one that was presented to Mayor Tom Bradley of Los Angeles in 1979 as a gift from the sister city of Nagoya. The small number of dolls and their $20,000 price tag reflect painstaking craftsmanship and the cost of rare materials. Tamaya, unlike Tatsukawa, uses real baleen for the wound spring. This comes from Right whales, currently protected by a 1936 treaty to which Japan is a signatory; it is therefore obtainable today only from beached animals or from pre-1936 materials. One sheet of baleen costs nearly $3,000, and only around five strips can be cut from it to fashion springs.

At sixty-three, with his face heavily lined from hard work and heavy smoking, Tamaya is the only person in Japan making true copies of the tea-carrying dolls and other automata listed in *Karakurizui*. In the tradition of Japanese craftsmen, he will keep making them as long as he can and then be succeeded by his sons, who will make them exactly as he does. The way this tradition has been restored after a century-long interruption symbolizes a major difference between the automata of East and West.

In Europe many of the makers of automata also applied their talents to industry. Vaucanson, who created the famous duck that digested its food, devoted the later part of his life to making useful machinery, such as programmable looms, and thus influenced not only the industrial revolution but even the computer revolution. Rechsteiner, another mechanician who later tried to duplicate Vaucanson's duck, went on to develop machines for making screws. In seventeenth- and eighteenth-century Europe, automata were also intrinsically linked with the quest for knowledge. In their steady progression toward more realism and complexity, at the extreme they represented an attempt to replicate life itself.

In isolated Japan, the technology for both clocks and automata evolved to a certain point and then stopped. Roboticist Ichiro Kato, writing about *karakuri* in 1982 in an engineering journal, contrasts the little tea-carrying doll with the automata of Europe, especially with an uncannily real piano-playing android woman created by Jaquet-Droz and sons. Unlike Europe, he concludes, the technology for automata in Japan fused into art, rather than representing a quest for more scientific knowledge. Extrapolating, he suggests that like the masked theater of Noh, this reflects both the Japanese love of the abstract, or deformation in art, as opposed to the Western emphasis on realism.[8]

Kato also mentions how in the Confucian mood of the day, social behavior was emphasized over technological prowess. During the Edo period Japan was governed by a ruthlessly totalitarian feudal regime. Society was rigidly stratified into four classes—warriors at the top, followed by farmers, craftsmen, and merchants. Feudal authority, which depended on a static social structure for its survival, abhorred radical change. Technology and mechanisms, especially things that moved, could be a threat in the wrong hands. Yet the government could not control everything. *Karakuri* masters, who began by developing entertaining spectacles for the masses and exotica for the rich, survived in between the cracks of a social structure that creaked with contradictions.

Why, though, if *karakuri* became only a form of art and entertainment, are they given so much attention in Japan today? Tatsukawa, the professor partly responsible for re-popularizing them, suggests that modern people, being surrounded by cold, impersonal machines, long for technology with a more human face. The cute, simple *karakuri* help satisfy this craving. He also notes that since our computer age has made us reliant on millions of automatic and mechatronic devices, there is an overpowering interest in simple, easy-to-understand automatic and autonomous mechanisms. Finally, he points out how Japanese "used to think that automata only existed in Europe. Realizing that Japan also had this technological capability in the Edo period has increased interest, because *karakuri* can be seen as a point where Japan's machine civilization began."[9]

The Roots of Modern Japanese Technology

When Commodore Perry and his fleet steamed into Uraga Bay in 1853, demanding trading rights at the point of a gun, Japan's nearly two hundred and fifty years of isolation was effectively ended. Perry found a quaint feudal nation that had seemingly been evolving at its own pace and had entirely missed the industrial revolution of the West. Japan was nearly devoid of sophisticated mechanisms.

Japan in 1853 had simple spinning wheels, a few Archimedean screw pumps for irrigating fields, some wheeled carts for transport on superb roads, and a few mostly wooden mechanisms. But there were no telegraphs, trains, steamships, or stage coaches (or even, for security reasons, many bridges), and there were no screws. Large ships that could navigate open seas were banned; transportation overland was mostly by foot. Guns had nearly disappeared, and those that were left were antique matchlocks (Japan had never learned how to make flintlocks, let alone cartridge-firing rifles). The main weapon was still the sword, and the old-fashioned brass (as opposed to iron) cannon. And mining technologies, so critical to the industrial revolution in the West, were primitive.

When the new technologies were first introduced, the gap between Japan and the West was almost humorous. As the stories go, people removed their sandals—in accordance

YORINAO HOSOKAWA ON INVENTIONS AND LEARNING FROM THE WEST

In the introduction to *Karakurizui*, a 1796 Japanese manual of automata, author Yorinao (Hanzo) Hosokawa advises budding inventors to carefully observe the natural world around them. "The rudder, for example, was made by observing the action of a fish tail; oars were created by observing the sideways motion of its fins. Zhuge Liang [a second-century Chinese politician] observed the doll that his wife made and created an automatic ox-cart. Omi Takeda observed children playing with sand and used the idea to power his mechanisms." Hosokawa was clearly influenced by Chinese ideas, but he was not in favor of all foreign ways. The Confucian scholar Jozan Yuasa (1708–81), records him as warning that "while Western calendrical sciences and mathematics are worthy of learning, one should avoid the ways of the red hairs [i.e., the Westerners]."

---

with custom on entering a house—to board the first train between Yokohama and Tokyo and were shocked when they arrived without them; two-sworded samurai, fearing they might lose their souls, shielded themselves when they encountered the first electric lights; and when telegraph lines were strung between Tokyo and Nagasaki, there were attacks on construction crews and rumors that it was a Christian plot, that the blood of virgins would be spread on the wires.

But more than anything else, the technology gap was a national humiliation to a proud people, and it triggered a political, social, and economic revolution—the downfall of the Tokugawa shogunate in 1867, the end of the feudal system, the end of Japan's self-sufficiency, and the beginning of a madcap race to catch up to and surpass the technology of the West, a race that continues to this day. Humiliation is one of the most powerful teachers of the human psyche, and in this case the lesson driven home in the minds of many intellectuals was that technology is a type of power.

In 1905, only fifty-two years after Perry arrived in Japan, Japanese soldiers armed with the latest weaponry and Japanese sailors manning modern battleships trounced Imperial Russia in a modern war. The world, especially the European world, was stunned. Overnight it seemed a tiny feudal Asian land had become an industrialized nation, and had smashed the technological hegemony of the white colonialist powers. How could this have happened?

One of the first of only a few Westerners to see Japan's potential behind its feudal veil—British envoy Sir Rutherford Alcock—arrived in 1859. Swallowing his national and racial pride, he conceded that "but for the fact that their mechanical

Hisashige Tanaka in his later years.

appliances are inferior, as well as their knowledge of the applied sciences connected with mechanical industry and arts, they may rightly claim a place with nations of European race." Moreover, if the shogunate adopted a more open policy, he foresaw a day when Japan would use its cheaper labor and ingenuity to compete equally with England in trade, "not withstanding all our advantages of funded knowledge and civilization of a higher order—our stream and river machinery, and the marvelous perfection to which all mechanical appliances have been brought."[10]

At least one Japanese already knew quite a bit about mechanisms. In 1867, the year the shogunate collapsed, British interpreter Ernest Satow visited Nagasaki, where he took part in a typical Japanese evening of eating and drunken carousing. Somehow he remembered enough later to record in his diary his impression of a man named Hisashige Tanaka: "Originally a Kioto clockmaker, [who] had developed into a skilled mechanical engineer, and had constructed engines and boilers for a couple of Japanese steamers."[11] Tanaka was actually one of the last great *karakuri* masters. In an age when there were no universities in Japan, let alone "mechanical engineers," he had mastered basic Western mechanical principles through sheer effort. In doing so, he symbolically created a technological bridge between feudal and modern Japan.

Born in 1799 in Kurume, a town on the southern island of Kyushu, Tanaka was the son of a tortoise-shell craftsman, by birth therefore in the second class from the bottom in Japan's four-tiered social hierarchy. From his father he learned metal working. Living close to the port of Nagasaki, he may even have seen Dutch clocks, telescopes, and Leyden jars (which generated electrical shocks for "health purposes"). Like many Japanese of his time, he was literate—often children of all classes attended *teragoya*, or temple schools—and it is said that he impressed his schoolmates by making *karakuri*, particularly trick boxes. It was also a tradition in his area for people to compete in making *karakuri* as offerings to the local shrine. Perhaps aided by Hosokawa's manual, which had appeared only a few years earlier, Tanaka made saké-carrying dolls, musician dolls, and other automata powered by springs or water. In honor of his talents he was given the name Karakuri Giemon. Eventually, in the tradition of Omi Takeda, he took *karakuri* shows throughout Japan. He even began experimenting with steam to power them.

Had Tanaka simply limited himself to *karakuri* dolls, he would long ago have been forgotten. Unlike most *karakuri* masters, who were often eccentric craftsmen in a feudal technological darkness, Tanaka went on to become a Japanese Thomas Alva Edison. At twenty-one he improvised an air gun of Dutch type, and at twenty-five he invented a pocket-size lamp for travelers. Later, using technology from his air gun, he also invented an "endless" oil lamp that used compressed air to keep the sticky vegetable oil burning as it went up the lamp wick. He built a type of fire extinguisher, and some say he may have made the first wound steel spring in Japan.[12]

A replica of a *karakuri* doll that pushes a cup of saké toward a drinker; made by Hisashige Tanaka and displayed at the Toshiba Science Institute.

Not all of his creations were practical. Moving to the Kyoto–Osaka area, in 1847 he began making clocks of increasing complexity and even developed a miniature "planetarium" based on the prevailing Buddhist theory that the sun revolved around the earth, instead of the reverse. Then in 1851 he made what was perhaps the last significant "Japanese" clock—the Mannendokei, or "Eternal Clock," an enormously complex but precise contraption with six faces that told, among other things, Japanese time, Western time, the phase of the moon, the day, and the date. On top it had a glass dome, inside of which the sun and moon revolved over a map of Japan. Once wound, Tanaka's clock would run for 225 days.

In contrast to another *karakuri* master of the time, Benkichi Ono, who depended on a wealthy merchant patron for survival and was then ruined when his master was thrown in jail, Tanaka became a technical and commercial success and enjoyed an independent livelihood. In part this was possible because of the times. In the early nineteenth century, Japan's highly static feudal society was groaning at the seams. Whereas mobility was legally very restricted, Tanaka was able to travel widely and sell his products to the newly monied urban class. With sales from clocks and toylike *karakuri*, he could finance other ventures and even form his own company.

Tanaka's curiosity, moreover, eventually led him to Western technology. Even during Japan's isolation, it was impossible to keep out all information from the West. Some intellectuals advocated *wakon-yosai*, or "Japanese spirit—Western learning," which asserted the superiority of Japanese race and spirit but acknowledged the merits of "barbarian" technology. The *rangakusha*, or "Dutch Scholars," painstakingly translated books obtained from the Dutch at Nagasaki and tried to absorb the wonders they saw within, particularly in medicine. At the official Bureau of Astronomy, others studied Western calendars and translated books to help in observance of eclipses. Tanaka, despite his class, studied under a local astronomy master and from the *rangakusha* in particular gleaned as much information as possible on Western technology. His efforts paid off when, in 1852, he reportedly used a Dutch reference book to build a model steamship before ever seeing a real one.[13]

Toward the end of the Edo period, the wheel of history really began to turn in Tanaka's favor as Western technology came to be seen as a threat by many leaders. Despite isolation, news had reached Japan of the Opium War in China in 1839 and of the West's carving up of that once-great nation. And near Nagasaki, one could occasionally see the cast iron cannons and steamships of the Dutch. Later, even die-hard samurai, who thought the "southern barbarians" could be repelled with Japanese swords and "spirit," were convinced when in 1864 British, French, Dutch, and American warships bombarded the town of Shimonoseki.

Japan needed desperately to arm itself, both on land and sea, but to do so it had to to obtain machine tools and master Western navigation, mathematics, and physics, and it needed to do all these things in a hurry. Perry's visit was therefore followed by a massive infusion of Western expertise and technology, but there was a critical need for Japanese who could make sense of it. Because of its years of isolation, Japan in effect had to "reverse engineer" the achievements of Western science and technology, taking apart machines, rebuilding them, and copying them in order to learn. In these circumstances, the *rangakusha*, the scholars from the Bureau of Astronomy, and anyone with mechanical skills such as Tanaka's became instant stars.

At age fifty-five, in 1854, one year after Perry arrived, Tanaka was invited to Saga, a technologically progressive fiefdom near Nagasaki that had built Japan's first reverberatory furnace and had also realized the critical need to develop steel cannon, better gunpowder, and steam warships to navigate the open seas. Along with two other guest experts—a *rangakusha* and a chemist—Tanaka presided over a sort of research laboratory, where he was able to try his hand at the manufacture of ammunition and a model of a steam ship, at telegraphy, and even at photography. In addition, he

MURDER IN THE DOLL HOUSE

A 1969 whodunnit film, *Midare Karakuri* (with the English title *Murder in the Doll House*) incorporated both a tea-carrying doll and historical fact. In the story, members of a wealthy family who own a toy company are being killed one by one. Among the victims is a collector of old dolls, including a tea-carrying doll. While demonstrating the doll, he is jabbed and poisoned by a hypodermic hidden in its mechanism. A private eye (played by Yusaka Matsudo) hired to solve the murders investigates the doll's history and discovers it had been made by Benkichi Ono (1801–81), an actual *karakuri* craftsman who

lived in the city of Kanazawa in western Japan. Benkichi's patron was a merchant named Zeniya Gobe-e (1773–1852), who had made a fortune by smuggling. In 1852 Zeniya was accused of poisoning the local water supply and was crucified along with his family, thus ending Benkichi's career as an inventor. The movie cleverly ties this true story into the plot by imagining that Zeniya's fortune lay hidden in a special trick labyrinth beneath the toy-making family's house, which had been designed by a former disciple of Benkichi. Shoji Tatsukawa, a *karakuri* expert, worked as a consultant on the film.

worked in the port of Nagasaki at a new Naval Training Center, the incubator for Japan's first navy and another focal point for the latest Western technology.

Shortly after arriving in 1859, envoy Alcock visited Japan's first steam engine repair factory, which was associated with the center, and was astounded. Although the Japanese were under the tutelage of the Dutch, he writes,

> we saw one of the most extraordinary and crowning testimonies of Japanese enterprise and ingenuity, which leaves all the Chinese have ever attempted far behind. I allude to a steam-engine with tubular boilers, made by themselves before a steam-vessel or engine had ever been seen by Japanese; made solely, therefore, from the plans in a Dutch work. This engine was not only put together, but made to work a boat. . . . [It is] worthy of being preserved as a national monument of Japanese capacity and enterprise.[14]

Tanaka later went on to supervise construction of a small paddle-wheel steamer and to oversee boiler repairs and construction for other ships, and cannon building as well. But his pursuit of technical knowledge did not stop at heavy industry. At seventy, after the feudal government fell and Japan began modernizing, Tanaka began experimenting with ice makers, bicycles, and even rickshaws. In 1873 he moved to Tokyo to study telegraphy. In the Ginza he formed a company, Tanaka Seizojo, to manufacture and repair telegraph equipment, putting up a sign that boldly announced, "Orders Taken for Design of Any and All Machines." In the later years of his life, when asked to make a *karakuri* doll for a street performer, he is said to have replied, "We have civi-

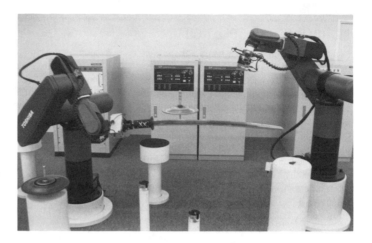

A modern *karakuri* spectacle: at the Toshiba Science Institute, vision-equipped industrial robots put on a show with swords and spinning tops.

lized gadgets all around us that use *karakuri* principles; dolls alone will no longer attract a crowd."[15]

What was Tanaka's real significance? In a global context he may not have been a creative genius. But like the dolls he once made, he symbolizes the larger relationship between Japan and technology. As Kenji Imazu, his foremost biographer, notes, feudal Japan was an airplane ready to take off, lacking only wings. The wings were the two critical technologies for the industrial revolution: navigation-inspired clock technologies and mining-derived waterwheels and steam engines. Tanaka, with no formal training, symbolized the ability of a nation without an industrial base and scientific skills to absorb and internalize these technologies.[16] Since he was not a member of the ruling elite, he also symbolized, along with the dolls, a grassroots infatuation with technology and mechanisms that smoldered throughout two hundred and fifty years of isolation.

Although Tanaka never lived to see it, his Tokyo firm was the seed that would eventually sprout into Toshiba, Japan's second largest electric and electronics manufacturer—and the fourth largest maker of industrial robots. At a conference room at the Toshiba Manufacturing Engineering Laboratory today, nearly everything in the room including the television, video cassette recorder, and electronic-copier blackboard is made by Toshiba with the help of Toshiba robots. Conspicuously displayed in a glass case, however, is one of Shobe-e Tamaya's hand-crafted replicas of the seventeenth-century tea-carrying doll.

Robots of the Imagination

*Science fiction
masterpieces in Japanese
comics and animation
. . . planted the idea of
robots as friends in the
minds of young Japanese
and helped create the
psychological conditions
for the current explosion
of [industrial] robots in
the "Robot Kingdom."*

GOVERNMENT SCIENTIST
EIJI NAKANO

Science fiction robots began appearing in Japanese literature shortly after the Tokyo performance of Capek's *R.U.R.* in 1924, but they did not capture the public imagination the way they did in the West. Perhaps it was just as well. Before World War II, most robot science fiction in the West adhered to the formula "man makes robot, robot kills man." In Japan, the most popular robot stories and characters have been visual and, instead of novels, have emerged mainly from postwar comics and animation. As a result they have also had far greater influence.

Comics, once mainly for children, now are read by nearly all ages and comprise nearly 30 percent of all printed matter in Japan; several robot characters created in them have become icons of popular culture. Similarly, since 1963 more than one hundred serialized robot animated shows for television (not to mention movie theaters) have been produced.[1] Unlike the humble *karakuri* dolls of feudal Japan, these imaginary robots are an exuberant assertion of a collective technological fantasy.

One of the first prewar "robot" characters in Japan was Tanku Tankuro, the hero of a children's comic story (with the same name) created by artist Masaki Sakamoto in 1934. A pseudorobot, Tanku's human head sat atop a cast iron body that looked like a bowling ball with eight holes. He operated on what seemed to be magic, and readers never knew what he would pull out of the holes in his body. Sometimes he waved swords or guns, at other times he sprouted wings and a propeller and transformed into an airplane or even a tank. He was drawn in a naive style and given an endearing personality, and when he fought he was always on the side of good (Japan). Often he was involved in wars, which reflected the climate of the times.

At Kyodo Printing, one of Japan's largest printers, industrial robots palletize magazines and comic books. Kenichi Natsume, one of the developers of the system, holds the "teach box," which operators use to program the robot.

Tanku Tankuro in an airplane configuration, in a 1935 work titled *Dai senso* ("The Great War"). © 1976 Humi Sakamoto.

Kagaku senshi Nyu Yoku ni shutsugen su ("The Science Warrior Appears in New York"), a 1943 propaganda cartoon drawn by Ryuichi Yokoyama, probably in frustration over Japan's inability to counter U.S. air raids. © 1943 R. Yokoyama.

Since the end of isolation, Japan had pursued a policy of *fukoku kyohei*, or "rich nation, strong military." To avoid being swallowed by the colonialist powers of the West, it tried to catch up to them on all levels of technology, especially military might. In the process, militarists gained control, and Japan (emulating the West) embarked on an imperialistic course in Asia, in the 1930s becoming embroiled in a war in China that eventually led to the disaster of World War II. In 1939 both Sakamoto and Tanku moved to the puppet state of Manchuria. Sakamoto worked for the Manchuria Development Agency as a cartoonist. Tanku appeared in the local newspaper.[2]

Atom and Iron Man

The most famous Japanese robot character of all time appeared in an utterly different social environment after World War II, when comics were beginning their explosive growth in popularity, when militarism was replaced by an ideology of peace, and when science and technology took on a new, civilian significance.

Tetsuwan Atomu, or "Mighty Atom" as he was called, was created by a young medical student/artist named Osamu Tezuka in 1951. He proved so popular that he went on to be serialized for eighteen years as a comic book story, starred in Japan's first animated series for television in 1963, and was then exported under the name Astro Boy. In his basic form (he changed slightly over the years) Atom was a little boy robot in a normal family—of other robots—who went to a normal school with real human children, but unlike them he had a nuclear reactor for a heart, a computer brain, searchlight eyes, rockets in his feet, and a machine gun in his tail. Instead of waging war, he fought monsters and bandits in the name of peace. He became one of the most popular fantasy heroes ever, and his image—that of an android robot with feelings that helped man—was permanently etched into the national consciousness. Japanese children had discovered a new hero: the machine.

Tezuka claims that as a youth the robot stories which influenced him most were the translated copy of *R.U.R.* he read in 1938 and the prewar works of a Japanese science fiction novelist named Juza Unno (1897–1949). Unno, called the "father of Japanese science fiction," worked in an electronics lab in the prewar Communications Ministry and wrote novels on the side, many of which had robot characters sometimes used as weapons in wars with the Chinese. He, in turn, may have been influenced not only by *R.U.R.* but by *Metropolis*, a famous German film that played in Japan and featured an evil robot character named Maria.[3]

Given these dark influences, Tezuka's robot had an extremely original, humanistic bent. In a 1986 article in the *Journal of the Robotics Society of Japan*, Tezuka explained that he created Atom to be a type of twenty-first-century reverse "Pinocchio," a nearly perfect robot who strove to become more human (i.e., emotive and illogical), and also to be an interface between two different cultures—that of man and that of machine.[4] Although Tezuka had never read American novelist Isaac Asimov, who worked hard to overturn the

Osamu Tezuka's Mighty Atom, showing his atomic reactor, computer, searchlight eyes, and other attributes. © 1950 O. Tezuka.

"evil" image of metal men in the West, his creation—Atom—was a friend of man and lived according to strict rules of robot behavior remarkably similar to Asimov's Three Laws of Robotics.

In Tezuka's story, Atom was invented by a top scientist at the National Science Agency as a replacement for a son lost in a traffic accident. Later, Tezuka placed him in a family of robots who were all androids and quite normal in most respects. This had the brilliant effect of making him immediately identifiable to all the children in Japan. Atom became the little boy next door, except he lived in the future where science and technology had created a world of clever gadgets and a standard of living that Japanese could only dream about. Furthermore, since Atom was, according to the lyrics of the animation theme song, "a child of science," over the years in the public mind, he—and robots—became linked with a wonderful future that science and technology could provide.

Tezuka claims this was not his intention at all. As a licensed physician with a strong background in the sciences, he had intended a character that was more cynical and more of a parody. But publishers, the public, and the times pushed him to a more romantic depiction of the future, and as is often the case his character took on a life of its own. "In the days after the war," says Tezuka today, "the publishers wanted me to stress a peaceful future, where Japanese science and technology were advanced and nuclear power was used for peaceful purposes. At the time, Japan was so poor that most of the patients I was treating as a medical student were suffering from malnutrition; the technological world I depicted was utterly fantastic. Since most of the technology did not yet exist, I had the freedom of drawing whatever I pleased."[5]

One result of Tezuka's science background was a great deal of pseudoscientific realism. Atom had seven special powers (sometimes the number changed), such as the ability to speak over sixty languages, but unlike the magical powers of American superheroes or earlier fantasy robots in Japan, they were all based on what seemed to be scientific electromechanical principles. Schematics of Atom's body were published, showing a maze of wires and circuitry. Sometimes, in the story, he would be damaged or malfunction and have to be repaired.

LAWS OF ROBOTS AND ROBOTICS

Isaac Asimov's Three Laws of Robotics, presented in 1942 in his short story "Runaround":

1. A robot may not injure a human being, or through inaction, allow a human being to come to harm.
2. A robot must obey the orders given it by human beings except where such orders would conflict with the First Law.
3. A robot must protect its own existence as long as such protection does not conflict with the First or Second Law.

Osamu Tezuka's Ten Principles of Robot Law from the *Mighty Atom* series:

1. Robots are created to serve mankind.
2. Robots shall never injure or kill humans.
3. Robots shall call the human that creates them "father."
4. Robots can make anything, except money.
5. Robots shall never go abroad without permission.
6. Male and female robots shall never change roles.
7. Robots shall never change their appearance or assume another identity without permission.
8. Robots created as adults shall never act as children.
9. Robots shall never assemble other robots that have been scrapped by humans.
10. Robots shall never damage human homes or tools.

Part of the pressure put on Tezuka was related to a change in attitudes to technology. The carnage wrought by technology in World War II had deepened distrust of it among many intellectuals in the West. In Japan it had a decidedly different effect. Perhaps in reaction to the adulation of all Western technology in the late nineteenth century, prewar conservative Japanese forces had convinced themselves that any technological gap between Japan and the West could be more than offset by the superiority of Japanese "spirit," a vaguely defined, antirational concept with roots in myths of Japanese racial uniqueness. It was a costly error. In a book whose translated title reads "Technoland Japan's Technology Is By Far the Most Interesting," technonationalist Takemochi Ishii, a professor at the University of Tokyo's Department of Engineering, claims that the very roots of Japanese postwar progress lie not only in political changes but in the fact that Japan was overwhelmed by being a guinea pig for Western military technology. "World War II was technological competition between nations," he writes, "like that between corporations today. Japan, which had not even fully mastered the mass production of automobiles, never had a chance." The result was a bloody lesson, pounded into the brains of every man, woman, and child.[6]

Ishii is by no means alone in his view. The emperor, in a letter to the young crown prince at the end of World War II,

An Iron Man No. 28 bicycle in Tokyo.

bared his soul and wrote that Japan had lost the war because of overconfidence and because "our armed forces put too much emphasis on the spiritual side and forgot science." Even the antiwar Tezuka was affected. "I realized very clearly that Japan lost the war because of science and technology," he says today. "While the U.S. was dropping atomic bombs, the Japanese military were trying to light forest fires in America by sending incendiary balloons made of bamboo and paper over on the jet stream. We developed an inferiority complex about science and technology."[7]

In 1956, soon after Tezuka began drawing Atom, another artist named Mitsuteru Yokoyama created a rival series starring a robot of an entirely different nature. Called Tetsujin 28go, or "Iron Man No. 28," he, like Atom, could fly through the air (with rockets on his back). But he was actually a step backward technologically. A giant metal monster (eventually "20 meters tall and weighing 25.08 tons"), his main power was his brute strength, used to kick and punch in fights. Instead of being an autonomous android endowed with artificial intelligence, he was operated by a remote-control device. Usually this was in the hands of Shotaro Kinta, a young boy "private detective" who used Iron Man to foil nefarious criminals of various sorts. If the device was stolen, Iron Man could be employed for evil ends as well. He was, in a sense, much closer to today's industrial robots than Atom. He was neither good nor bad; he was only a machine.

In 1982, in a publication called *Robotopia: The Magazine for Man & Robot Relations* (put out by the industrial giant Hitachi with the English subtitle "Mechatronics, Science & Society in Robot Age"), artist Yokoyama explained how he conceived Iron Man. He says he was influenced by three things in his youth. "One," he writes, "was the sight I saw when the war ended and I returned to [my home] Kobe from my rural evacuation site. Everything as far as I could see had been transformed into scorched earth and piles of rubble. . . . I was . . . stunned by the destructive power of war. Second was the V1 and V2 missiles that the German Nazis developed. I had heard that Hitler tried to use them as an ace in the hole to reverse his waning fortunes. The third influence was from the American movie *Frankenstein*."[8]

In the story he devised, Iron Man was given the number 28 because, like the V1 and V2 rockets, he had originally been designed by the Japanese military as a last-ditch secret weapon to reverse its sinking fortunes. All the models up to

LYRICS TO THE THEME SONG OF THE *MIGHTY ATOM* SERIES (*ASTRO BOY*)

Music by Tatsuo Takai
Lyrics by Shuntaro Tanikawa
[Translated by Author]

1. Through the sky—la la la—to the distant stars
    Goes Atom, as far as his jets will take him.
    The oh-so-gentle—la la la—child of science
    With one hundred thousand horse power, it's Mighty Atom.
2. Listen carefully—la la la—and watch out
    That's right, Atom, be on your guard.
    The pure-hearted—la la la—child of science
    With his seven powers, there goes Mighty Atom.
3. On the street corner—la la la—or at the bottom of the sea
    There's Atom again, protecting mankind.
    The oh so cheerful—la la la—child of science
    Everyone's friend, Mighty Atom.

No. 28—and the end of the war—were failures, however, so Iron Man No. 28 became a civilian robot. It is hard to imagine a robot more different from the humanistic, family-oriented Atom, but both characters resemble each other in that they were used to help mankind, and both have competed for fans until this day. Like *Mighty Atom*, *Iron Man No. 28* was serialized for years in comic magazines, and then turned into toys, picture books, records, radio shows, and television shows and exported to the United States (under the name *Gigantor*). Also like *Atom*, a new animated *Iron Man* series was created and broadcast in 1980.

Atom and Iron Man are the ancestors of all subsequent Japanese fantasy robots, particularly two distinct genres seen today—truly autonomous robots and those that require human intervention for their operation. In this sense, they parallel laboratory research trends that aim at developing advanced robots which operate on their own or by remote control. This, however, is where most similarity with the real world stops.

Autonomous Robots

A 1981 survey of robot animation (mostly based on stories first created in comic magazines) revealed that around 20 percent of the cartoon heroes fell into the category of autonomous robots.[9] The most successful of these are in the tradition of Tezuka's Atom, but by extrapolating and expanding on Atom's little-pal-next-door qualities and adding humor, several artist/writers have created robots that are cuddly

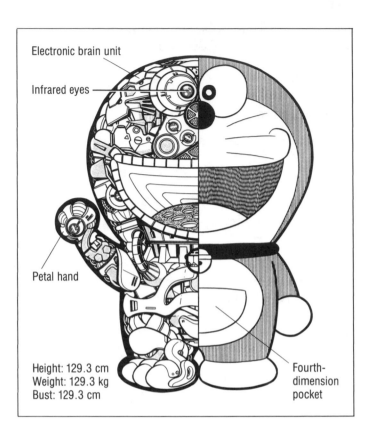

Electronic brain unit

Infrared eyes

Petal hand

Height: 129.3 cm
Weight: 129.3 kg
Bust: 129.3 cm

Fourth-
dimension
pocket

Fujiko-Fujio's Doraemon, the robot cat. © 1970 Fujiko Fujio.

machines. The influence of such characters on the national psyche far outweighs their number.

Doraemon, created by comic artists Fujiko-Fujio in 1970, is an example. A cute, endearing robot cat, Doraemon lived with a young boy named Nobita in a normal family setting, having materialized in Nobita's desk drawer one day after being sent through the fourth dimension from the twenty-second century. Nobita was rather clumsy and a poor performer in school, so much so that he had created great problems for his descendants. To correct this, his great-great-grandson sent him Doraemon, a robot cat that children of the future used as guardians. Doraemon was extremely intelligent and always looking out for Nobita's best interests, but he was of flawed construction and prone to error. Taking a hint from Tanku Tankuro of the 1930s, the artists made Doraemon a walking toy box and gave him a kangaroo-style pouch from which he could produce exciting technological gadgets, which he would share with Nobita. This always

resulted in humorous problems and proved immensely popular among young children.

Within a very short span of time Doraemon became a household word, what the Japanese call an "idol." By 1985, over fifty-five million copies of the story had been sold in paperback form; the series had been animated for television and theater; Doraemon dolls and toys were everywhere; and the original artists were millionaires.[10] In a land where space is at a premium and where animals have traditionally been few and far between, Doraemon symbolized a popular fantasy among Japanese young children—the little robot as "pet."

The same thing occurred with Arare-chan, a little girl android robot created by comic artist Akira Toriyama in 1980. Arare-chan, even more than Doraemon, achieved that rare status all creators of fantasy hope for—a character so popular it appeals to people of all ages and both genders. In the original story, Arare-chan was created by a slightly dingy inventor named Dr. Slump (also the title of the comic story). Arare-chan looked like any other little girl, except that she would occasionally take her head off at the wrong time and had difficulty controlling her herculean strength. Her appeal lay in her funny mistakes, her cuteness, and the utterly zany world of her inventor. Grammar school children as well as office workers became her fans, and in one year, with the films and merchandising that followed, her twenty-seven-year-old creator earned $2.4 million.[11]

There are, of course, scores of other autonomous gag robots found in comic magazines, animation, and cheap-special-effects TV shows. There are robot dogs, cats, birds, tape recorders, and trains—in short, something for everyone, of any age group. The most successful of these stories, however, always bring the machine into a very mundane, average Japanese environment. Because they rely on a Japanese cultural setting, and often use wild, zany Japanese humor that includes puns, scatology, and eroticism, they are the genre least well known outside of Japan.

Warrior Robots: The Man-Robot Symbiosis

The most famous, original, and prolific type of fantasy robot character in Japan is the giant warrior robot. The vast majority of these are the descendants of Iron Man No. 28 and require human intervention for their operation. The 1981 survey of robot animation shows that 73 percent of all works at the time fell into this category.[12]

The popularity of giant warrior robots in comics and animation in Japan should not be misconstrued as a love of war. Unlike the United States, where military applications have become a major theme of robotics, in Japanese laboratories scientists to a man are still steeped in peace ideology. Japan's American-authored constitution, after all, "renounces war" and— technically speaking—all "war potential." And in the world of Japanese comics, American-style "war stories" have never been very popular. In the immediate postwar period, Japanese literature, films, and even comics containing scenes that smacked of militarism or samurai warrior ethics were censored by the Occupation authorities. "Besides," as one robot artist confesses, "if we drew comics about World War II, we'd always have to show the Japanese losing, and who'd like that?"[13]

In this context science fiction and the giant robot genre of comics and animation have become a healthy outlet for the aggressive tendencies of normal young boys. Heroes—very average human beings unendowed with "superpowers" or the bulging muscles of Greek gods—battle not other actual nations but monsters and evil robots from other planets, and they augment their strength with technology, with insectoid, samurai-style machines.

————

The first major step in the evolution of the giant warrior robot genre after Iron Man No. 28 was taken by Go Nagai, an artist raised on both it and Atom. Nagai had a reputation of being a "bad boy" in the industry. In 1968 he had scandalized the country by drawing erotic comedies for children's comics

RESEARCHERS TALK ABOUT ATOM

Osamu Tezuka's *Mighty Atom* has not only influenced the general public's attitude to industrial robots; it has also motivated a younger generation of researchers.

The October 1983 issue of the scholarly *Journal of the Robotics Society of Japan* includes a debate on bipedal robots in which Ryozo Kato of Toa University comments, "We are of the Mighty Atom generation, and we were brought up looking at Atom in comics and animation, so it just seemed like it would be a great deal of fun to create something that can walk."

Similarly, the June 1986 edition of the same journal included a roundtable discussion among robot scientists and Tezuka himself on the links between Atom and the real world of robotics. Yuji Hosoda of Hitachi Ltd. was involved in the design of a rather anthropomorphic four-legged nuclear power plant robot for the Ministry of Trade and Industry. While the robot may not resemble Tezuka's creation, Hosoda notes that one goal of the design is to achieve similarly fluid motion and control.

"I have always created robots," he says, "in the belief that someday they should be like Mighty Atom."

(although by today's standards his stories would be tame). In 1969 he began developing a new robot series called *Mazinger Z*. "All the robot comics," he says, "were either like Atom—humanoid—or like Iron Man No. 28—remote controlled. I wanted to create something different, and I thought it would be interesting to have a robot that you could drive, like a car."[14]

This was not an entirely new idea. In Isaac Asimov's 1942 short story "Runaround," some of the robots are ridden like horses by men, who use the robot's "ears" to steer with. Tezuka, also, had created a story for the *Atom* series in 1954 in which robots were "driven" by people inside them. There have even been drivable robots in real life. In 1968, General Electric built a four-legged vehicle called a "walking truck" that could be driven over obstacles. But no one ever articulated the concept in visual fantasy as well as Go Nagai.

Koji Kabuto drives Mazinger Z into battle. © 1972 Go Nagai and Dynamic Pro.

In Nagai's tale, a young hero named Koji Kabuto pilots a type of hovercraft, which docks in the head of a giant robot and serves as a cockpit from which to control it. Like many other robot works, the plot revolved around fights, in this case between Mazinger Z and an assortment of monsters and evil robots, usually created by an archenemy named Dr. Hell. But the man-robot symbiosis that Mazinger Z symbolized helped solve an old problem in robot fiction—the problem of personifying the machine while still preserving its mechanical identity. When the robot became, like a car, a machine that could be jumped in and driven, it had a powerful appeal to young boys. When animated, and when toy companies began issuing faithful reproductions, the *Mazinger Z* series became a smash hit.

"Mazinger Z," says Go, "comes from the Japanese word *majin*, or 'genie.' The basic concept was of a machine that can be used for either good or evil, that when human will is transferred to it, becomes even more powerful than a human." Go admits that when a child he liked the scenes in Tezuka's series where Atom destroyed the evil, big robots. "Atom basically follows Asimov's Three Laws of Robotics," he says. "Mazinger Z inherited Atom's destructive power— he is basically a type of tank."[15]

Mazinger Z's shape was also a trend setter. Atom had simply been a little boy, and Iron Man No. 28 was a clunky metal giant distinguished mainly by his neo-European knight's helmet. Mazinger Z also incorporated a knight's visor, but was very brightly colored, and had wing- and horn-like protrusions on his helmet. The latter evoked some very Japanese images, of samurai and insects, that have become a trademark of the genre. Most Japanese artists, including Nagai, incorporate these images unconsciously. For young boys in Japan, samurai and samurai armor images have always had a romantic air about them, and so have insects. Traditionally beetles, cicadas, and fireflies have been caught, kept in cages, and played with by young boys, with horned armored beetles especially prized for their strength.

Nagai went on to create innumerable robot stories, most of which were animated for television, and he made one other major contribution to the warrior robot genre in 1974. "The toy companies," he recalls, "said they needed more characters in each story so they could sell more toys, so I complied by creating a series called *Getta Robotto*, where one hero robot disassembled into three smaller ones." This was the start of "combining robots."[16]

There remained one element to finalize the giant warrior robot genre—*henshin*, or transformation, a popular ingredient in Japanese fantasy. In Japanese myths, foxes, even cats, transform into beautiful women, and ninja warriors often transform into other entities to foil their enemies. In the comics, Shotaro Ishimori, in particular, had created many popular characters in the 1960s and 1970s who switched from one form to another, and often they were robots. *Jinzo ningen kikaida* ("Kikaida, the Artificial Man"), a series created in 1968, was an example. The hero, whose name was a contraction of *kikai* ("machine") and *raida* ("rider"), was a bell-bottomed young man who rode a slightly futuristic motorcycle with a guitar slung over his back. When danger threatened, he

JAPANESE ROBOT SHOWS AND AMERICAN TITLES

In recent years Japanese robot films have swamped the American and European television markets, accompanied by heavy merchandising of toys. In the United States, the animated shows are dubbed and so heavily edited that their origin is betrayed only by art styles, backgrounds, and a few Japanese names in the credits among long lists of American "executive producers" and "production managers." Sometimes the rights to several shows are purchased, with all of them being edited into one show upon which is overlaid an entirely different, locally produced script. Examples of dubbed series appear below, with the name in Japanese followed by its literal translation into English (where appropriate) and then by the name under which it was broadcast in the United States.

Tetsuwan Atomu ("Mighty Atom"): *Astro Boy*
Tetsujin 28go ("Iron Man No. 28"): *Gigantor*
Eitoman: *Eighth Man*
Mazinger Z: *TranZor Z*

COMBINED AS *FORCE FIVE*
Getta Robo G: *Starvengers*
UFO Robo Grendizer: *Grandizer*
Ozora Maryu Gaikingu ("Great Sky Demon-Dragon Gaiking"): *Gaiking*
Wakusei Robo Danga-do A ("Planctary Robo Dangard Ace Λ"): *Dangard Ace*
SF Saiyuki Stajinga ("Starzinger: The SF Monkey King Legend"): *Spaceketeers*

COMBINED AS *VOLTRON, DEFENDER OF THE UNIVERSE*
Hyakujuoo Goraion ("Go Lion, King of the Beasts")
Kikokantai Dairaga XV ("Armored Fleet Dairager XV")

COMBINED AS *ROBOTECH*
Chojiku Yosai Makurosu ("Super Dimension Fortress Macross")
Chojiku Kidan Sazan Kurosu ("Super Dimension Cavalry Force Southern Cross")
Kiko Soseiki Mosupida ("Armored Genesis Mospeada")

would touch both shoulders and activate a switch that transformed him into his fighting robot identity. Like many of Ishimori's stories, instead of being animated, *Kikaida* was produced as a live-action, special-effects series on television, part of a huge genre of programs where actors in rubber suits portraying good robots battle other actors in rubber suits portraying bad robots. In these films, transformation based on "mechanical principles" is obviously difficult and is therefore preceded by a ritualistic movement or dance, or by flashing lights and explosions. Often the robots are humanoids.

Because transformation is infinitely easier to depict in animation than in live action, artists have had a field day. Ever since Yusha Raideen ("Brave Raideen") in 1975 changed into a fighter plane called "God Bird," animated giant warrior robot characters have been folding, combining, and disassembling in increasingly complex and ridiculous patterns, into cars, robot lions, fighter planes, and trucks, with the toy companies struggling valiantly to keep up and reproduce them in three dimensions. Even the human-robot interface is varied. Some robots are driven by joy sticks, some have steering wheels, some are operated by telepathy from inside the cockpit or remotely, and some are driven by amplifying the muscle movements of the human driver.

———

By and large, the plots of the giant warrior shows adhere to a simple formula. A young boy is leading a normal life, going to school or playing with his friends, when giant robots or alien monsters attack, threatening destruction of the world or, at the very least, Japan. Usually the boy's parents are killed, but before dying his father (sometimes his uncle), who is a top scientist, hands him the keys (or blueprints) to a secret weapon he has been building—a giant robot more powerful and technologically sophisticated than anything else. Then the boy hero gets in his robot, and the plot degenerates into fights between robots and monsters, with a young girl and a few cute little animals or "mascot" robots thrown in as a softener. In the end the world is saved. At their worst, giant warrior robot shows are thirty-minute toy commercials, filled with explosions and fight scenes; as industry personnel lament, they are a "synonym for bad taste."

Increasingly, production companies specializing in robot animation work directly with toy companies. They rely on directors who are masters of the genre rather than simply animating existing stories created by artists in comic magazines. The challenge for these directors is to devise an original idea within the constraints of the medium. After years of laboring without recognition, a couple have actually become minor celebrities in Japan. But it wasn't easy.

In his autobiography, robot animation director Yoshiyuki Tomino (who had worked on the *Mighty Atom* TV series) describes the advice he was given when he first worked for Nihon Sunrise for the *Raideen* series: "You introduce a powerful opponent for Raideen, show them fighting the first round, and then show how Raideen polishes him off. That's the basic ingredient. Then you add a little story each episode. The most important thing is to show what weapons Raideen uses, and . . . you have to have lots of scenes that the kids think are cool—showing Raideen finishing off his enemies, and posing."[17]

Tomino swallowed this bitter pill. But in the end he had his artistic revenge when in 1979—still adhering to the essential formula—he created the TV series *Mobile Suit Gundam*, by far the most influential show in recent years. Whereas most television robot shows had degenerated into hyped battles between sword-wielding machines thirty stories high that tromped through cities and slugged it out with their opponents with karate chops, Tomino took a different tack. He called his robots not robots but "mobile suits," and he (temporarily) abandoned combining and transforming techniques that defied the laws of physics. These robots were weapons, developed and used by a distant colony in revolt against the forces of Earth. It was a grand *Star Wars*–type conflict set in outer space.

Tomino claims his idea for mobile suits was influenced by Robert Heinlein's 1959 novel *Star Troopers*, a hard-boiled science fiction classic in which mobile infantrymen wear "power suits" that surround their bodies and amplify their movements. Like "drivable" robots, the idea of powered armor or exoskeletons has a precedent in reality. Around 1968 General Electric in America had built a mock-up of what it called Hardiman, a steel skeleton with powered joints that

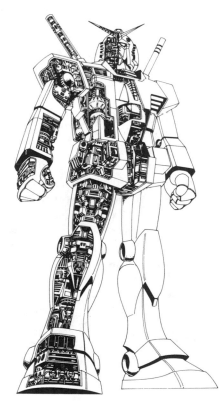

Mobile Suit Gundam.
© 1978 Sunrise; Sotsu Agency.

surrounded an operator and amplified his every move. In the *Gundam* series, however, most of the mobile suits were really part of the drivable robot tradition; operators sat in a cockpit and manipulated levers and pedals. The difference between *Gundam* robots and others was the level of mechanical detail and the aura of realism.

To rationalize the idea of huge machines fighting in close quarters, Tomino postulated that something called "Minofski particles" had rendered radar inoperable. Additionally, he worked to blur the traditional conflict between good and evil. The humans he depicted had complex characters with both good and bad traits, and heroes as well as enemies sometimes died. To audiences raised on lesser fare, it was shockingly believable.

Although the original television series had low ratings, *Gundam* created a groundswell of enthusiasm among fanatic fans, especially junior and senior high school students. When plastic models of the robot went on sale, several people trying to purchase them were injured in a riot at a Tokyo department store. Tomino thereafter went on to make *Gundam* a national institution. Over the next eight years he created not only *Mobile Suit Gundam*, but *Mobile Suit Z [Zeta] Gundam*, and *Mobile Suit Gundam ZZ [Double Zeta]*. In the Japanese tradition, the shows were also, of course, accompanied by feature films, comics, novels, records, toys, stationery, and books lavishly detailing the *mecha* inside the various robots.

Nihon Sunrise has subsequently made a virtual trademark out of fairly serious giant warrior robot animation. But *Gundam* has been a hard act to follow. "Tomino's realism created problems for us," jokes Takeyuki Kanda, another successful robot show director for the company, "because now when a robot runs out of energy it's like a car without gas, and just a piece of machinery." Kanda tries to distinguish his films by stressing young heroes who are victims, caught up in wars created by their elders; his robots are armor, or protection, with an emphasis on beauty in function and shape.

Ryosuke Takahashi, the director responsible for *Layzner* and other popular shows, stresses highly realistic robots with limited functions; he took construction equipment as an inspiration. Takahashi's father was killed in World War II, and until high school he could not bear to watch a movie that dealt with war. Today he makes a living with action-oriented

GIANT WARRIOR ROBOT FACTS

Heights of Various Giant Warrior Robots
  (1 meter = 3.3 feet)
  Dangard A: 200 meters
  DynaRobo: 53 meters
  Gundam: 18 meters
  RV Bi-form: 17.9 meters
  Scope Dog: 3.8 meters

Heaviest Robot: 60-meter-tall Sunbot 3, at
  100,000 tons

**Robot Capable of Greatest Number of
  Transformations**: Trider G-7 (7)

Fastest Robot: Diapron (Mach 50)

Strongest Robot: Ideon (capable of slicing a
  planet in two with his ideo-sword)

Smallest Robot: Gold Raitan (built as a ciga-
  rette lighter, he is pocket-size until he trans
  forms into his "giant" entity)

shows that he admits are more violent than many. He feels that robots have aided his creativity. "The robot world we portray doesn't really exist yet," he says, "but it seems as though it could if science keeps progressing. The unknown variables are a stimulus to young people's imagination; we use the robots as a bridge to a fantasy world."[18]

Who watches giant robot shows? The main fans of the more simplistic stories are clearly young boys, who love the karate chops and thrill of stomping through cities. The more sophisticated shows, like *Gundam* or *Layzner*, appeal to an older audience in junior and senior high school, and even college. On the surface they depict a very masculine world of action and awesome power, but they also have women characters and love scenes. As the directors joke among themselves, the boys tend to watch the scenes showing the *mecha* and the girls pay more attention to the characterization and to the love subplots, going to the bathroom or kitchen when the fighting starts. "Few people," Tomino laments, "watch the whole shows." "Japanese viewers," adds Taka-hashi, "have become very good at simultaneously watching TV and doing other things."[19]

Because of Japan's enormous success in exporting warrior robot animation, very Japanese images are today very inter-national. When asked to draw a picture of a robot, for example, young children in San Francisco unwittingly draw the image of robots conceived in Japan. There's nothing sinister here. With their outer-space settings, futuristic sur-roundings, and emphasis on machines, warrior robot shows avoid frequent, direct references to any particular culture. Also, due to an idiosyncrasy of Japanese comics and animation, the human characters are often depicted as having blonde hair and blue eyes, even if they are meant to be Asian. When dubbed into English, and given new names, they can appear as any nationality the producers like.

In 1979, after Go Nagai's *Gurendaiza* ("Grandizer") show was shown in Italy, *Variety* magazine reported that the character had been condemned in the Italian parliament as an "orgy of annihilating violence, a cult of allegiance to great warriors, a worship of the electronic machine."[20] But this was certainly an overreaction. In the context of Japanese history and of the Japanese relationship to technology, giant warrior robots are closer to being an antidote for a deep-seated fear of elemental destruction, a high-tech version of the Nio, the twin Deva Kings whose giant, muscled forms stand at the gates of Buddhist temples and protect the faithful from evil.

As with all the other myriad fantasy robots that exist in Japan, warrior robots have only helped to promote acceptance of machines and technology. Says Eiji Yamaura, senior vice-president of Nihon Sunrise, "Japan has a long history of robot shows, and the robots themselves sometimes appear as enemies, sometimes as friends. But the basic concept of a robot was formed with Atom—a robot is fundamentally a friend, and, as in Asimov's Laws of Robotics, will not harm us."[21]

The Toy Robot Kingdom

*The toy industry is a
miniature of all industry.*

JOURNALIST
SATOSHI KAMATA

*During the first stage of
technological innovation,
technology takes the path
of least resistance.*

JOHN NAISBITT,
IN *MEGATRENDS*

The first generation of Japanese robot toys was made of tin and contributed to the rebirth of postwar Japanese industry. Atomic Robot Man, the oldest robot in the Tin Toy Museum in Yokohama, dates back to the late 1940s. About five inches tall, and "Made In Occupied Japan," its body and haunted, expressive face are rendered in a style somewhere between futuristic and archaic. The crude wind-up mechanism permits only a stiff-legged shuffle and the uneven seams suggest that the robot may have been made from tin cans discarded by American GIs. Tin was in short supply right after the war. Toy makers recycled cans by banging them flat and then cleaning them with boiling caustic soda, which often burned holes in their clothes and temporarily removed their fingerprints.

As with 80 to 90 percent of first-generation toy robots, Atomic Robot Man was not made for Japanese children but for export. Defeat of the Japanese empire in 1945 forced the repatriation of over six million overseas military and civilian residents to a ruined homeland that had long ago lost its self-sufficiency. Only by the grace of several billion dollars of American food over the next few years did millions avoid death by starvation. In exchange for American taxpayer generosity, however, at the end of 1945 Japanese toy industry representatives were summoned to the headquarters of the Occupation forces in Tokyo and asked to begin making toys for American children.[1]

Among the American authorities, some may have correctly reasoned that the toy industry was a form of light manufacturing that could easily be revived. Before the war Japan had had a thriving export-based tin toy industry with many clever wind-up toys (including a design based on the tea-

Atomic Robot Man.

carrying doll). But after Pearl Harbor, members of the Tokyo Metal Toy Industry Association sorrowfully held their last meeting and, with the chairman in tears, shifted to production of military goods. When given their marching orders by the Americans after the war, instead of feeling resentment, toy makers realized they would be indirectly helping to feed the nation. According to toy historian Ryosuke Saito, "a great racial rejoicing spread [in their hearts], and they were shaken by a new self-realization and courage."[2]

Export or Die

For postwar Japan, it was export or die, and only ten years after the war, toys topped the miscellaneous category of exports. Many of them were tin robots. Like most exports, the robots were made with a very practical purpose—to please American consumers and thereby earn the foreign capital needed to purchase food and raw materials for survival. Along with toy cars and planes, hundreds of different models of tin robots were shipped to the U.S. Despite the fact that Japan had fantasy robots of its own, most designs reflected the American craze for robots in live-action films. In the Tin Toy Museum, for example, by far the most common robot model is Robby, the metal hero of the 1956 science fiction film *Forbidden Planet*. Today, with the nostalgia boom, some of these tin robots—such as a mint-condition "Mr. Atomic"—are worth up to $10,000 among American collectors. Originally, however, their real attraction was novelty and low cost, certainly not quality.

In the late 1940s and early 1950s, Japanese toys were virtually synonymous in the American mind with shameless copying and shoddy construction. Springs broke too easily, flammable celluloid caused public warnings to be issued, and paint was alleged to contain toxic lead (a charge investigated by the U.S. Surgeon General's Office and found to be untrue). Atomic Robot Man, for his part, was primitive even compared with the seventeenth-century tea-carrying doll. But in the Tin Toy Museum, subsequent robots show a steady evolution in wind-up, friction-powered, and eventually battery-powered, remote-controlled mechanisms, and in increasingly colorful and original designs, including transformation (one early robot turns into a television set). As Teruhisa Kitahara, the owner of the museum, proudly claims in a passage deleted from the English edition of his book

RIOTS OVER ROBOTS

On a Sunday morning in 1982, nineteen elementary and junior high school children were injured on an escalator at a major Tokyo store. They were on their way to purchase model kits of Mobile Suit Gundam robots. The kits were so popular that stores had to ration their stock by selling it only on Sunday mornings. Writer Yutaka Sasayama describes what happened: "That morning, the instant the opening bell rang, about 250 children rushed desperately at the escalator en masse. Most of them, unable to hold up under the press, lost their footing and toppled over on top of each other like dominoes, piling up on the second floor landing as more came up from behind, while some 40 more stormed onward, treading over their fallen comrades as they made their way to the second floor where Gundam was going on sale."

Wonderland of Toys: Tin Toy Robots, "Japanese industrial robots are currently grabbing the world's attention, but between 1955 and 1965, Japanese toy robots had already surpassed others in technology."[3]

Tin toy robots were an ideal product for Japan to make at the end of the war for the same reasons they initially had so many problems. Toys have traditionally been a form of light manufacturing by which industrializing nations can compete on the world market. In 1945, Japan was so ruined and poor it could not match the United States in industries that required a heavy investment in equipment or where a great deal of specialized hard automation was already in use, churning out single products that rarely changed. Tin toy robots, however, like all toys, changed constantly with the season and fashion and required little more than stamping presses and a work force with a modicum of skills, willing to work for low wages. As a result, the robot toy makers were essentially a cottage industry, with a type of mass production only a few steps removed from one-of-a-kind manufacturing. Hundreds of loosely organized companies often consisting of five or six people operated on shoestring budgets. Many of the companies were family-run, and the whole industry was almost feudal in structure.

Like the rest of Japanese manufacturing, robot toy makers were aided by the establishment in 1949 of the Japan Industrial Standards. The JIS system, by coordinating standards of manufacturing nationwide, serves to "rationalize production and consumption, increase productivity, and even promote exports." In 1950, the toy industry formed its own program of self-inspection and regulation. Throughout the next decade the government and the toy industry association worked together to promote modernization and cooperative efforts among the smaller firms. In 1965, in a classic example of Japanese competitors joining forces, eleven companies (eventually over forty-four) relocated to a government-financed zone outside of Tokyo called Omocha no Machi, or "Toy Town," where they shared warehouses, employee dorms, and some modern manufacturing facilities. The consortium's brochure, with a photograph of a long line of young women assembling robots by hand, notes that in 1980, with 2,091 employees, the town produced ¥30 billion, or over $164 million, worth of toys.[4]

The toy makers—as did other sectors of Japanese industry—made a vigorous attempt to learn from the United States. During the Occupation (1945–53) the U.S. military had sometimes advised Japanese toy makers of designs that might prove popular overseas. But the bigger companies soon took the initiative. Tomy, one of the larger toy and robot toy manufacturers today, hired a part-time worker to translate articles on toy trends in American magazines, and in 1955 it began sending employees abroad to do market research. In 1958, when Japan was swept with "modern" American ideas on management (and even old-fashioned companies began using English acronyms to describe them), Tomy adopted and adapted MTP, a "Management Training Program" developed by the U.S. Air Force. Managers initiated discussions at the plant level and tried to disseminate conclusions throughout the company, while also centralizing information from manufacturing, sales, and headquarters. Later, in the research department, brainstorming techniques were introduced to further creativity.

These ideas from America were soon given a special Japanese twist. In the Tomy plants, slogans and goals for "quality control" were displayed, and workers tried to live up to them. Quality control was a company objective, but rather than being imposed by management, many specific ideas for improvements were initiated by workers on the floor. Reflecting its founder's belief that "quality will conquer the world," in the late 1970s Tomy, like companies in other industries, would hold "Quality Control Circle Competitions."[5] Today these are a ritual throughout Japan in which teams of workers from manufacturing plants present reports on ways to improve quality to a panel of experts.

The toy industry in Japan merits attention because, being export-based, it is extremely sensitive to labor costs and is often a weathervane for the rest of manufacturing. Improvements in the toy industry eventually had to be made because of increased international competition and because Japan's dramatic postwar economic recovery had indirectly created a problem. In 1963, the year before the Tokyo Olympics, Japan exported more toys to the U.S. than any other nation. At the same time its economy was growing at an annual rate of over 10 percent, and standards of living as well as wages were improving dramatically. American wholesale buyers were starting to bypass Japan for cheaper toys in Hong Kong, and Japanese makers were starting to complain about copying and low wages among their new competitors. By 1970, America was importing more toys from Hong Kong than Japan.[6] The Japanese toy industry is a microcosm of all manufacturing, but, for the reasons noted earlier, it is extremely difficult for it to counter rising costs with hard automation. Flexible automation, in its infancy in 1970, was out of the question. The one thing, therefore, that Japanese toys could offer over low wages was the added value of quality and originality of design. This was to characterize the next wave of toy robot exports.

Machine Robos and Transformers

The second generation of robot toys appeared in the 1960s. Unlike the earlier box-shaped tin toy robots, these robots used smooth plastic and die-cast materials. Again, the raw materials (scrap metal and resin) were often imported from the U.S. Instead of mechanisms, the new toys stressed articulation, and instead of American images, they mirrored Japan's unique and fertile robot culture in comics and animation. Also unlike tin toy robots, most were first created for Japan's domestic market and then exported almost as an afterthought.

The largest Japanese toy makers today all manufacture and export their own version of these toy robots. Bandai, Japan's most famous robot toy maker, had made tin versions of Mighty Atom in 1963, but in 1974 it began manufacturing a toy robot that replicated Mazinger Z—artist Go Nagai's giant "drivable" warrior robot that thrilled young Japanese boys in comics and animation. Company designers made the toy "realistic." It could not only pose, but with plastic parts and a die-cast zinc metal alloy body, had a feeling of weight and power. In clever advertising, the toys were said to be made of *chogokin*, or "super-alloy," the same mysterious ultra-high-tech metal skin that Mazinger Z had in the story.

Mazinger Z was a huge success, and the sales of similar *chogokin* robots subsequently helped propel Bandai to the top of an estimated two thousand toy companies in Japan. The company then began replicating the combining robot characters popular in animation, such as, in 1976, the Super Electro-Magnetic Robo Combattler V, which combined five separately sold robot toys into one. It also created "machine-robo" vehicles—ordinary-looking little cars, helicopters, and dump trucks that could transform into menacing robots. As Satoru Matsumoto, the head of Bandai's First Development Division notes today, "Essentially our robots must incorporate three elements: they must look 'cool'; they must look 'strong'; and they must be movable and have some function."[7] Within these constraints, the wild imaginations of Bandai's young designers—raised on robot comics and animation—have created a vast assortment of three-dimensional puzzles and have helped stimulate a playful trend of intricate interlocking and modularization in many areas of Japanese design.

Bandai was also the source of the tremendously popular Mobile Suit Gundam plastic dolls in 1980, whose realism and complexity caused such a riot among Tokyo children. These robots were precision-scale models of the seemingly endless varieties of robots in the ever-expanding Gundam animation universe, plus some extras, and by 1984 a total of one hundred million had been sold, nearly one for every man, woman and child in Japan. Most were assembled from kits, but some were also sold in completed form. One, the Deluxe Mobile Suit MSZ006 Z Gundam, retailed in 1986 for around thirty dollars and, as the box design shouts in English (for advertising effect), is a "perfect detailed super heavy version." It is also designed with the complexity of an origami masterpiece: to transform it into a fighter plane requires nearly forty different twists and turns. But if a boy cannot figure out the complex movements, all is not lost. Bandai was one of the first Japanese toy makers to guarantee its wares in 1958 and like most major toy companies today has a national network of walk-in service centers where specially trained staff answer questions and complaints from consumers—and demonstrate how to properly transform robots.

In affiliation with the toy manufacturer Tonka in the U.S., Bandai's Machine Robo series pioneered the transforming

Forty twists and turns
transform a Mobile Suit
MSZ006 Z Gundam
doll into a fighter plane.

robot craze in America in 1984, when millions of its little
vehicle-robots reached the hands of American young children under the name of Gobots. Many of Bandai's larger,
more complex models are today sought after by adult American collectors, who wax ecstatic over "attention to detail,"
"realism," and the "amazing tolerances" of their joints.

The eventual winner in the transforming robot market in America, however, was Bandai's archrival, Takara, which became serious about toy robots relatively late in the game. In 1974, it came out with robot-linked toy lines called Microman and Diakron. Unlike Bandai it did not use "super alloys." Also it developed its own characters rather than use existing heroes from comics or animation. These toys sold well in Japan, especially at the beginning of the 1980s when the company developed cars that transformed into robots in the Diakron series. Then, as Hideaki Yoke, chief of the Boy's Toy Division Research and Development Department at Takara, explains, "The transforming idea was so popular among children that we decided to expand the core concept from cars to things that children actually had around them, like tape recorders, model guns, and even cameras. The idea was to suggest to children these could actually be a robot."

Yoke claims that today the robots are designed with a deceptively simple formula. "We select an object already familiar to us in daily life—a car, for example. Obviously, we all know what it looks like. Now, as designers we also know exactly what Japanese children think makes for a cool-looking robot. Then all we have to do is design the mechanical process that allows the transformation from one to the other."[8] As a parody item for all ages, Takara today makes a series of little robots that transform from famous-brand instant noodle containers.

At the end of 1983 Takara linked up with the American toy company Hasbro-Bradley, a strong marketer in the industry. Under the name Transformers, Takara's robots became the most successful toy introduction ever in the United States, reaping over $100 million worth of sales for Hasbro-Bradley in the first year.[9]

———

The actual process of creating a second-generation robot toy is much more complicated than its tin predecessors. It consists of eight stages and may take up to ten months: (1) conceptualizing the design, (2) creating a dummy in styrofoam, (3) reanalyzing the design, (4) creating a plastic and wood mock-up, (5) finalizing the design, (6) creating the master model, (7) carving the dies, and lastly (8) actually manufacturing the robot. Bandai and Tomy both use limited computer-aided design, or CAD, to create their toys. Bandai, as secretive about its manufacturing operations as a state-of-

From an egg, into a robot.

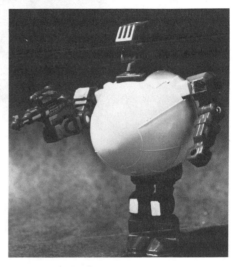

the-art computer maker, claims it uses simple pick and place robots to remove parts from high-speed plastic injection machines. But at all toy robot manufacturers the high-tech stops at the assembly stage. There would be a certain poetry if toy robots were actually made using real industrial robots, but in the factories of toy robot manufacturers in Japan today there are none, just as there are no automatic warehouses, no artificial vision devices, and no automatic guided vehicles.

The reason for this lies in the nature of both the real robot and the toy robot. Industrial robots are ill suited for true mass production because they are too slow and too expensive. Nor are they suited for one-of-a-kind items, because they lack versatility; they excel at relatively simple tasks, creating small batches of a limited number of models that do not change too rapidly. Second-generation toy robots, unfortunately, have a myriad of parts, springs, and screws that have to be attached at different angles. They are made in small lots, seasonally (which idles equipment), with each model having a very

Yukio Tanaka, Fuji Bussan's president, and Tetsuro Sugawara, plant manager, proudly display their Ultra Magnus robot and quality control award.

short life, thus requiring frequent and radical design changes. They therefore thwart assembly by industrial robots, just as their first-generation cousins defied hard automation. Even worse, since most customers are children with fixed allowances, retail prices cannot easily be raised to compensate for the cost of the equipment. The final assembly of these toys, therefore, still depends on the most versatile tool of all—the human hand.

Fuji Bussan, located in the city of Matsudo not far from Tokyo, is a typical example of a firm that assembles transforming toy robots. It is one of fifteen "primary subcontractors" for Takara, which like many large Japanese manufacturers makes only around 10 percent of its products at its own factories and farms the rest out to a huge family of subcontractors—"primary subcontractors" and hundreds of "secondary subcontractors." The scene inside the Fuji Bussan factory is a throwback to assembly operations in other industries thirty years ago.

In the spring of 1986, Fuji Bussan's forty-eight employees were assembling the Ultra Magnus plastic robot (which transforms into a truck-trailer) for the British market. As is generally true throughout the world, all those doing delicate assembly operations were uniformed women, lined up beside a conveyor belt. With parts supplied by a myriad of different "secondary subcontractors," they could assemble 380 plastic robots every hour. As in many small Japanese

TRANSFORMERS IN JAPAN AND THE UNITED STATES

For the Transformer line of robot toys, Takara in Japan supplied Hasbro-Bradley with its robots, while retaining copyright on them in America and receiving royalties for their design. Japan does not recognize copyrights on toys, so for Takara this was a great honor—and a huge source of income. Hasbro-Bradley handled the packaging and marketing of the robots in the United States, creating dualistic "stories" with characters like "Heroic Autobots" and "Evil Decepticons" to fit American play patterns.

Many of these Transformers in the United States had been sold earlier in Japan as part of Takara's Microman and Daikron lines. In 1986 Takara began "reimporting" them into Japan timed to the broadcast of the *Transformers* animated TV series, also from America. The imported toys of course had actually been made in Japan, as was the bulk of the animation. The only thing really imported was the marketing concept and the name Transformers.

Are the robots Takara makes for the Japanese and U.S. markets any different? According to Hideaki Yoke, chief of the Boys' Toy Division in Takara's Research and Development Department, what is popular in America are combinations of purple and yellow, as well as gradations of colors not common in Japan. "I first thought the colors were horrible," says Yoke, "but now I've gotten used to them." Also, in Japan robot heads are usually small to make the robot itself look huge, as in Japanese giant warrior robot animation. "But in the United States," says Yoke, "children thought the robots were stupid . . . and the designers needed bigger heads to distinguish between characters. It's hard for us to design them with big heads—where do we put them when the robot transforms?" Reflecting greater concern over safety and product liability laws in the United States, robots for the American market also lack many of the weapons and projectiles that come with the Japanese models.

factories, many of the women were part-time workers, often local housewives supplementing their family income. And as in most Japanese companies, they were organized into quality control teams, or "circles"; quality is an important part of robot toys.

"Robots are one of the most difficult toys to assemble," lamented Tetsuro Sugawara, the plant manager. "The initial design and the specifications are critical. Ultra Magnus, for example, has fifty pages of specifications. It contains nearly fifty parts if screws are included, and the metal molds for many parts take nearly forty-five days to carve, as opposed to around thirty days for other toys. If the parts don't have exact dimensions, assembling them is impossible and the line stops, and I have to instruct the secondary subcontractors who supply them."[10]

An even greater problem with the robot toys was the fact that the wages of the women averaged around ¥600 an hour, or over $4, roughly what their counterparts in a nonunionized industry in America might expect to earn, and one of the highest in the world. Since the fall of 1985, the yen had increased in value over 40 percent against the dollar in the world currency markets. Like an atomic bomb going off in the economy, this revaluation wreaked havoc with manufacturers of export-oriented, low-priced, labor-intensive goods. Especially toys.

Toy manufacturers, as in other industries, can eliminate inefficiencies and cut costs. But without access to automation, if labor costs climb too high, too fast, exports face disaster. Only with great difficulty can advanced nations with high labor costs and a free market continue to manufacture toys. United States toy manufacturers, therefore, were one of the first industries to abandon domestic manufacturing, moving plants to Hong Kong, Taiwan, China, and Mexico, or—as in the case with most American firms that sell transforming robot toys—simply shedding their skins and becoming marketing companies for Japanese manufacturers. The Danish, with Lego toys, and the West Germans, with Marklin trains, could still make toys domestically for export on a limited basis by stressing high quality at a price. Until recently, the Japanese toy industry, despite rising wages, had an advantage in that it was buffered from the outside world, not by tariffs as much as by an arcane distribution system that shut out imports and by consumers who sniffed at anything that fell below perceived Japanese quality standards. Under the normal logic of economics, Japan should long go have been swamped with inexpensive toys from Taiwan and Hong Kong. But this has not happened. Toys for the Japanese market are still almost all made in Japan. Still, to compete in the world market on the basis of quality *and* relative low price is asking too much. In 1970 toy makers became one of the first Japanese industries to build plants overseas.

In 1986, as more and more Korean and Taiwanese copies of Japanese transforming robot toys began to appear in the American market, and at a lower price, Hasbro-Bradley began to look beyond Takara for many of its Transformers. Toward the end of the year, Tomy closed two of its factories in Japan and reduced its labor force 40 percent, while an executive intimated to the media that all toy production must be moved overseas. The head of Bandai said his company might resort to producing 15 percent of the toys for the domestic market offshore. Fuji Bussan, Takara's subcontractor, stopped manufacturing robots for export, as its president considered doing more design and development.[11]

Robot toy manufacturers, like all Japanese manufacturers, nonetheless have a more than sentimental attachment to the idea of making what they sell, and they are strongly committed to maintaining plants in Japan. An ideology of manufacturing has emerged in Japan because of the lessons of history, but the attachment to domestic production also has its roots on a very personal level. Many of the larger Japanese toy companies are still run by families, and these companies in turn have long been knit together with hundreds of tiny subcontractors in quasi-family relationships. The idea of toy companies moving factories overseas fills these subcontractors with terror.

At Bandai, in 1986, Akira Murakami of the Sales and Planning Division noted that "we try to keep manufacturing in Japan. For the domestic market we need the factories close by simply because of the speed with which we have to make changes in the product, not to mention the pressure we have from our subcontractors." At Takara, Yoke, while acknowledging that his firm might have to shift more production to Southeast Asia, revealed the pain involved. "In Japan we are close to the factories," he said, "and we can just call them up and talk about specifications for the robots. When using overseas plants, it's hard to know what foreign workers are thinking. Sometimes they blame problems on the designs and don't try to make improvements on their own, and they are hampered by their own divisiveness. Countries like Singapore and Hong Kong, unfortunately, have imported some of the negative 'rational' attitudes of the West. Unlike Japan we can't just say, *tanomuyo*, or 'we leave it up to you,' and have the work done right."[12]

At Tomy, however, Yoshiro Yamazaki, a marketing manager at the Tomy High-Tech Center, reflected his company's particular strength. "If we have expensive labor," he says, "we may have to have simpler products made overseas. But to foster domestic industry we must keep developing a higher level of technology, and keep adding even more value to our products."[13]

Robots As Advanced Mechatronic Toys

The third generation of toy robots, which appeared in the early 1980s, uses advanced mechatronics. Several toy companies make these robots, but Tomy has been notable in their development. A manufacturer that started making robots in their tin days and now makes transforming robots, Tomy has historically emphasized action and mechanisms.

Workers test the voice-recognition circuitry for Verbot at a Tomy plant in Nagareyama in the early 1980s.

Tomy may be best known among the younger set today for its Zoids series, a clever fusion of the prehistoric world with the future in which (at the top of the line) intricately articulated robot dinosaurs and other animals are powered by tiny electric motors. But the company also makes Armatron toy industrial robots, with scores of internal gears and six degrees of freedom. In addition to these electromechanical creations, it also makes robots that use integrated circuits.

In 1983 Tomy created Ki-ku-zo (meaning "I hear" in Japanese, called Verbot in America), a toy robot that recognized up to eight human words telling it to go forward, turn left or right, pick up an object, set it down, stop, start, and "smile." Since then Tomy has generated a variety of cute little toy robots that sharpen pencils, sweep eraser shavings off of desk tops, and perform comical human or animal-like "actions."

These toys represent a Japanese fascination with robots as an idea or image, and an insatiable love of gadgetry, but they also are part of a new category of desktop emotive mechanisms that entertain bored workers, encourage students preparing for entrance exams, and amuse visitors to homes. Tomy is, of course, not the only firm making them. Bandai, while specializing in robot toys without mechanisms for the younger set, makes a little remote-controlled, motorized, and gyroscope-equipped two-legged "walking robot" as well as a little "God-Jesus" robot. Equipped with sound sensors, this latter marvel of Japanese flexibility cleverly fuses Christianity and Japan's native Shinto faith; when someone claps his hands as if to make a wish in the Shinto ritual, God-Jesus emerges from a cardboard church and either nods or shakes its head in response. One of the best sellers of 1986, however, was Tomy's Rakuten-kun, or "Mr. Optimist," a toy robot that

TOY FRICTION

runs around happily waving its arms and swinging its head until scolded, whereupon it hangs its head as if to apologize, cries, and then takes off again merrily—the perfect companion, it is suggested, to the rank-and-file "salaryman," or office worker, who is always being bossed around and needs an underling to torment.

Tomy's Omnibot series of robots, designed initially for export in 1984, stretched the word "toy" to the limit. The Omnibot robots incorporated voice recognition, photo sensors, infrared sensors, ultrasound, remote control, and automatic guided vehicle (AGV) technologies. The Omnibot 2000, the top-of-the-line model, retailed in Japan for nearly $600, was twenty-six inches tall, programmable, and self-powered; it also had a motorized jointed arm widely advertised as being able to pour drinks into a glass, although it was really far easier to do it by hand.

A poster for Tomy's Omnibot line of robots.

Ever since the abolition of slavery, robots like the Omnibot 2000 have been a part of the human dream for a personal robot to tend the lawn, walk the dog, and wash the dishes. As an inventor's dream, however, it has yielded precious little fruit. In 1983, the first so-called commercial personal robot, Heathkit's Hero I, appeared in the United States, but with a price tag of nearly $2,500 it was really aimed at hobbyists with enough technical skills to master its idiosyncrasies. Hero I was really a teaching tool. Subsequently, several other American companies also put out what were hailed as "personal robots," but none had the functions or ease of use that the name would imply, and many of the companies have disappeared.

Tomy's Omnibot 2000 was no closer to being a true personal robot. Its real significance lay in the fact that it was made by a major toy company, rather than by an electronics firm, a venture business, or a garage tinkerer; that it was far more reliable and easier to use than most similar hobbyist products on the market; and that it had so many advanced functions—at such a low price. This was the robot of which a former president of America's Robotic Industries Association, once joked, "If we made that thing, you KNOW it would cost $80,000!"

While the Omnibot 2000 final assembly was entirely manual, Tomy was able to bring the manufacturing cost down to a fraction of what it might otherwise have been by using mass-produced high-tech components from some of Japan's most automated factories and by exploiting its own established manufacturing skills and the economies of scale. Still, with development costs of nearly a million dollars for the metal molds for the first robot in the Omnibot series, and with retail prices clearly beyond the reach of most children, many in the industry said that the Omnibot line of robots was not profitable.[14]

There are other reasons toy manufacturers make high-tech toy robots. As Tomy's Yamazaki said in 1986, "We don't ignore the profit factor, but one reason we make toy robots is symbolic. They are also one of the best vehicles for the application of new technologies." Making robots has opened up many new possibilities. Tomy's High-Tech Center has no formal links with Japanese electronics manufacturers, but as a member of the high-tech community it has frequent contact with, and receives advice from, Oki Electric, Sankyo Seiki, and Matsushita. When Matsushita approached the center several years ago with a newly developed voice-recognition integrated circuit, the result was Ki-ku-zo, one of the first nonindustrial applications of this new technology.[15] The Omnibot 2000, moreover, uses tiny electric motors made by Mabuchi Motors, which creates the miniature high-tech motors used in today's consumer electronics. Mabuchi, in turn, has used a picture of the Omnibot in its ads. Finally, in 1985 the Omnibot series won for Tomy the much-vied-for *Nihon keizai* newspaper's Superior Product of the Year Award, and with it a great deal of free publicity.

The robot toys are also an attempt on the part of toy manufacturers to develop new markets. In recent years high Japanese wages and trade friction have made toy exports more difficult, while the domestic market for children's toys has stagnated because the ratio of children to the rest of the population is shrinking. Caught in this double bind, the companies, in order to grow, need to find new kinds of customers. New markets targeted by Tomy for its high-tech robots include not only well-heeled young adults and families but also businesses looking for what are called "amusement robots." Too expensive for most individuals, and of no value to factories, amusement robots are the bridge between toys and the real world.

Amusement robots in Japan are usually made in limited quantity to entertain customers, to promote newly opened stores, and to hawk products at trade fairs. Traditionally, they have been made not by toy companies but by ten or so firms with names like Taito, Namco, and Sega—game machine and software manufacturers, old friends to millions of teenagers around the world who hang out at video game parlors. Until its 1986 bankruptcy, their ranks included Dainichi Kiko, one of Japan's largest industrial robot manufacturers. Dainichi Kiko made amusement robots to complement its regular line for industry. The game companies, like the toy companies, make them to raise their own technological level and to create a high-tech image.

One of the biggest amusement robot manufacturers is Namco, best known today for Pac-Man, the video arcade game designed by Toru Iwatani that took the world by storm in 1980. Established in 1955, Namco has a long relationship with robots. It originally built amusement attractions and rides of the sort commonly found on the tops of Japanese urban department stores—often in the shape of popular cartoon character robots like Arare-chan and Doraemon. Thus far, it has produced nearly four hundred amusement robots, ranging from Atomic Robot Atom, which greets visitors to the Science Museum in Tokyo with flashing lights, waving arms, and voice recognition and synthesis, to Robot Theaters and Robot Circuses, where microcomputer-controlled mechanical robot characters perform in front of audiences.

Namco's president is also a director of the Japan Foundation to Promote Science and Technology, a trustee of the Robotics Society of Japan, and Vice-Chairman of the Japan Micro Mouse Association, which sponsors amateur competitions to see whose computer- and sensor-controlled robot "mice" can navigate an elaborate maze in the shortest period of time. (Namco produces a commercialized version of a

A boy driving an amusement robot at Expo '85.

Namco's robot receptionist gives directions to visitors.

"mouse," available in kit form, and sells it to corporations as an educational tool.) What really demonstrates Namco's commitment to robots is that it was the first corporation in Japan to replace the receptionist at its headquarters with a microcomputer-, ultrasound-, and infrared-sensor-controlled android woman—one that bows and orally greets each visitor and then gestures to a touch-sensitive computer terminal that will provide more information.

True personal robots may not yet exist, but when they do their ultimate acceptance in the market and in the home will probably require more than a broad range of functions and affordability. The companies that make toy and amusement robots may help provide the extra ingredient required.

Yoshiro Yamazaki of the Tomy High-Tech Center, where the Omnibot robots are made, explains that "we are trying to create a special playfulness, a type of interaction that can only be achieved between humans and robots. Our robots use high technology, but we are creating emotive rather than functional toys, ones that react more like dogs or cats."[16]

"Japanese are very indebted to industrial robots today," says Hideki Konishi, section chief of Namco's Amusement Robots Division. "The products they make, like cars and televisions, are all around us. . . . But these robots are largely invisible. Namco doesn't make robots for industry; we give them sentiment, and we sell dreams. It is with these dreams that robots will enter the home. Cleaning robots, for example, already exist in Japan for industry, but a vacuum cleaner robot won't be a success in Japanese homes if it is only a machine. It doesn't have to be perfect. It might do its work, and then say 'I'm tired,' to which a housewife could respond, 'Go ahead and take a break, then.' Communication will be critical for acceptance."[17]

Toy and amusement robots appeal to our dreams of a future far beyond the present technological horizon, although the industry that manufactures them is trapped in an older, labor-intensive world. It is to the unromantic industrial robot we must now turn—and to the manufacturers that have so enthusiastically put them to work.

PART
THREE

After Industrial Robots:
Building the Kingdom

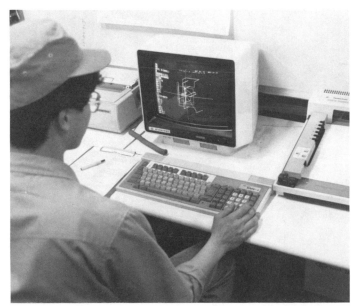

The 25-ton Fanuc Man humanoid, first displayed at Expo '85. With a vision system and two coordinated Fanuc industrial robots for "arms," it can lift a 440-pound barbell and assemble tiny models of itself.

At Kato Seiki, a robot manufacturer and subcontractor for Matsushita Electric, only two of sixteen workers at its Meishin plant are college graduates, but all are capable of programming the CNC machine tools that make the robot parts.

6
Japan Manufactures the Industrial Robot

The companies that can make their own robots, that can manufacture the best industrial robots for their industries, they'll be way ahead of the other fellow.

GEORGE C. DEVOL, JR.

Early industrial robot technology was like a fragile flower that needed the right soil to grow, and when transplanted into Japan it flourished beyond anyone's wildest dreams. In 1967, Joseph Engelberger, who had already turned George Devol's invention into a product, visited Japan as a guest of the government. Having spent much of the 1960s trying to interest American manufacturers in "a solution looking for a problem," as he calls it, he was shocked. Expecting a poor turnout at his lecture in Tokyo, he found an audience of seven hundred, whose questions kept him on the podium so long he recalls having to be "dragged off." And they were not science fiction dreamers. Most were engineers and executives, and many were subcontractors in the very hierarchical auto industry, ordered to attend by their superiors. As Engelberger says today, when the Japanese met robotics they "jumped right in, ran with it, and didn't agonize over it either."[1]

An industrial robot was first exhibited in Japan that same year, but instead of Engelberger's company, Unimation, it was made by archrival American Machinery and Foundry, or AMF. Called the Versatran, it lacked the sophistication of the Unimate, yet nonetheless attracted tremendous interest. Japanese were familiar with robotics-related areas, especially mechanical hands and unprogrammable devices for manipulation, but few had seen a programmable, playback manipulator.

Many manufacturers around this time had a big problem. Unlike the toy industry, the auto, electrical equipment, and steel industries could afford, and already had invested in, hard automation, but their salesmen were being hounded by customers demanding an increased variety of products. The

Kawasaki Unimate 2600s performing spot welding in the early 1970s.

result was a push away from traditional specialized mass production toward a more flexible type of automation. It was a worldwide trend. American and European manufacturers, who had already made large commitments to traditional mass production, were not well positioned to take advantage of the new technology. To many Japanese manufacturers, however, the industrial robot seemed an ideal tool, one that could offer a quantum leap in flexibility.

Among the gawkers when the Versatran was exhibited was a forty-eight-year-old employee of Kawasaki Aircraft named Gensuke Okada whose responsibilities included new project development. He and his company (known today as Kawasaki Heavy Industries) would play a pivotal role in introducing the industrial robot into Japan. Two years later, Kawasaki would produce the first Japanese robot under license, not from AMF, but from Unimation.

Of the prewar generation whose sacrifices made Japan an industrial giant, Okada today is the only surviving Kawasaki employee who remembers how the agreement with Unimation was reached. "When I saw the AMF Versatran on exhibit at a Tokyo industrial fair in '67," he recalls, speaking in precise English, "I was intrigued by the intense interest of people from the auto industry. Industrial robots, it seemed, might be a good opportunity for my company. But was the Versatran the best model? A friend told me of the Unimate, and I decided to go to the United States to investigate both companies.

"I stopped at AMF first," he says, now unburdened by the ambiguity and layers of politeness of Japanese, "but they seemed very arrogant. At the time they were producing such things as snowmobiles and large-caliber gun shells for the military, and robots were only a small part of their business. The first person I met was extremely ill-mannered; the company, moreover, seemed to have no business philosophy, and to be interested only in making money.

"At Unimation, however, Joe Engelberger had his office in a trailer house in the woods, and he turned out to be a very interesting character with whom I had many discussions. I told him the Unimate looked much superior to the Versatran, but he asked me why I thought any robot could sell in Japan. I told him it is because we do not have slaves. No offense intended, but I had seen how many American companies would take people off the street and put them to work at the most menial, backbreaking jobs with no future. He understood what I meant, and after a few nights of discussion, and a few drinks, he liked my proposal."[2]

In 1968 an agreement was reached. Kawasaki first purchased a Unimate MKII for an in-house demonstration and then, in exchange for an initial payment of $130,000, followed by a 5 percent royalty on sales, took out a ten-year license to manufacture and market Unimates in Japan and Southeast Asia. In 1969 Japan thus manufactured its first true industrial robot, the Unimate, for quite a bargain. But why not simply import them? "We are a manufacturer," says Okada, bristling slightly, "and not a trading company. Furthermore, at that time neither Japan nor Kawasaki was wealthy. If we wanted to introduce a new product, we had to manufacture it. And we believed in our own work."[3]

Robots Take Root

A type of herd instinct exists among Japanese manufacturers, and Kawasaki was soon faced with local competition. In the late 1960s and early 1970s robot technology was introduced not only from Unimation but also through tie-ups with pioneering European firms such as Norway's Tralfa and West Germany's VFW. Following Kawasaki's example, almost all Japanese firms preferred to license the technology from the West and build the machines themselves rather than simply import them. Sometimes, in the early days, they produced clever imitations of foreign robots—a strategy that dramatically aided their technological development and irked their trading partners. The Unimate's rival, Versatran, was doomed. Instead of forming a licensing agreement like Unimation and Kawasaki, AMF tried to go it alone in Japan; but their robot was too expensive, too easy to copy, and too easy to improve.

From the start there was also a difference between robot manufacturers in Japan and the West. In the United States, most (with the exception of AMF) were venture capital businesses, small firms with innovative technologies dedicated to robot manufacture or tool makers who wanted to extend their line of products. In Japan, however, many were large corporations like Kawasaki, Yaskawa Electric, and Kobe Steel—established heavy industry conglomerates, electronics firms, and steel manufacturers—able to mobilize vast amounts of finances, resources, and personnel. Kawasaki, in addition to robots, made everything from supertankers to trains, planes, and of course motorcycles, and it could put its robots to work making them, thereby gaining experience and economies of scale.

Why were these corporate giants able to initiate projects in such radically new technologies that offered little immediate payback? And why was it so difficult for large U.S. corporations? Among the many reasons, Yukio Hasegawa, a professor at the Waseda University Systems Science Institute and winner of the RIA's 1977 Joseph F. Engelberger Award for his work in robotics, cites what is today almost a cliché: "Large American corporations," he writes, "are severely handicapped by the need to report corporate performance to the Securities Exchange Commission every quarter, and also by the high turnover in managers and executives in the company. It is difficult, in other words, for them to take the lead and enter a new field like robotics, which has little immediate prospect of turning a profit; managers instead tend to aggressively pursue policies which yield immediate results." Or as Engelberger himself says, more succinctly, "In our country we have a very short attention span."[4]

But there was another aspect to this. In the early days, even the most advanced robots were quite primitive. As an immature technology they required great patience and effort

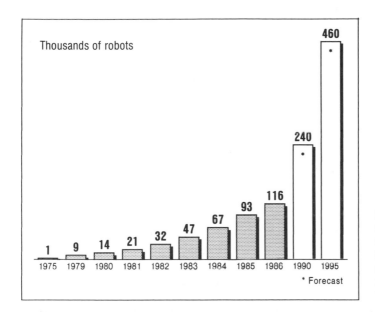

Thousands of robots

1975	1979	1980	1981	1982	1983	1984	1985	1986	1990	1995
1	9	14	21	32	47	67	93	116	240*	460*

* Forecast

Number of industrial robots in operation at the end of each year in Japan (excluding manual manipulators and fixed-sequence robots). Source: JIRA, July 1987.

to use properly; to develop they needed nurturing. Large Japanese manufacturers, in an export-or-die economy, with a national goal of catching up to the West economically and in science and technology, may have better grasped the potential of robots, and thus have been predisposed to giving them more attention.

Selling robots in Japan was still difficult. As Naohide Kumagai, currently the senior manager of Kawasaki's Industrial Robot Sales Department describes it, "At the beginning of the 1970s if a customer like Nissan bought four robots we yelled *Banzai!*—we were only selling about twenty or thirty a year. Marketing was difficult. There were no videos like today. We had to lug around 16mm film projectors to show people what industrial robots were, because many thought they were like Mighty Atom and Iron Man No. 28, robot cartoon characters then popular on TV. And they complained about the expense. In 1971 a robot cost ¥12 million, or around $34,000, at a time when the average worker's annual pay was around $3,000. Nowadays a robot may cost about the same, but it has vastly improved functions, and a worker's salary is about $26,000 a year."[5]

After buying an expensive robot, moreover, a customer might find that the arm would suddenly begin flailing wildly at the wrong time or simply stop working for no apparent reason. Worker performance, in addition to output, is often measured by absenteeism; robots are measured in colder terms—by what is called the MTBF, or "mean time between failure"—the average time it can keep working before it breaks down. By the end of the seventies, Unimate robots made by Kawasaki had a higher MTBF than those made by Unimation in America, but it took work. "Precision and reliability were really a problem," says Kumagai. "In the early days, robots often stopped after 150 hours and we were lucky if we could get an MTBF of over 1,000 hours. Today it's up to around 10,000. That means that working two shifts, 18 hours a day, the robot won't break down for two years."[6]

Even allowing for a salesman's exaggeration, this is a remarkable improvement considering that the average human is probably off work once every 500 hours for colds, hangovers, or trips to the dentist. As with the robot toy industry in the early days, it was accomplished by strict control of the individual components that went into robot manufacture; by use of quality-control techniques introduced in the 1950s from the West; by adoption of national standards and goals; and by demanding nothing but the highest standards from suppliers and subcontractors. Other factors were the rapid advances in microcomputer technology in the 1970s, including the dramatic decline in the cost of memory chips in Japan, and the shrinking of electronic components. Early robots had extremely limited memory and could therefore only "remember" a limited number of points in space to which their arms were supposed to move to perform a task. With more memory and better software, they could be programmed to perform tasks with far greater precision.

In Japan, customers are not called king, but god, and as in other industries, in robotics much of the momentum for improvement came from them. In the beginning, as in other nations, they were auto manufacturers. "Nissan, Toyota, and so forth," says Kumagai, "kept asking us for this speed or that speed, and feeding us specifications. They demanded improvement, so we had to try to please them."[7] But the companies that purchased the robots also made great efforts on their own to make them work properly. In Japan, unlike in the United States, the customer does most of what is called the "systems engineering"—the configuring of the robot to the particular manufacturing process, whether it be welding, painting, or material handling.

Nissan's first robot was a Kawasaki-Unimate used for spot

welding at its Oppama plant in 1969; overhauled, it is still at work today. As the general manager of Nissan's No. 3 Engineering Department, Kosei Minami, recalls, one of the biggest problems with robots, in addition to expense, safety, and quality of work, was reliability. In those days robots worked with many people around them, and if one stopped working on the line, hundreds of people might be idled. "When we had problems," he remembers, "we of course gave the robot manufacturer the specifications and improvements we wanted, but we also found that about 30 percent of the solution lay not in the robot but in such things as the welding gun position, the jig used, and the conveyor. All these required modifications and careful adjustments, which we did ourselves."[8] To make the robot work right, in other words, required a thorough understanding of the work it had to do.

Often the workers themselves played a major role. According to Joseph Engelberger, in the U.S. one person normally services around 10 or 12 robots, doing programming and maintaining the hydraulics or the electrical system. But at a Mazda plant he visited, he was told that each shift had only five people servicing 150 Kawasaki-built Unimates. After protesting this seeming impossibility to his guide, he learned that people from other shifts came in to learn and to help on their own time. "It's a matter of dishonor if the robot stops on their shift," he says. "They were there on their coffee break, polishing the things. Every machine was shiny, and they knew it was theirs, and they were proud to be able to go home and say they knew how to program it. Now in the States, you run it till it breaks. If you need time off, maybe you kick it till it breaks. The whole attitude is different."[9]

The problems Japanese auto makers encountered in using robots were no different from those faced by users of welding robots in the United States. But in Japan, as in several European auto firms, the solution was often different—to make their own. About ten years ago, Nissan, for example, began making two models of its own, and today nearly a quarter of its robot population—over five hundred—are made in-house. Why? As Minami says, "The manufacturers' robots are very sophisticated, so much so that often we can't use all their functions. At the same time they are very expensive. We therefore build our own robots with the speeds, movements, and specifications *we* need. Sometimes, for example, the robots are too big, and we simply need something smaller. . . . But manufacturers don't like to customize robots—they like volume sales of one type or another."[10]

Nissan's approach was duplicated throughout Japanese industry and is one reason so many companies make robots in Japan. Large corporations in the auto and electrical industries, musical instrument makers, bicycle makers, and even pen manufacturers eventually found that they could make their own robots for specific applications. Often these were very simple models that cost far less than those sold by specialized robot companies. Because they made them themselves, they learned how to use them better. And because they knew how to use them better, it was easier to turn around and sell them on the market and compete with the specialized robot companies.

This do-it-yourself approach has exacerbated the tension that sometimes exists between robot users and robot vendors. Japanese manufacturers often compete on the basis of process, as opposed to product, technology; the way a radio is made, rather than the innards of the actual radio itself, is a jealously guarded secret. "We are reluctant to show the robot companies how we use the robots," says Nissan's Minami, "because applications know-how is a type of technology, a corporate secret. They are not so cooperative either, since they know many of the users will make their own robots. Robots are still expensive, and many companies just buy a few, copy them, and make their own. These days we're not on such good terms with the robot vendors."[11]

Larger Forces at Work

Many Japanese like to attribute the sudden profusion of robots in their nation to human and cultural factors—to the lifetime employment system and job security, the high educational level of the workers, the cooperative labor unions, the large ratio of engineers, and even religion. All of these may be important, but there were larger, more immediate forces at work. In order to sell robots, there has to be a demand for them.

The aggressive, early utilization of robots in Japan was practically assured not just by the need for flexible automation, but by the relative high cost—and shortage—of labor.

MR. AROS

The technology for Japan's first industrial robots may have come from the United States, but important innovations were made in it much sooner than is commonly known. Spot welding joins metal parts together by fusing them at a limited number of locations along a seam. Arc welding, which joins metal parts along the entire length of the seam, requires far greater control over the robot arm doing the welding, and far greater accuracy. One of the world's first micro-computer-controlled, "intelligent" arc-welding robots, Mr. AROS was developed by Hitachi in 1974 and used a vision system and a noncontact sensor attached to its wrist. These allowed more accurate welding by sensing both machining errors and errors in the position of the workpiece.

Experiencing the crush of people in Tokyo's subways or the teeming crowds in shopping areas makes it difficult to imagine a labor shortage of any sort, and it is this, perhaps, which has continually reinforced the Western impression of Japan and Asia as a place of unlimited, cheap labor. But if economic growth rates are high enough, labor shortages can occur anywhere. In 1969, when the first true industrial robots were introduced into the Japanese auto industry, the economy had a real growth rate of 12 percent per year, nearly triple that of the U.S. But the population growth rate was under 1 percent; as early as 1965 a Ministry of Labor survey reported that Japan needed 1.8 million more skilled workers. Workers' wages, moreover, while perhaps low by Western standards, rose relative to production cost, and more and more young people, unlike their parents, chose to continue their education and to attend university; they were reluctant to do dirty, dangerous, and dull work. As Nissan's Minami recalls, "We simply couldn't find enough people at the time. Sales of our cars were exploding: we went from 21,767 a year in 1955 to 2,077,447 in 1970, a tenfold increase. We tried using seasonal workers and farm workers, and scoured Japan for people."[12]

It was a problem common to all industry, and Japanese immigration policy did little to help. A 1973 book with the remarkably prescient title of *Mujinka kojo e no chosen*, or "Challenge of the Unmanned Factory," recorded a freewheeling discussion of Japanese roboticists on the subject. Said Jun Oizumi of Toshiba Electric's Automation Promotion Center, "Japan has the worst labor shortage in the world. In the U.S. they have Blacks, Puerto Ricans, Italians, or whatever, but we're different. . . . We have to find some way to overcome this. In my company we say that 'if you don't automate assembly, you'd better get ready to move to Southeast Asia.'" Speaking slightly more elegantly and to the point, Waseda

University scientist Ichiro Kato elaborated, "We have an unwritten law that only allows Japanese residents to work here. But this is not the case in other countries, which gives them access to far more plentiful human resources."[13]

Unlike the United States, Europe, or even the oil nations of the Middle East, postwar Japan has never resorted to foreign "guest worker" programs, immigration programs, or the use of illegal aliens to solve its labor shortages. Prior to 1945, it is true that thousands of Koreans were brought to Japan, often as forced labor, but their descendants (who form nearly 80 percent of Japan's less-than-1-percent minority population) are still victims of discrimination and regarded by some as a blemish on an otherwise pure racial complexion. In recent years, some Southeast Asian prostitutes and laborers have illegally entered Japan, but their number is minuscule. Japanese immigration law today technically allows only foreign workers who are diplomats, scholars, teachers, researchers, athletes or entertainers. To manufacturers needing extra hands, robots are a gift from heaven.

Soon after robots were introduced into Japan, manufacturers had yet another reason to try them—the 1973 oil crisis, or *oiru shokku*. With nearly 90 percent of its raw materials imported and producing only 30 percent of the food it needs, Japan survives by manufacturing goods to sell to the world— a fact pounded into the head of every citizen. But when, as in 1973, the price of a key raw material—oil—rises drastically, so too does the cost of manufacturing, all other variables being constant. That year, the growth rate of the economy plunged from nearly 11 percent to 4 percent. As the Japan Industrial Robot Association Handbook describes it, "International competitiveness is absolutely essential to Japan, and without it our economy would be ruined. . . . To counter the skyrocketing prices and wages that ensued, and to maintain international competitiveness, Japan had to try any means of increasing productivity. This was a major stimulus to the introduction of industrial robots."[14]

Subsequently, the 1978 oil crisis and, recently, the exchange rate crisis have provided additional stimuli. Some manufacturing industries, like the toy makers described earlier, were obviously not in a position to take advantage of the flexible automation robots could provide. But if any industry could benefit from robots and despite all these incentives still could not figure out what to do on their own, help was on the way.

COMPARING JAPAN AND THE U.S.

Toru Hamaya, an executive director of Hi-Tech Seiko, has this to say about manufacturing with robotics: "Japan has tried to enforce control over its systems with hardware. It has not put so much emphasis on software, which is where the U.S. has concentrated its efforts. When automating in the U.S., the people in the company who truly understand the software tend to be an elite engineering minority, and the company depends on them. But in Japan, since everything hinges on the hardware, even those with fairly low-level engineering skills can use robots. Also, when told to automate, Japanese want to try working with robots, even if the goal is not entirely clear to them. They start using robots right away. The result is that in the factory, Japan has been more successful than America at increasing productivity with robots.

The Japan Industrial Robot Association, or JIRA, is located in Tokyo next to Tokyo Tower in the official-looking Machinery Promotion Building. The former, slightly higher than the Eiffel Tower, was designed to lift both tourists and postwar Japanese spirits. The latter houses associations that engage in a different sort of boosterism. The JIRA, formally chartered in October 1972 with forty-four corporate members, has the lofty goal of "promoting the manufacture of industrial robots and systems products, investing in automation and labor-saving in industry, and thereby contributing to a healthy growth of the national economy."[15] As part of this process, it also actively conducts surveys and promotes the use of new technologies, trade, research, and standardization. The JIRA was the first association of its sort in the world and a model for those that sprang up later in the United States and Europe.

As Yukio Hasegawa remembers it, the association began informally. An official from Kawasaki who had contracted with his laboratory to study the performance of early Unimate robots complained that the problems of robots could not be solved by one company alone and that there should be an industrial association. Starting with seven or eight key men from other large corporations making robots, such as Mitsubishi, Hitachi, and Toshiba (men Hasegawa jokingly refers to as "the Seven Samurai"), a group was formed. It then expanded, and to increase its influence made an application for recognition to the Ministry of International Trade and Industry, or MITI, the agency often said to have masterminded Japan's postwar economic "miracle." When MITI approved, the JIRA's role as an official industrial association was legalized, and the group became eligible for government financing.[16]

From the beginning, the JIRA differed from its cousin, the RIA in the United States. Chartered in 1974, the RIA, like most U.S. industrial associations, serves mainly to further the interests of its members. As the name change it once went through—from Robot Industries of America to Robotics Industries Association—hints, any national identification has been diluted. Not so the JIRA. It is in fact a quarterback in a national strategy. In Japan the robot industry was designated as a "target" industry under the 1971 Extraordinary Measures Law for Promotion of Specific Electronic and Machinery Industries, and again in 1978, under the Extraordinary Measures Law for Promotion of Specific Machinery and Information Industries, robots were designated as equipment promoting research, industrialization, and "rationalization." As an English translation of a JIRA brochure says in one gasp, "Our Association has been promoting the manufacture of industrial robots under advice and support of governmental and academic circles and cooperation of users and related industries and evolving undertakings . . . for automated and safe operations in the industries."[17]

The current executive director of the association, Kanji Yonemoto, is a former employee of MITI. In 1973 the ministry asked him to head the association, and he has ever since. In the U.S., the RIA has no such well-connected members on its board. As Engelberger grumbles, "You never see anyone who's a big wheel. . . . It's always working stiffs like us."[18]

Decision making in Japan can be agonizingly slow, but when an industry-academia-government consensus is achieved, things can happen quickly, thoroughly, and with little argument. If the late 1960s represented the infancy of the industrial robot, the 1970s were the decade in which it finally became practical. By 1980 Japan had over 14,000 U.S.-defined robots, as opposed to 4,000 in the U.S. itself. But this was only a beginning. For the year 1980 Yonemoto coined the term *robotto fukyu gannen*, which was subsequently turned into a national buzzword by the Japanese media. It translates inelegantly into English as the "first year of the robot diffusion era." That same year the government also aggressively began to promote robotization.

Under the direction of MITI, and with the support of the Japan Development Bank and other financial institutions, in 1980 the Japan Robot Leasing Company (JAROL) was formed, its shareholders consisting of most of the major robot manufacturers of the day. Like the JIRA, JAROL has become a model for many other nations. Its purpose in Japan has been to stimulate the use of robots in smaller companies that would normally not be able to afford them. Leasing offers many advantages. It frees the money that would be needed to purchase a robot for other projects. It is a largely deductible expense. It allows users to upgrade to more advanced robots easily. And it is a fixed expense, a blessing for companies trying to plan for the future. A $50,000 welding robot can be rented for seven years at a fee of $850 a month. It will run for two or three shifts a day, and unlike a human worker will never ask for more pay, benefits, or holidays. JAROL even provides advice on how to use the robot; by 1984, it was also leasing complete FMS, or flexible manufacturing systems.

The government, too, is active in promoting the use of robots in small businesses by giving low-interest loans to those who employ new robots for otherwise dangerous work, and to spur modernization of production. Tax benefits, moreover, are available through what are called the "Mechatronics" and "Technopolis" tax programs. The former gives small manufacturers special depreciation allowances of 30 percent or a 7 percent tax deduction; the latter provides a special depreciation allowance for manufacturers in what the Japanese call "technopolises"— currently nineteen cities designated as host areas for high-tech research and manufacturing facilities.

The result of all this, as noted before, is that whereas in most nations most robots are still used in the auto industry or large corporations, in Japan robots are increasingly found at work in a great variety of industries, even in the plants of small subcontractors. These small companies are the true driving force behind the Japanese economy, usually belonging to the corporate fiefdoms or huge industrial pyramids that support the elite giant manufacturers such as Toyota, Sony, and Honda.

Takumi Kojima, of the Small Business Research Institute (under the jurisdiction of MITI), has identified three ways in which small manufacturers introduce robots. In the first case, subcontractors with little independence are virtually forced to robotize when their parent companies automate. In return they may be given considerable technical assistance and know-how. Often these subcontractors are very small family-run firms, what are sometimes called the three *chan* factories—*chan* being a term of affection applied to people's

Seiji Furihata of the Tokyo Technical Center proudly shows off a cylindrical-coordinate robot developed with his students.

Workers at Kato Seiki, a subcontractor for Matsushita Electric, developing a robot that simultaneously mounts four components on a printed circuit board.

names—for *to-chan*, *ka-chan*, *robotto-chan*, or "Mom, Pop, and baby robot" plants. In the second case, companies with more than twenty employees and multiple parent companies will introduce robots to gain flexibility in work cells and to shorten delivery times. In the third case, if the companies are larger and have enough resources, they will develop their own robots.[19]

Small companies can also obtain outside help and training from regional governments. The Tokyo Metropolitan Industrial Technology Center, for example, gives free advice to local manufacturers on their technical problems, including robots, and sends advisors to the plants themselves. For a small fee these companies can also send employees to the Tokyo Center for intensive training in manufacturing technologies, such as mechatronics and robotics. Sometimes they do research there as well, building their own robots.

"Many small manufacturers," says Seiji Furihata, the resident robotics expert at the Tokyo Center, "deal with a large variety of products, all at very low volume, and therefore have great difficulty using robots. . . . Still, many of the employees are very eager to learn and to use robots in their companies, and many try to make their own—simple ones

DIVERSIFIED PRODUCTION

When nations reach a certain level of wealth and social maturity, consumers demand more products of a greater variety. Historically, however, manufacturers have responded to increased demand with mass-production methods that made their goods ever more simple and specialized. When Professor Yukio Hasegawa, currently at Waseda University's System Science Institute, took part in a survey of Japanese manufacturers in the late 1960s, he found that resolving this contradiction in interests was invariably their main concern. The solution lay in what the Japanese call *tahinshu shoryo seisan*—literally, "multimodel, small-batch production"—the automated production of many different models of a product in small volumes. In 1970, Hasegawa published a highly technical book on the subject that described how robots could help; it sold out in a month and later went through nine printings. Today 80 percent of the output of all Japanese machine manufacturing is said to fit into this type of diversified production; robots, because of their programmed flexibility, are one of the ideal tools for the job.

of course. Obviously the success rate is highest in larger firms; in those with under a hundred employees we see a lot of failures. Nonetheless, the prevailing attitude toward factory automation and mechatronics is that in order to increase the level of technology in the factory, you have to make things yourself. Where companies can't make a robot, therefore, they often make improvements or improvise peripheral devices. If they are successful, they often later market them.[20]

Robots Reach Critical Mass

If 1980 was the year when industrial robots officially began to diffuse throughout Japanese industry, it also was the start of a period of national consciousness raising in which the many facets of the so-called Robot Kingdom fused into one monolithic entity. Over the next few years the mass media spewed forth what seemed like an endless number of feature articles, books, and television specials on industrial robots, all of which were gobbled up by a populace already conditioned by robot cartoons and toys. A 1981 industry exhibition drew 300,000 people, mostly average citizens responding to the hype. It was what the Japanese called *robotto feebaa*, or robot "fever," a term taken from the title of the popular American film *Saturday Night Fever!* and now used to describe a frenzy of energy.

The industry also engaged in its own frenzy—of manufacturing robots. In 1981 over ten new firms, mostly large corporations, began making and marketing robots that incorporated their own particular strengths. They included such diverse giants as Sankyo Seiki, the world's largest manufacturer of music box mechanisms, among other things; NEC, a leader in the electronics field; Nitto Seiko, a major manufacturer of industrial screws; and Komatsu, one of Japan's largest construction machinery manufacturers. Most of the new robots produced were for arc welding or for the new field of electronics assembly; many were electrically powered rather than hydraulic (and therefore smaller and lighter); and many used a new, uniquely Japanese design.

Like the first industrial robot, the first so-called assembly robot in Japan had come from the United States. In 1978, Unimation built a model called the PUMA (Programmable Universal Machine for Assembly) and delivered it to General Motors—later, even Kawasaki made it under license. The PUMA was a very advanced design, yet its roots were not in manufacturing but in a machine made by a Stanford University graduate student, Victor Sheinman, in 1975, as part of an artificial intelligence project to develop a robot arm for microsurgery. It was modeled after the human arm, had many degrees of freedom, and was capable of intricate movements in three dimensions (today, in addition to its use in industry, a PUMA model in fact assists brain surgeons in Long Beach, California).[21]

The Japanese design took a radically different approach, and as a result had a much greater influence on industry. Called the SCARA, it was designed and developed in 1978–79 by Professor Hiroshi Makino of the Yamanashi University Engineering Department, and first manufactured in 1981 by Sankyo Seiki. It was small and specifically created for light assembly.

The SCARA, whose name is short for Selective Compliance Assembly Robot Arm, had been inspired by a Japanese folding screen. With only four degrees of freedom, it was highly flexible horizontally, but rigid vertically, and ideal for light assembly work, especially in electronics. Whereas most robot arms had been slower than a human arm, the SCARA was as fast or faster, with a positioning accuracy of 0.05 millimeters. It was also less than half the price of other robots on the market. In a very real sense, the SCARA design symbolized the new approach to robotics that Japanese industry was taking. Instead of creating anthropomorphic arms that relied on complex controls and software, more and more manufacturers chose to simplify the robot mechanism and the robot task, and to augment this with stricter control over the apparatus that controlled or held the work pieces— the jigs, conveyor belts, and parts feeders.

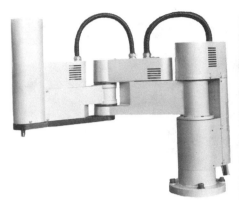

As Makino stated in a 1983 interview in a Japanese magazine, "Most robot manufacturers . . . like to create robots with a lot of joints that can move in a complex fashion, but this makes the control difficult and slows down the speed; it hinders productivity. Robots like this may be good for going to the moon and picking up rocks, but they are not very useful in a manufacturing environment."[22]

If the Japanese were once accused of merely licensing Western technology for their robots, or worse yet simply "copying" them, the SCARA design ended most criticism. Japan now exports far more robots and robotics technology than it imports, and SCARA design robots dominate in the electronics assembly industry around the world today. Most major robot manufacturers in Japan today make a SCARA design robot, and the technology has been licensed to European and American firms. In the United States, IBM robots are mainly a SCARA design manufactured in Japan by Sankyo Seiki. GE, until it withdrew from the robot business in 1987, used SCARA robots made by Hitachi. Even most of the robots marketed by a firm called United States Robots are SCARA designs made in Japan by Yamaha. As for Professor Makino, he has received awards from Japanese industry and government, and even the RIA's Joseph F. Engelberger Award, for outstanding contributions to the field.

Sankyo Seiki, one of the first firms to develop a SCARA robot, now markets the SK-5407, a streamlined model with a "folding screen" structure (photo does not show the end effector, or hand).

Hiroshi Makino, inventor of the SCARA robot, receiving the RIA's Joseph F. Engelberger Award for Technology Development from Engelberger in Tokyo, 1985.

And what of Unimation and Kawasaki, the two firms that pioneered industrial robots in the United States and Japan, respectively? Unimation shows how some technologies may need special attention in order to really thrive; in the laissez-faire U.S. environment, the logical customers for robots have been slow to understand their importance, and robot man-

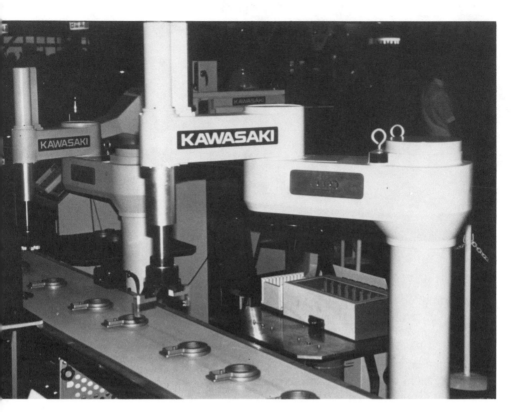

Kawasaki's vision-equipped Adept One robot at work, sorting parts coming down the assembly line.

ufacturers have never had much help from anyone. For years the largest U.S. robot manufacturer, Unimation was never able to achieve the critical mass and economies of scale of Japanese robot makers, and, falling behind in technology and expertise, began getting more and more robots made and designed by Kawasaki to sell under its own name. Losing money, and unable to find enough financing, in 1982 Unimation was purchased by corporate leviathan Westinghouse. After Engelberger resigned as president, its huge market share promptly disintegrated. In 1987 Westinghouse sold off the original Unimate line of hydraulic robots.

Kawasaki has fared far better, but it, too, has been slow to keep up with technological change. In an attempt to bolster its competitiveness, in 1985 it once more turned to a U.S. firm and took out a license for a new generation of robots made by Adept Technology, a small California firm founded by former Unimation employees.

The current star of the U.S. robotics industry, Adept Technology was the first to manufacture a commercial

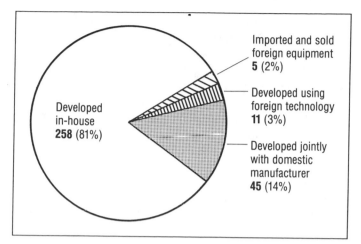

Developed
in-house
258 (81%)

Imported and sold
foreign equipment
5 (2%)

Developed using
foreign technology
11 (3%)

Developed jointly
with domestic
manufacturer
45 (14%)

In a 1986 JIRA survey, 279 Japanese firms claimed they had manufactured robots (Japanese-defined); 13 percent for in-house use only, 87 percent for outside sale. The chart shows how firms developed their robots; some firms gave multiple responses and sell imported machines as well as their own.

"direct-drive" robot, which uses special electric motors that eliminate the need for almost all gears and is exceedingly fast and accurate. Employing the latest in computer vision and American software, the Adept robot shows how American firms can still have an advantage over Japan in state-of-the-art technologies, and also how thoroughly intertwined the Japanese and American robotics industries have become. The first experimental direct-drive robot arm was developed in 1981 at Carnegie-Mellon University in the U.S., mainly by two Japanese scientists, Haruhiko Asada and Takeo Kanade. In 1984 Adept manufactured the first commercial direct-drive robot for light assembly, and for its basic structure it used a SCARA design. The firm that developed and made the new generation motors central to the Adept robot, and was for a time its sole supplier, was purchased in 1986 by a Japanese company, NSK, which moved all manufacturing facilities to Japan. Adept Technology today builds the motors under license from Japan and is the only U.S. firm making direct-drive robots. In Japan, over eight firms have them under development.

In keeping with the Japanese industry tradition of make-it-yourself, Kawasaki of course manufactures the Adept robot in Japan rather than importing it, just as it did with the old Unimate MKII. But licensing designs from the U.S. has a major drawback; it can hinder exports to the U.S. In the world of industrial robots, the United States market is enormously underdeveloped. For Japanese makers it has become a potential gold mine, a chance to achieve even greater economies of scale. Until 1987, though, when Kawasaki dissolved its relationship with the ailing Unimation, it was unable to compete in the American market directly.

On the home front today, thousands of Kawasaki-made Unimate robots toil away in Japanese factories. But onetime lone-runner Kawasaki now has a horde of competitors. The same environment that had helped it thrive had, by 1986, spawned around three hundred other manufacturers of industrial robots in Japan, as opposed to around fifty in the United States—a nearly fivefold difference, even accounting for separate "robot" definitions. One of these local competitors is particularly formidable. Its bright yellow robots have already stormed into the American market, and its president, if he can only have his way, will someday conquer the entire industrial robot world. . . .

An Empire of Yellow Robots

Awesome . . .

FORMER GMF
ROBOTICS EMPLOYEE,
COMMENTING ON FANUC

It is easy to understand how Japan's Mount Fuji became famous and sacred. When snow frosts the cinders atop the now-dormant volcano, Fuji's size and symmetry dominate the landscape and the mind. But today, in the woods at the mountain's foot, a huge, glaring yellow complex of buildings competes for attention. This is the home of Fanuc, one of the world's largest and most modern manufacturers of industrial robots, and one of Japan's most aggressive and eccentric corporations—the maverick child of postwar Japanese industrial culture.

The Fanuc complex includes housing and dormitories for employees, a research laboratory, a training center, a fortresslike headquarters, and factories for the manufacture of industrial equipment such as machine tool control devices, pulse motors, and robots themselves. Nearly everything in the complex screams yellow. Machinery is yellow. Building walls are yellow. Vehicles are yellow. And employees wear identical yellow uniforms with yellow hats and carry yellow notebooks.

There are two robot plants, designated "F" and "R," together capable of creating a thousand robots a month. In F, the largest, built in 1980, Fanuc Man—a giant two-armed humanoid robot once displayed at Expo '85—greets visitors at the entrance. Inside, parts for robots are being manufactured. Materials are stored in a towering automated warehouse, and loaded onto pallets on giant stacked shelves. As needed, pallets are brought to ground level, where they are picked up by AGV, or automatic guided vehicles, which carry them around the factory floor to staging areas, where they are later transferred to one of fifty "work cells." These cells are usually clusters of automated machining tools—called NC

The Fanuc complex
beneath Mount Fuji.

(numerically controlled) and CNC (computer numerically controlled) tools—and yellow industrial robots, whose job it is to unload the material from the carts and feed it to the tools for processing. When an operation is completed, the robot then returns the work piece to the AGV cart, which takes it to another work cell for yet another operation, or to the automatic warehouse to be retrieved at another time. Almost no human help is required.

The Western press has frequently described Fanuc's Mount Fuji plant as "robots making robots," unfortunately creating an impression of SF-style humanoid machines cloning themselves. The robots being made are, of course, the plain old one-armed industrial variety. Humans are still involved in the staging of parts, and most of the initial work is done by computerized machine tools rather than robots. Final assembly and inspection of the robots is a task still more suited to human hands than machines.

But reporters can be forgiven their hyperbole. Robot Factory F has an eerie, futuristic air to it. On a spotlessly clean floor the size of two football fields, the fewer than ninety workers look like ants, lost among yellow robots, NC tools, and AGV carts. Most of the robots are in the work cells, loading or unloading the parts that will make their comrades, but since they only cycle (or move) as needed, at first glance little seems to be happening. Much of the actual grinding,

Inside the Fanuc Motor Factory, robots are configured with machining tools in "work cells" and supplied by AGV from an automated warehouse.

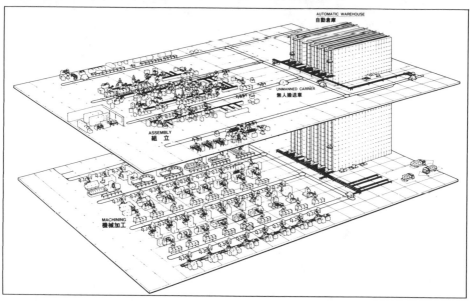

The Fanuc Motor Factory.

drilling, or boring is done by machine tools that are partially enclosed and make little noise. The factory almost seems on vacation. At night, human workers actually disappear from the floor, manual assembly and testing operations cease, and the machining operations in the cells continue automatically, with a solitary worker monitoring progress from gauges and terminals in the central control room.

The robot factories are actually some of the least automated in the complex. Fanuc's real pride and joy is the factory that manufactures motors for robots and NC machine tools. Nearly 80 percent automated and connected by computer network with CAD/CAM design facilities in the research

Dr. Seiuemon Inaba shows his Fanuc complex to Prime Minister Margaret Thatcher in 1982.

labs, with sales, and with the other factories in the complex, it is one of the most advanced facilities of its type in the world, close to being what is called the "Factory of the Future" in the United States. "We used to have somebody here monitoring the place at night," says the manager, "but now we just let it run by itself, unmanned." After everyone goes home, the lights are dimmed. Machines, unlike humans, need little rest, and they work fine in the dark.

Every month almost two thousand people visit the Fanuc complex near Mount Fuji. They include not only prospective clients, journalists, and gawkers, but heads of state such as Prime Minister Margaret Thatcher of Great Britain and Deng Xiaoping of China. Roboticist Joseph Engelberger, after touring the facilities, joked that Fanuc should invite its American competitors to the complex. "They'd lay down and die," he says. Mrs. Thatcher left gushing with enthusiasm for high-tech as a means of energizing her stalled economy, leading a London columnist to use the headline "Iron Lady Riveted by Robots."[1] Fanuc's Fuji complex has become a symbol to the world of the strength of Japanese manufacturing and of the futuristic world into which Japan has so aggressively plunged: flexible automation, unmanned factories, and robotization. Locating the showroom complex beneath Mount Fuji was a brilliant, symbolic act.

———

The Fanuc headquarters building, at four stories, is the tallest on the property and affords a view of both Mount Fuji and a small Japanese garden in the back. Its walls are thick concrete, and its interior is spacious and sparse, almost Zen-like—a high-tech samurai castle. A visitor is greeted at the door by an impeccably coiffed and mannered young woman (dressed in yellow), and escorted inside.

Exiting from the elevator on the floor where the reception rooms are, a visitor might encounter employees, standing at attention, scattered throughout the long, wide hall—all, including the chefs, dressed in bright yellow. Japanese are known for their bowing, but when a portly little man dressed in a yellow lab coat strides energetically by, these employees will bow deeper, and with greater respect, than almost anyone else in Japan. The person they revere, or fear, is Dr. Seiuemon Inaba, president of Fanuc.

Fanuc stands for Fujitsu Automatic Numerical Control. It first became independent from its giant parent, Fujitsu, in

1972. As the name implies, Fanuc has traditionally concentrated on automatic numerical control devices, primarily for numerically controlled (NC) machine tools. Machine tools are the "mother machines" that prop up modern industrial society, the lathes, grinders, planers, and boring devices used to create other tools. Compared with manual operation, the numerical and computer control of machine tools uses essentially the same servo technologies as today's robots and has enabled vast increases in the precision and speed of machining. Save for the fact that NC and CNC machine tools do little external manipulation of objects, they are essentially robots. And while the technology for them was developed in the United States, Japan has become the NC and CNC machine tool kingdom of the world. Fanuc, for its part, is said to monopolize an astounding 75 percent of the market for machine tool computer control devices in Japan, and 50 percent of the entire world market.[2]

Dr. Eng. S. Inaba, who insists on being called by his title of Doctor of Engineering, was born in 1925, spent the war trying to design better cannons, and entered Fujitsu in 1946, where he remained until the division he headed became independent. It is a mystery how he lasted so long in a subordinate position to anyone in a Japanese corporation. In a 1982 autobiography proudly titled *Robotto jidai o hiraku: kiiroi shiro kara no chosen*, or "Pioneering the Robot Age: The Challenge from the Yellow Castle," Inaba humbly confesses that he was always regarded as somewhat of a maverick at Fujitsu. In case anyone misses the point, the book has a glaring yellow jacket and is emblazoned with the author's proclamation that this is his personal *Mein Kampf*. Some have suggested that Inaba's dynamism and drive are attributable to internal rivalries in Fujitsu. Fujitsu is today Japan's premier computer company and one of IBM's few true rivals. In the course of its fanatical race to catch up to IBM, there was a period in which machine tool controls were looked upon as less glamorous. Perhaps even more significant, in the early days they were less profitable.[3]

Gensuke Okada of Kawasaki, who helped shepherd industrial robots into Japan, claims Inaba was not interested in them at first, a charge which Inaba denies. "I was in charge of computer controls at Fujitsu in those days," Inaba says, "and I thought that a licensing agreement with Unimation would restrict us, but that we should enter the robot business at a future date." Around the same time, however, he wrote an essay called "My Dream," in which he noted that his goal of the "unmanned factory" was impossible solely with NC and CNC machine tools. Eventually, he stated, "a robot becomes essential." And he went on to envision a futuristic robot with one arm, one eye, and a means of propulsion that would enable it to retrieve material from the factory stockroom, take it to a lathe, give it to a handling robot that would attach the work to the lathe, and then when the work was finished return it to the stockroom.[4] Robots were an inevitable extension of Inaba's lifelong work in factory automation, and his dream proved remarkably similar to the reality of the automated Fanuc plants today.

Fanuc was a latecomer to the robot market, but its background in servo-control technologies and secure position in the machine tool controller market gave it a big advantage. It manufactured its first in-house robot in 1974 and marketed its own model in 1978. Since then its rise has been meteoric, leaving most of Japan's hordes of robot manufacturers behind in the dust. In 1981 it was sixth in sales value; in 1985 it was second only to Matsushita. Matsushita, however, includes automatic component inserters—specialized machines that insert electronic components in printed circuit boards—in its definition of robots. If these machines are excluded and the U.S. definition of a robot applied, in 1985 Fanuc was Japan's largest robot manufacturer. To understand how it came so far so fast requires a further look inside the company.

Fanuc the Maverick

American and European robot manufacturers regularly complain that they "are not making any money" partly because the Japanese are selling their products at such low prices. But the Japanese companies—and this also applies to makers of televisions, semiconductors, and toys—are often simply willing to settle for drastically smaller profit margins (usually half that of their American counterparts, according to a recent survey).[5] There are many reasons for this, including stiffer competition, large conglomerates that are willing to run a division at a loss, banks that are more cooperative in their financing, and some basic differences in attitudes toward capitalism. Sometimes, however, Japanese companies and their aggressive employees seem to be conducting business as if it were more a sport, or even a group war, with the

MY DREAM

In the early 1970s, Seiuemon Inaba wrote an essay called "My Dream" in which he envisioned the robot his industry would need in the future as something like Tangezaemon, a fictional samurai from the Edo period, impoverished, fond of alcohol, and having only one arm, leg, and eye. An excerpt: "Tangezaemon," Inaba said, "need not be as powerful as a real samurai. He need have only one eye, and it can be near- or far-sighted, as long as he can vaguely see ahead. The arm, for that matter, need not be particularly powerful, but should at least have the sensitivity and re-sponse of an old man. And as for the leg, well, it need not walk all over the place, but simply slide along a fixed path. . . . [In the unmanned factory,] the computer would order him to take materials for processing to lathe no.5. After retrieving them from the materials warehouse, he would slide toward his destination, and when it hazily came into view, he would stop. Then he would gingerly hand it to the automatic supply robot next to the lathe. When work was finished on it, he would slide back to the warehouse, and store it."

winner receiving market share, power, prestige, a chance to shape the future, and a guaranteed living wage for its workers. But even in the Japanese context, the robot business is regarded as particularly unprofitable, cutthroat, and treacherous. In 1986, high-flying Dainichi Kiko, one of the largest Japanese robot manufacturers, with links around the world, scandalized the industry by crashing into bankruptcy.

Fanuc, while engaging in the same battles as its competitors, has been one of the world's most efficient and profitable corporations. In fiscal 1985 it had only around 1,600 employees, yet sales of nearly $660 million and a net profit of more than $103 million. Its pretax ordinary profit was 36 percent of sales, the highest of all manufacturers in Japan, towering above such industrial giants as Toyota, with its measly 10.6 percent. To investors, Fanuc has at times looked more like a gold mine than a manufacturer. On January 22 1981, for example, shares temporarily reached an astronomical price of ¥7,150, or over $32 each—the highest ever in Japan at the time—and they have remained relatively high.[6]

These enormous profits permit two things. First, although Inaba himself owns almost no stock in the firm (Fujitsu is the majority shareholder), he can run it as a virtual "one-man" company, as the Japanese say, and do practically whatever he likes. Second, he can use the money to finance his vast ambitions. Most of Fanuc's profits in reality come from sales of CNC controllers; industrial robots form less than 10 percent of the total and thus can be subsidized if necessary as a strategic technology.

If Fanuc is an unusual Japanese company because of its profit margins, it is also unusual in the way these are

Dr. Inaba examines models of new robots with his employees.

achieved. Japanese companies are renowned for the discipline and loyalty of their hardworking employees. But even the Japanese are awed by Fanuc's workers. The *Nikkei Business* magazine, for example, in a 1985 feature article on reasons for Fanuc's success, said that "discipline in the Fanuc army led by Inaba is no less than that of Genghis Khan's. It is an ironclad discipline requiring absolute subservience of not only executives, but also regular employees; no exceptions are allowed."[7]

Genghis Khan is said to have exterminated the entire families of commanders who failed him. Inaba, reportedly an admirer of the Mongolian general, takes much milder measures. As the media delight in pointing out, however, all employees going overseas on assignment must personally report to him, before departure and on return, even though Inaba rarely makes himself available to meet them; researchers need written permission to leave the plant premises during lunch, and those who return late have their pay docked. But it is unlikely that Inaba ever has to visibly demonstrate his anger or even invoke the rules. Most Japanese are raised in a hierarchical environment and are used to obeying authority; besides, anyone joining Fanuc has a good idea of what to expect. Employee discipline shows itself most clearly in small ways—in the spotless quality of the factories themselves and in the demeanor of the workers. Fanuc chauffeurs, for example, rush to open the door for passengers and always place a gloved hand below the edge of the car roof, protecting poorly aimed heads from a potential bump. It is a simple gesture, but executed with a machinelike precision that is awe-inspiring.

Normally Japanese corporations are said to stress group harmony and a bottom-up type of management, a system with a strong, clear vertical hierarchy on the surface, but with a tremendous amount of innovation and policy formulating actually welling up from the rank-and-file. Everything depends on consensus and the *ringi-sho*, a paper circulated throughout the organization to be stamped by all concerned as an expression of approval or disapproval of a policy. Often the company president will be little more than a genial, aging figurehead who spends much of his time golfing and greeting people.

The showcase item of Japanese bottom-up management is the QC circle, or quality control circle. To improve quality on the factory floor, groups of employees pool and discuss ideas and try to solve them on their own. Quality control may have been pioneered in America, but in Japan it has been elevated to a religion (and Dr. W. Edward Deming, who helped make quality control a science, to near-God status). The circles are in use not only in factories but in supermarkets and even among receptionists in office buildings. Not supporting the notion of QC circles is virtual heresy in today's Japan.

Fanuc has no QC circles. "I hate *matsuri*," says Inaba, sarcastically referring to Japan's carnival-style traditional festivals. "They're nothing but a waste of time. . . . But we do have banners in all our factories proclaiming, 'Quality is Number One,' and to handle quality control we have a special Quality Control Department, the head of which has the same authority as I do, for quality. He checks not only the factories but also the research and development labs, and he has access to all the data, so if there is a problem he will issue a warning. If there is a defect in a semiconductor chip or an electronic component he will go directly to the subcontractor or manufacturer and complain. He is extremely powerful."[8]

Inaba's last sentence is said with great emphasis. His pride in his company's quality control, even without democratic QC circles, is more than justified. Usually factories test or check the quality of the components they use on a sampling basis; instead of checking every item in a batch of a hundred, every tenth one might be examined. Fanuc, however, checks a hundred percent of the electronics components it receives from its subcontractors and suppliers. "We stress quality over everything else," proclaims Inaba, "and as a result our CNC controls have a 0.02 failure rate, which means they will break down only once in fifty months of operation. But it took us four years to get to this point."[9]

Inaba speaks with what sounds almost like a slur but is really a mild dialect from the rural region of Ibaraki Prefecture, where his samurai ancestors lived for sixteen generations. Because of the influence of national television, dialect is rarely spoken in official situations today, and it is unusual for someone of Inaba's education and status to still use it as it sounds somewhat unrefined. But Inaba speaks in a soft voice without a trace of embarrassment and without a hint of the authority he wields. Rumor has it that he is a devoted father and husband. Unlike many Japanese of his age, he neither smokes nor drinks, and even more shocking, has sworn off golf as a waste of time. Some say, however, that he avoids the game because he dislikes losing.

Inaba insists that his company, and not his employees, have strong character. The color yellow is an example. Many companies have corporate colors—in the United States IBM uses blue, and Kodak and Caterpillar both use yellow. But no one employs such a glaring yellow as aggressively as Fanuc. Fanuc uses yellow throughout the company and goes to great lengths to apply it even to everyday items, such as menus, chopstick holders, and Yves Saint Laurent–designed *o-shibori* —the hot hand towels Japanese give guests. A summer visitor, presented with an orange drink, is liable to feel he is in the midst of a hallucination.

Yellow was supposedly chosen to distinguish Fanuc from its parent, Fujitsu, which uses green. But in his *Mein Kampf*, Inaba writes that "yellow is a fighting color for Fanuc. . . . I think that a company needs an element of orneriness. If all the employees have a strict understanding of a single, clear ideal, and carry it out, then there will be no easy compromises and actions won't be affected by appearances." Some, however, have suggested that the pervasive yellow is really a means of annihilating the individual egos of employees. The *Nikkei Business* report on Inaba quotes him, for example, as stating that "the strength of Fanuc lies in the fact that none of the employees has a sense of 'me.'" And unlike many Japanese factories, where banners strewn with cute cartoons merrily proclaim the benefits of group harmony and working together for peace and human happiness, Fanuc's robot plant is decorated with the undemocratic slogan "Plant Operations Are Based on Employees' Serious Efforts and the Strict Leadership of Executives." This reflects one of Inaba's mottoes for management, that "a rational, imperialistic method is better than an irresponsible democratic one."[10]

But Inaba does not treat his employees as brainwashed zombies. When he abandoned Tokyo and began moving his company to Mount Fuji in 1980, it must have seemed an extremely radical act. Tokyo is the political, technological, economic, and artistic epicenter of Japan. To urbanized Tokyoites, the Fanuc Fuji complex is an island in a sea of near-wilderness, and in its early days it was especially so; to many young people, living there would be a fate worse than death. To avoid a near rebellion among young researchers—one of the most valuable assets of the company, and hard to hire locally—Inaba reluctantly but deliberately delayed moving his main research lab for eight years until 1988.

Inaba also has a strict rule about employees not working at night, despite the fact that modern industry often works around the clock on a two- or three-shift basis if needed. Launching into the type of generalization his tribal countrymen are prone to make, he says, "We Japanese, unlike you Americans and Europeans, who are hunters, are traditionally a farming people, and we always sleep at night. At Fanuc we only hire machines that can work at night, and we run the factories unmanned." Ostensibly the entire factory is on a single eight-hour daytime shift, but as Shinpei Kato, a senior vice-president, grudgingly admits, "We do work overtime when necessary." In fact, the *Nikkei Business* report on Fanuc speculated that for managers in the research labs, between sixty and one hundred hours a month in overtime is not uncommon. As for Inaba, another magazine notes his eleven-hour days.[11]

In modern Japan, where more and more young people each year are spoon-fed a diet of materialism, Fanuc's spartan, almost militaristic environment would seem to be very unappealing. It is hard to imagine Fanuc employees whistling while they work, or even smiling very much, but they all look fiercely proud. The real payoff may be the opportunity to belong to an elite group of technology storm troopers led by a charismatic general, Dr. Inaba.

The military analogy would certainly not surprise anyone in Japan, for a vestigial warrior ethos still lurks in the heart of many an organization man. A popular genre of management publications in Japan, for example, displays covers of company presidents in heroic poses superimposed on famous battle scenes from Japanese history, or on ghostly images of legendary warrior-generals; inside, articles emphasize strength of character and compare modern business tactics with those used in ancient wars. In a recent publication of this ilk, Inaba noted his admiration for another Japanese general, the sixteenth-century warrior Nobunaga Oda, whose systematic use of a new technology—guns— enabled him to conquer all his enemies and unify the nation under his rule.[12]

Like Nobunaga, Fanuc is "technology driven," but not in the sense of inventing radically new products. Like most of Japanese industry, many of its machines still depend on basic technology licensed from America and Europe. The Fanuc approach stresses development and engineering, as opposed to research and development, and its focus is on the marketplace, rather than the distant future. The Fanuc Automation System Laboratory, which no one is allowed to enter save researchers (even company executives are forbidden), reportedly has the words "Reliability Up, Low Cost, and *Weniger Teile*" plastered all over its walls. The last item in this list is German coined by Inaba to mean "the fewest number of parts." The Fanuc philosophy is therefore to first survey the world, determine a price lower than that offered by any competitor, and then design the product to that price to maximize profit, with the fewest number of parts possible. Engineering for the lowest price, in Inaba's view, is the ultimate state-of-the-art technology.

The next step is trial by fire. "I have always thought," writes Inaba in his autobiography, "that the Japanese market is one of the most fiercely competitive. In military terms, it is where all the heaviest action takes place. If our product is victorious here, and the necessary marketing preparations have been done diligently, then I am fully convinced it will be victorious in any market in the world."[13]

First the World, Then Japan

In January 1986, there occurred a little-noticed but highly symbolic event in the history of the world robot industry. Among the swimming pools and tall saguaro cacti of the wealthy city of Scottsdale, Arizona, the U.S. Robotic Industries Association crowned Eric Mittelstadt as its new leader. The president of the RIA is usually the head of one of the largest American robot firms, and Mittelstadt was no exception. He is president and chief executive officer of GMF Robotics, which currently ships over 30 percent of all robots sold in the U.S. and is sometimes called the largest robot maker in America, even in the world. Yet nearly all of GMF's robots are bright yellow, and save for one painter robot, all the arms and the controllers are actually made by Fanuc in Japan.

Mittelstadt, moreover, technically reports to Dr. Inaba, who is in fact the chairman of GMF.

GMF Robotics stands for General Motors–Fanuc Robotics, and was formed in 1982 as a joint venture uniting GM—at the time the world's largest auto manufacturer—and Fanuc, the world's largest maker of NC controls. It was a convenient marriage for both. GM, like other American auto manufacturers, had suffered badly in competition with the Japanese, and robotics was seen as a means of restoring competitiveness, both in quality and price. It had also developed in-house a highly sophisticated painter robot, but had not yet brought it to market. With plans for the introduction of over 14,000 robots into its factories by the end of the decade, GM needed a source of high-volume, low-cost, reliable robots, and it needed it in a hurry.

For Fanuc, the arrangement provided a chance to tap the software expertise that Japan lacks in artificial intelligence and machine vision. It was also a chance to absorb General Motors' new manufacturing automation protocol—MAP—a communications standard that allows different makes of automated equipment on the factory floor to all "talk" to each other. Most of all, though, the deal meant an entry into the huge, just-now-awakening market for robots in America. Unlike other equipment, robots require so much on-site adapting that sales are almost impossible without a strong local presence for service and engineering.

Eric Mittelstadt, president of GMF, describes the relationship between GM and Fanuc as "an elegant strategy" and a "beautiful synergism." A tall Scandinavian who spent most of his life working in management for General Motors, Mittelstadt differs from many heads of robot firms in the United States in that he has no background in robotics. Relaxing beside the pool after his inauguration in Scottsdale, he could savor the satisfaction of GMF's—and his own—stellar ascendancy in the industry. Scarcely making any of its own robots, GMF danced to the top of the U.S. robot market in a mere four years, while traditional U.S. robot firms stumbled and steadily lost share and money. In terms of dollar sales, GMF did more business, he claimed, than Fanuc itself, and even more than ASEA, the Swedish robot firm sometimes said to be the world leader.

If it doesn't make the robots, what does GMF do? "We put the systems together," says Mittelstadt, obviously used to the question. "The robot and the controller come from Japan.

We tie it all together. We do the specific programming that's required and handle all the peripherals, like the parts positioners, manipulators, and end effectors, robot positioners, tracks, and all the other things."

With more and more hardware imported, and more and more emphasis on robots as part of a system for manufacturing, the RIA and companies such as GMF emphasize sales dollars rather than "robot units." "To put it into perspective," continued Mittelstadt, the sun glinting off his sunglasses, "of our $186 million sales in 1985, less than 25 percent was the robots that we imported from Japan. The rest of the content, in addition to our painter robot, was the value that we added such as the systems for all of the products that we sell, as well as the training."

"We've got to stop thinking about where we import the hardware from," he emphasizes. "That's not where the action is. If my competitors think that cutting the iron is what making a robot is all about, then I'm in good shape and will continue to dominate the market for a long time."

According to Mittelstadt, before GMF was formed, General Motors considered eight or ten different companies as partners, all of which were American except for Fanuc and a European firm. Most, however, disqualified themselves because they wanted to concentrate on expensive robots, did not have a broad product line, or simply didn't want to be swallowed up by General Motors. Fanuc's lead, in the end, was clear. "They've got a tremendous cost and reliability advantage over anybody else who could possibly be in robotics," asserts Mittelstadt, "because they are the world leaders in NC controls, and a lot of the control hardware is common between the NC controls and the robots."[14]

In the American tradition, after accepting his new position as president of the RIA in 1986, Mittelstadt presented the outgoing president, Walt Weisel, with a farewell gift, a video camera. Opening the package before the crowd, Weisel, with exaggerated humor, exclaimed, "Oh, no, Eric, it's Japanese!" whereupon the audience roared with laughter, fully aware of his meaning.

Weisel's firm, Prab Robots, like other U.S. robot manufacturers, has been damaged by the influx of Japanese robots, particularly by the GM-Fanuc joint venture. His criticism, however, is not aimed at GMF so much as at one of its parents, General Motors. Weisel doesn't mince words. "Many U.S. robot companies feel cheated by General Mo-

INABA ON MECHATRONICS

" 'Mechatronics' is a word invented by mechanicians. Robots are actually products based on electronics technology, with a minimum of mechanisms added. At Fanuc we believe in 'electro-mechanics.' . . . Assembly robots are an example of the increasing emphasis on electronics. Currently 60 percent of the technology relies on electronics, and in the future, with the advent of truly 'intelligent robots,' this proportion will probably climb to 90 percent, with the mechanical portion of the robot comprising only 10 percent of the total."

---

tors," he says with an edge in his voice. "I mean there was twenty-some years of waiting and development and plodding along, and base-building for this robot explosion. . . . All of a sudden GM decides to do the right thing, and it cost a lot of companies dearly who had GM as a star in the crown for future work. . . . We used to do millions of dollars of business with GM in robots, and now we do practically nothing."[15] Despite GM and GMF denials, from the perspective of outside robot and component manufacturers, the joint venture with Fanuc drastically narrowed their access to what is still the largest market for robots in the United States—GM and the auto industry. In short, the deal was a disaster for the United States robot hardware industry.

Thus far, unlike semiconductors, machine tools, cars, and motorcycles, Japanese robots themselves have received relatively little criticism in the United States. Unimation once complained that many Japanese robot firms should be paying royalties on their technology, and others grumble of overly low prices, but the United States government has never asked Japan for restraints on exports or advocated protection. One reason may be that many of the large companies—such as IBM, Unimation, and General Electric—are already just as dependent on Japanese hardware as GM and GMF. Unlike the Japanese, they did not develop their own hardware as part of a strategic manufacturing exercise, but instead have concentrated on software and systems engineering. For them, using foreign robots is extremely pragmatic, at least in the short term. As a GMF employee at an American robot exhibition whispered in 1986, "These yellow Fanuc robots sure are ugly, but they work great."

In Japan, joint ventures are entered into gingerly, and simply supplying foreign firms with hardware to sell under a different name (called OEM, or original equipment manufacture) is sometimes regarded with unease. If industrial robots weren't so difficult to sell without a strong local presence, most Japanese companies, like those in other industries, would certainly sell their own products directly for increased profits and prestige.

For Fanuc, however, the alliance with GM is a logical step in its global strategy, which the Japanese media often describe as "world conquest." Fanuc has subsidiaries all over the world to market and service its NC machine tool equipment, and usually these are a hundred percent owned and controlled by headquarters. But its huge market share in NC devices means Fanuc must grow with caution. Inaba was bitterly disappointed when in 1985 his company and the West German firm Siemens were fined by the European Commission for monopolistic practices in selling NC controllers. Since then avoiding trade friction has become a top priority. To his credit, Inaba asserts "friendship before business" and emphasizes local alliances and compromise.

For example, although the buildings of Fanuc's subsidiaries around the world are generally painted yellow, in France, where the company offices are in a residential area, the color of the side facing the neighbors has reportedly been toned down. In the case of the GMF joint venture, where capital investment is evenly split between General Motors and Fanuc, employees do not wear yellow uniforms except when loaned to Fanuc for exhibitions in Japan, nor is the GMF headquarters building itself yellow. Instead of iron-fisted control from Inaba, Mittelstadt could marvel in 1986 that "we've never had any direction from him. Even in 1983, when we didn't make as much money as hoped, he never told us what to do. He realized we're aggressive, and also that in the States you've go to do things in a different way."[16]

Inaba, for his part, was clearly influenced by the GMF joint venture. In 1985 and 1986, the Japanese industrial news media reported on delays in domestic delivery of Fanuc robots and complaints from old customers that they were being ignored. Fanuc, they said, was becoming arrogant. In his speeches, Inaba began sounding more and more American, stressing the superiority of American applications engineering, particularly in software, and suggesting the need for an international division of labor, as in the GMF arrangement, where the U.S. handles software development and Japan the hardware. Fanuc advertisements also began using the word "electromechanics" instead of the "mechatronics" most domestic competitors stress. And on a more immediate level, Inaba traded in his Japanese-made company helicopter for a U.S. one.

GMF employees wait for orders at the Robots 11 fair in Chicago, 1987.

What started out as a huge success for Fanuc soon became a major test of Inaba's policies. In January 1986 he was quoted as confidently saying that "I'm dissatisfied with a 30 percent share [of robots in the U.S.]. After all, we have 75 percent of the market in NC [in Japan], so I expect to gain at least 50 percent. It's only a matter of time."[17] Then, just when it seemed that GMF was about to sweep the robotics world, and plans were proceeding for a Fanuc-style showcase robot factory in the United States, the joint venture fell victim to bad luck and a strategical error.

Unlike diversified Japan, most robots in America are used in the auto industry, and almost all GMF's automatons were being sold to their biggest user—General Motors—which wanted to use them to compete with the Japanese automakers. GMF, therefore, was virtually captive to the fortunes of a single client. But as the *Wall Street Journal* reported on May 13, 1986, the 250 robots and other high-tech equipment that were supposed to presage a car "Factory of the Future" at GM's showcase plant in Hamtramck, Michigan, instead suffered software and systems engineering problems that resulted in robots painting each other instead of cars, in windshields being sealed in the wrong places, and in the bodywork accidentally being smashed. Subsequently, GM canceled $80 million worth of robots ordered from GMF, and GMF was then forced to lay off 200 of its 690 employees. For Fanuc, which depended on GMF for 80 percent of its business, it was a disaster. But it was not the only one. In 1985–87 the yen also gained over 50 percent in value relative to the dollar, making all the robots Fanuc was exporting to America vastly more expensive. Fanuc's much vaunted profit margins plummeted (while still remaining the highest of all Japanese manufacturers) and, in the ultimate Japanese industry embarrassment, its market share fell to sixth place.

One advantage of an authoritarian leadership, however, is an ability to make dramatic decisions quickly. In the summer of 1986, Fanuc formed another joint venture, creating GE-Fanuc Automation with the U.S. firm General Electric to market factory automation equipment other than robots. In keeping with Fanuc's global strategy of international alliances and a division of labor, Fanuc would supply its NC controllers and other hardware while GE would provide engineering know-how, communications software, and computer technology. In the early 1980s, GE had been a contender for world leadership in factory automation and robotics. But six months after signing its agreement with Fanuc, in January 1987, GE announced that it would abandon the robot side of its business. For Fanuc, this meant the elimination of another competing robot manufacturer and the transformation of it into one more software-oriented ally. Fanuc, it was reported in Japan, would assert much greater control over the joint venture than it did with GMF.[18]

And as for Fanuc's now expensive robots? Inaba turned to his development engineers and ordered them to redesign them to absorb the 50-percent increase in the value of the yen versus the dollar. To the consternation of domestic competitors, Fanuc robots suddenly became dramatically more competitive within Japan. At the same time, Inaba vowed to reduce his dependence on overseas sales from 80 to 60 percent, and to concentrate more on his customers at home.

The RIA's Eric Mittelstadt presents Dr. Seiuemon Inaba with the Joseph F. Engelberger Award for Technology Development in Chicago, 1987.

In the long run, Inaba's alliances with foreign firms may really be a way of strengthening himself in the Japanese market. On a global level, the forces of Fanuc and GMF are arrayed against ASEA, the Swedish world giant in robotics. But within Japan, Fanuc has weaknesses and faces stiff competition from established Japanese firms like Toshiba, Matsushita, and Yaskawa Electric. Furthermore, Fanuc has relatively little experience in electronics assembly, the fastest growing segment of Japan's robot market, and its emphasis on engineering for low cost and reliability makes it vulnerable to rivals using new innovative technologies. In the spring of 1986, Inaba claimed that the small American firm Adept Technology was his main competitor. "They've got a lead over us with their assembly robot, but with GMF we're racing to build one better."[19] Adept's software-enhanced, vision-equipped, direct-drive robots are a real threat in Japan because they are made and marketed by old archrival, Kawasaki.

The robot industry, to survive, must be as flexible as a mechatronic iron arm. Returning to the Fanuc headquarters building after inspecting the robot plants in the spring of 1986, vice-president Shinpei Kato lamented that "with all these new technologies, the one thing that impresses me is how fast they become out of date. The only thing around here that doesn't change is Mount Fuji."[20]

The Man-Machine Interface

In order for a new technology to diffuse throughout society, the people who use it must accept it. In Japan the excellent relationship between industrial workers and some 116,000 robots is touted at home and abroad. But even little Japanese children know there are always two realities: the *tatemae* and the *honne*, one of appearance, and one of true feelings. Both coexist. Both are important. Only one, however, is shown to the outside world.

In other nations, workers have at times been very frank about their opposition to robots. The General Motors plant at Lordstown, Ohio, which in the late 1960s became the first factory in the world to use Unimate spot-welding robots on a large scale, is a particularly notorious example. A showcase of automation built to compete with low-cost Japanese and German imports, it could spit out one hundred Vega compacts per hour. During an ugly strike in early 1972, however, some of the workers (like the English Luddites who smashed the tools of an earlier industrial revolution) sabotaged both machines and cars. The main issue was not wages but—as a result of automation and robots—management's firing of 350 employees, an increased work load, and sheer boredom. The *New York Times* in an editorial called it the "Revolt of the Robots."[1] At Lordstown, instead of robots helping men, the men were turning into robots.

Japan has had no Lordstowns. Yet robots are specifically designed to replace workers. In theory, one welding robot can unemploy three welders. If one welder who works an eight-hour shift is replaced by one robot, running the robot around the clock replaces two more. Furthermore, the goal of replacing workers in Japan has never been hidden from labor, but loudly and proudly proclaimed. Industrial newspapers help everyone keep score: "Kubota Steel Works Plant in Utsunomiya Reduces Work Force by One Hundred" trumpets a typical headline in a column titled "The Unmanned Factory." At the Toshiba Manufacturing Engineering Lab an engineer shows off his latest creation—a lightweight, inexpensive robot—and comments matter-of-factly, with devastating logic, "In theory at Toshiba we don't replace our workers unless there's a major savings involved; so that's why we have to design these things to be cheaper."

How can Japanese industry act this way?

The Research Institute of Industrial Safety is developing a compliant robot hand with rubber tube actuators.

The Outer Reality

Robots are distinguished in manufacturing systems by their flexibility—by programming different instructions, they can be made to perform different tasks. Likewise, when working with robots and robotic systems, perhaps the single most important quality a workforce can possess is flexibility.

In Europe or the United States, if workers have resisted robots it is usually for fear of losing their jobs if a machine can do them cheaper and better. In unionized industries where workers cannot easily be fired, the company that wishes to retrain and transfer them to a new task confronts a different problem. To a trade union (and there may be several in one company), the idea that its members, who may all be welders, might suddenly be changed into robot operators or salesmen is anathema; members might have to change unions, resulting in a smaller membership, fewer dues, and a weakening of the original union. In Japan, however, the much publicized lifetime employment system virtually guarantees workers in large corporations jobs (in exchange for near-total loyalty), and unions are normally organized by company, rather than by trade or skill. To an employee convinced he will be with the same company for life, the introduction of a robot or other automation may mean a new assignment, but not the upheaval of unemployment. To a company union, it makes little difference what its members do, as long as they are happy and stay in the company.

On an individual level, Japan is also reaping the rewards of its huge investment of human capital in an educational system that has given many workers great flexibility. The percentage of Japanese who attend college is smaller than for Americans (at Nissan's Zama plant, almost none of the assembly line workers are college graduates), but Japanese

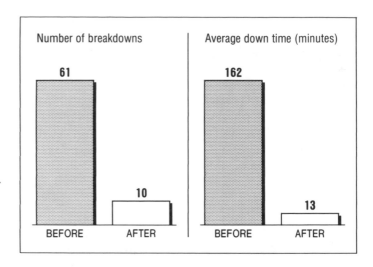

Improvements in welding robot performance at an automobile factory, comparing two six-month periods (July–December 1982 and February–July 1983), before and after the implementation of self-management techniques among maintenance workers. Source: Japan Management Association.

high school graduates have probably spent far more time studying than their American counterparts. Even if factory workers read mostly steamy comic books and sports newspapers, they are literate and are often equipped with the basic math and science skills needed to master new tasks as required. With company training widely provided, many skilled Japanese workers displaced by robots have been able to make the transition to the jobs robots create: robot operators, maintenance personnel, salesmen, and programmers. Flexible work rules also allow them to perform multiple tasks on the floor.[2]

Change almost always involves some form of sacrifice, but a flexible workforce can adapt to change. In the United States (and much of Europe) it was fashionable for years to blame problems of robotization on unions and plant workers; now it is fashionable to blame the managers. One real sticking point, however, has been the antagonistic relationship that exists in America between the two groups; when separated by dress, upbringing, education, and even race and language, it is easy to suspect that any change will be at one's own personal expense. The fears of workers are obvious, but as Eric Mittelstadt of GMF and the RIA notes, even managers are wary. "Robots threaten their status," he says. "They're used to controlling people, and hollering and yelling at them. You can't do that with a robotic system. . . . How can a foreman feel comfortable about a system that takes away a hundred people working for him when he's promoted by the number of people he commands?"[3]

The automated assembly line at JVC's Yokohama video products plant is nearly devoid of workers.

Only a few feet away, long lines of women still perform final assembly and checking. Many hands are still needed in most factories.

To insure the cooperation of a workforce it is essential to have both a perceived equity of sacrifice and an equitable distribution of future benefits that may accrue from robotization.

In Japan, achieving this kind of equity might at first seem even more difficult than in America. After all, Japan once had one of the world's most rigid class systems and is still so hierarchical it is difficult to carry on a proper conversation in Japanese without knowing the other party's age and social status. But equity does not imply a leveling of rank. It only means that within subgroups and age groups, workers can at least "feel" as though all sacrifices will be shared across the board, as will any long-term benefits. This sense of having one's individual fortune tied to that of the group is promoted throughout the very intense Japanese socialization process: school children wear the same uniforms and learn to clean their own classrooms; the hand-picked employees entering prestigious corporations may find their first job is to clean toilets. Thanks partly to the American Occupation and its idealistic "New Dealers," Japan today (like the other robot kingdom, Sweden) also has one of the most equitable distributions of incomes in the capitalist world; allowing for plenty of shirkers and corruption, a highly graduated tax system can take over 93 percent of the income of the top percentile (as compared to 35 percent in the United States).[4]

In corporations, equity is emphasized with the slogan of *Kaisha wa hitotsu, minna onaji* ("One Company, Everyone the Same"). Company presidents earn much more than floor workers, but the income gap between them is typically a fraction of that in the United States, and management usually takes pay cuts when times are rough. The ideal of lifetime employment also means that young workers are hired right out of college or technical schools as generalists, not specialists, with wages based mainly on seniority. Classmates generally start out at the same level, and maintain a rough parity with their peers throughout their careers. In the Toshiba Manufacturing Engineering Lab, an American graduate student on exchange from MIT marvels, "Even my boss helps sweep up the place."[5] And at Fanuc, although no one would dare think of him as an "equal," even Dr. Inaba usually wears the same uniform as the rest of his employees when in the factories.

To encourage a flexible response to change, the workforce must be prepared. To many U.S. corporations in recent years, a massive investment in robotics and integrated, futuristic factories has been seen as a way to leapfrog the Japanese. But sometimes this smacks of a quick fix, a way to wrest control from workers on the floor rather than involve them. As Brian Kuttner, writing in *Robotics World*, has noted, the U.S. approach has all too often ignored the importance of communication among humans before implementing the technology; the goal of total automation, by eliminating people, has been an "all or nothing approach. It may be compared with the nuclear option in military strategy."[6]

Generally speaking, both large and small Japanese companies have tried hard to smooth the introduction of robots. At thirty-man Yamasaki Seisakujo, mentioned in chapter 1, the president confesses that "when the top people in our company decided to introduce a robot for welding, some of the workers were a little worried. We basically have a top-dowr. type of management, so employee education was extremely important. We now have to show them how much easier work is with one industrial robot before we can introduce another. We have to have a consensus." At a huge Ricoh plant in Atsugi, where paper copier machines and other devices are manufactured by people and robots, an introductory video carefully emphasizes that "technology is for human beings, not the reverse," and a brochure illustrates factory automation with a pyramid—of software and hardware on the bottom, and humans on top. Even Dr. Inaba of

FOLLOW UP TO NISSAN'S MEMORANDUM ON THE INTRODUCTION OF NEW TECHNOLOGIES

Although the "Robot Agreement" between the labor union and Nissan Motor Company generated tremendous interest around the world and has often been spoken of as a model, it was never adopted by other automakers in Japan. Part of the problem is its vagueness. It calls for prior consultation on the introduction of new technologies such as robots, but says nothing about what type of approval is required for a management-labor agreement and nothing about the specifics of issues such as reassignments and reeducation.

Also, given the pace of technological change, some managers have reportedly suggested that the agreement should be renegotiated—requiring a detailed discussion every time a new technology is introduced might result in a fatal delay in Japan's competitive market. Nissan has already been losing market share.

Both Nissan management and labor claim the agreement reflects the fundamentally good worker-boss relations at Nissan. It may reflect just the opposite. Much of Japanese society functions on trust, and most Japanese manufacturing concerns would probably not put an agreement to paper unless there was considerable suspicion between labor and management.

In late 1986, Nissan was in the process of limiting the scope of the original agreement. In the future, says an official, consultations will be required only when a technology is likely to cause major upheavals.

Fanuc, the Genghis Khan of robots and automation, keeps in mind the limits of technology. In his 1982 biography, he stresses that "factory automation is not to be used to completely un-man the factory. It is a system to reduce labor, and shift people from monotonous to more creative work. It should only be used when this principle is clearly understood." When construction of a new motor plant with 101 robots produced a surplus of fifty engineers, "we had them do work," Inaba writes, "where they could apply their talents. Some, for example, went into design, some did tests and servicing as factory engineers, and some who were inclined to marketing became sales engineers. . . . It proved profitable for both labor and management."[7]

By far the most famous attempt to reassure workers was on March 1, 1983, when Nissan Motor and the All Nissan Motor Workers Union signed what came to be known as the "Robot Agreement." Officially called the "Memorandum on the Introduction of New Technologies," it called for the company to consult with the union in advance on its plans and their effect on the workers; to neither fire nor lay off workers; to neither demote union members nor decrease their pay; to insure worker safety; and to provide retraining and education in accordance with workers' abilities when work changes or reassignments were required.[8]

With such policies, written or unwritten, Japanese workers may not exactly clamor for more robots, but almost. In

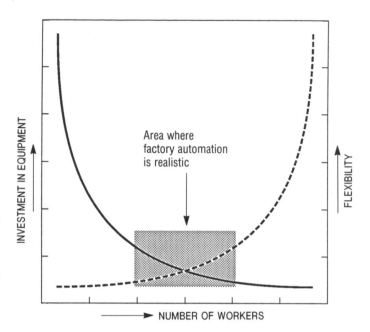

Inaba's graph of diminishing returns in automation. When automating a factory, trying to reduce the number of employees creates a need for greater investment in equipment (solid line), and less flexibility is gained. Since a totally unmanned factory is impractical, automation demands a balance between investment in plant and capital, flexibility, and number of employees. Source: Inaba, *Robotto jidai o hiraku*, p. 179.

INVESTMENT IN EQUIPMENT

FLEXIBILITY

Area where factory automation is realistic

NUMBER OF WORKERS

auto plants it is hard to hold a heavy welding gun for long hours and endure the heat and flying sparks. When robots were introduced in the early days, many workers therefore wanted to learn how to operate and service them; they wanted to shift jobs. When a poll was taken in 1983 among members of the All Japan Federation of Electric Machine Workers Union on the introduction of microelectronics (including robots), nearly 70 percent urged a cautious approach but not a single person replied in opposition.[9] And why should they? If being replaced by a robot means training for less grueling work, such as being a robot operator, and an annual bonus that fattens because of the increase in company productivity, who would say no?

On a macroeconomic level, Japan has provided a spectacular reassurance to those who fear that robots cause massive unemployment. In 1950 Norbert Wiener wrote that automatic machines are the equivalent of slave labor, and that those who compete with them must accept the economic conditions of enslavement. "It is perfectly clear," he confidently stated, "that this will create an unemployment situation, in comparison with which . . . even the depression of the thir-

HASEGAWA'S NEW LAWS OF ROBOTICS

Yukio Hasegawa, in his book *Robotto to sha-kai* ("Robots and Society"), introduces a revised, present-day version of Isaac Asimov's famous Three Laws of Robotics.

1. Robots shall be built and used to contribute to human welfare and development.
2. Robots shall never usurp work from humans that humans want to do themselves. Robots shall be used for work humans dislike and for work that is dangerous.
3. Robots shall never be built in a form or to specifications that physically or psychologically threaten humans.
4. Robots shall always obey human commands except when there is a danger of harming others or themselves.
5. Before robots take over human work, the humans affected shall be asked for their consent.
6. Robots shall be made so they are easy for humans to operate, and so they can easily help humans.
7. Robots shall remove themselves quickly from a site when an assignment is completed, so as not to interfere with humans or other robots.

ties will seem a pleasant joke." Differences in the way statistics are gathered inherently weaken international comparisons, but Japan's official unemployment rate has consistently been the envy of the rest of the industrialized world for the last decade. Naoyuki Kameyama, a researcher for the National Institute of Employment and Vocational Research, is typical of governmental optimism. In 1986, despite a jobless rate that was climbing to 3 percent, he could claim that robots and microelectronics had "zero" influence on employment. He does, however, admit that robots have changed the quality of work and required considerable sacrifices.[10]

The Other Reality

For a critical view of robotization in industry, one must look beyond the normal generalizations put forth by the industrial establishment. The outer reality in Japan—where human and machines coexist in a technological Lotus Land —applies largely to the elite workforce in Japan's giant corporations. These regular employees may enjoy lifetime employment and many other benefits that make working with robots easier, but their ranks rarely include women, people with physical or mental handicaps, or even awkward personalities. In fact, the number of such privileged workers in Japan's workforce is really only around 15 percent, perhaps not very different from the percentage in the United States.[11] The real difference is in the perceived reality. In Japan lifetime employment has been *tatemae*, or the surface reality. It is perceived as the social norm, but it is only a goal.

The human robot. At an older plant, a worker feeds red-hot metal parts into a press. If cost effective, this task could easily be done by an industrial robot.

Historically, much of corporate flexibility in Japan has actually been derived from nonregular employees. Spot welders and painters in the auto industry during its boom years, for example, were often seasonal workers brought in from the lesser-developed Tohoku and Okinawa regions under six-month contracts, which made it easy to replace them with robots. Also, most line workers in electronics assembly have been women, who work part-time or who as full-timers are expected to follow the traditional Japanese pattern of quitting at age twenty-three or -four to marry and raise a family. Journalist Biko Nano, writing in a 1982 book *Robotto shitsugyo* ("Robot Unemployment"), claims robotization ruined the formerly unbeatable Hitachi Musashi women's volleyball team. Most of its members came from a factory where they were employed by the hundreds to package large scale integrated circuits. With development of what the Japanese call "wire-bonding robots," or computerized machinery that connects the chip circuitry to its outside lead wires, these women disappeared.[12]

By emphasizing their own security, regular employees in elite corporations may actually desensitize themselves to the insecurity of others. A 1983 book with the sensational title *Ima robotto kojo ni haittara ikigai wa aruka* ("Is Life Worth Living in a Robot Factory Today?") contains a revealing interview with Ichiro Shioji, then head of the Federation of Japan Automobile Workers' Unions, who compared the perspective of Japanese workers with their counterparts in the West. "In Japan," he said, "everyone's talking about ME [Micro Electronics], ME, robots, robots . . . but in reality they're only worried about the macro situation; they're optimistic about the micro side. When they . . . think theoretically they feel uneasy, but believe they themselves will be all right. Overseas, people are uneasy about the macro and the micro aspects."[13]

The union's dogged pursuit of security may also have led them to ignore various internal contradictions. Journalist Satoshi Kamata, a former Toyota factory worker, has made blistering attacks on robotization with books such as *Robotto shakai no kanri to shihai* ("Management and Control in a Robot Society") and the even more lurid *Robotto zetsubo kojo* ("Robot Factory of Despair"). In a 1982 work titled *Robotto jidai no genba* ("On the Shop Floor in the Robot Age"), he lambastes Japanese labor unions that have marched under the banner of "protecting employment." To do so, he says, they must protect their company. To protect their company they must win in the struggle for domestic market share, and in the war for overseas exports. To do that they must promote computerization and robotization. Even the unmanned factory built with robots thus becomes a means to preserve employment; without it, threatens the Ministry of Trade and Industry, Japan's competitive position cannot be maintained. The result is that nary a voice is raised in opposition to FMS, which is really a revolution designed to sweep laborers from the factory floor."[14]

When one broadens the definition of robots to include automation outside the manufacturing industry, unions have not always been so cooperative. A classic example is the heavily overstaffed, debt-ridden 300,000-man Japanese National Railways (JNR) before it was privatized in 1987. In the Tokyo area JNR men always painstakingly punched the ticket of each rider—despite the fact that many private subways in Japan (and most subways around the world) had adopted automatic machines. Whenever reductions in the workforce were proposed, JNR unions trotted out red banners of protest. After a government commission recommended the JNR workforce be cut by between 60,000 and 100,000 men, several dramatic incidents of fire bombing and sabotage of JNR facilities and communications lines occurred, with speculation that union members were involved.[15]

"I, too, oppose rationalization." The Keisei train line labor union opposed economy measures in 1981 and used Iron Man No. 28 to make a point.

The sacrifices employees make for automation are often cloaked by industry to preserve the aura of lifetime employment. Sometimes the cost to workers and the intellect is such that one wonders if firing might not be a better fate. The words "fired" and "layoff" are virtually taboo; preferred terms are "rationalization" or "adjustment" of the workforce, or even the very vague *rishoku*, which literally means to "leave work." Most large companies do try to train employees and reassign them to other jobs, and to streamline by encouraging early retirements. But when times are really rough a common solution is *shukko*, a system by which employees are "loaned" for several years (perhaps permanently) to any companies with which the firm has a stock-holding relationship. Conceivably, an auto worker displaced by automation could therefore wind up working for a real estate agent for years in another city, but still be part of his original auto firm, keep his seniority, and still belong to the auto union. When the JNR was privatized in 1987, it created *ukezara*, or "saucer" corporations, which served mainly to contain the excess employees, and encouraged any and all affiliate organizations to hire them. Long-time railway men —burly train drivers and ticket punchers—suddenly found themselves operating ski lifts and working in restaurants. One company was called in to teach the rougher men better manners for dealing with the public in service jobs. Between January and November 1986, however, there were thirty-three suicides (some groups said sixty-two)—so many that the prime minister ordered a special commission to investigate.[16]

Several groups in Japan consistently spotlight the shadows of the man-machine interface. The Japan Revolutionary Communists League, Revolutionary Marxist Faction, known as Kakumaru, is an extreme example. This anti-imperialist, anti-Stalinist revolutionary group dates back to 1956 and claims followers in both the student and labor movements, including some factions of the JNR union—despite the fact that in the last decade its leaders' ranks have been decimated by police arrests and by deaths incurred in factional violence. Kakumaru writers condemn both capitalism and Stalinism. While they have a very sharp ax to grind, their writings on robots do reflect an antitechnological viewpoint shared by some elements of the general public.

Robots are as welcome to labor in recessions as droughts are in the Sahara, and ship building (and steel) in Japan has been in recession for several years. In a 1986 issue of the weekly *Kaiho* ("Liberation"), a shipyard worker named Kai Funado (presumably a pseudonym, since his first name means "paddle" and the second "ship's hatch") bitterly attacked the increased use of robots in his industry. Using plenty of rhetoric, he noted the many transfers and reassignments among his fellow workers, the increased work load for those remaining skilled workers who must do the touch-up welding work the robot cannot, their isolation, and their spiritual and physical fatigue. "The labor aristocracy and their ilk," he rails, "have no way of knowing the suffering that we workers experience on the shop floor. No, guided by management, they merrily go through the shop on their 'robot tour,' only expressing interest in the robot's movements."[17]

Yet another Kakumaru member, writing in a 1986 issue of the monthly *The Communist* on the introduction of robots into electronics assembly, describes a problem with robot-related transfers. "When a line worker—a skilled assembler—is shifted to office work, young women in their twenties and thirties have to show him how to use an unfamiliar word processor or terminal keyboard. But a man over fifty has a hard time learning this even if forced, and he will be gritting his teeth while the young women around him use the same equipment with ease. The workers who can't endure this have no choice but to leave the company—under the pretext of 'voluntary resignation.' Despite the capitalists' talk of 'no layoffs,' in reality 'firings' of this sort occur all the time."[18]

Workers who avoid the "humiliation" of working with young women in the office by becoming robot operators on the shop floor may still grit their teeth. Typing is alien to most older Japanese. So are many of the arcane foreign words used in modern manuals. But robot arms are often taught their motions by commands issued from a computer keyboard, using "off line" programming. And sometimes the commands themselves are in English. Kawasaki's Unimate robots use an American programming language called VAL that requires the operator to memorize over one hundred very foreign English words.

———

Robots affect people in far more ways than simply replacing them. In theory, robots should help humanize work and liberate us from dangerous and dirty tasks, and even from monotonous ones. Someday, they should even free us from the assembly line, a modern industrial grotesquerie that sucks humans into a machine system and forces them to become part of it.

Sometimes, however, the actual results are different. Vocational researcher Kameyama likes to tell the story of a very modern garment factory that employed handicapped people and then introduced microelectronics technology and robots. "Those with ambulatory problems," he says, "were aided by the technology, and able to do more complex, interesting work. Work for those with emotional and mental handicaps declined. As a researcher, I had assumed that advanced technology would liberate us from boring, repetitive work, and lead to greater happiness. But some people like—and need—simple, repetitive physical work."[19]

For the average employee in modern factories, the simple work may actually increase. The movement of a painting or arc-welding robot's arm is a digitalization of that of a skilled worker; it is programmed to imitate and usurp his actions. One result is a polarization of skills. More and more people with advanced skills are needed to maintain the equipment and to program it, but others find themselves doing tasks that have been "de-skilled"—merely stacking widgets for the robot to handle, or pushing a button.

De-skilling carries with it special hidden dangers for Japan. Many Japanese pride themselves on their craftsmanship, and in conversation the expression "we Japanese are clever with our hands" is used to imply the superiority of everything from Japanese products to the Japanese race itself. And Japanese are dexterous: foreigners marveling over Japan's postwar economic miracle would do well to look not only at books on management but also at clerks carefully wrapping gifts in department stores. But like many things in life, craftsmanship and manual dexterity are largely learned traits. Traditionally, tiny Japanese children learned to manipulate chopsticks as soon as they could hold them, and grammar school children learned to carefully hand-sharpen pencils with razor blades. But today, as their elders lament, children use spoons in school cafeterias and show bad chopstick form at the dinner table at home; the proliferation of battery- powered pencil sharpeners has made beautifully hand-carved pencil tips a thing of the past. Among adults, cheap word processors threaten to demolish decades of carefully nurtured calligraphy skills.

It is a syndrome from which industry is not immune. At the video cassette recorder assembly plant of the Victor Company of Japan (JVC) in Yokohama, a highly automated line with sixty-one robots puts together the mechanical subassembly of the machine—most of the moving components except the recording head itself. When the robot arms solder some twenty-one connections, they do not merely spit a glob of molten metal onto the connection; they are programmed to duplicate the hand motion of an experienced worker, lowering the solder tip to the contact point delicately but quickly, and then raising it slowly to avoid tiny balls of unwanted solder spilling off and damaging the connection.

As Katsuhiro Kawasaki, general manager of the Video Division says, "One of the basic philosophies of our automation is to make the work so easy even an amateur can do it."[20] But in the process workers are gradually being distanced from direct contact with the work piece itself. In one sense this is merely part of a long historical trend, but computerization and robots have accelerated it to the point where man is increasingly a spectator. It is also a trend that contradicts the postwar Japanese manufacturing ideology of *genba shugi*, or "shop floorism," and the glorification of "hands-on experience," often credited for major improvements in worker skills, process technology, and quality. How will workers know how to solder if the skill survives only as a memory of a long-since-retired worker, now encoded in the program that drives the robot arm? It conjures up amusing images of young workers traipsing to the factory, where they learn how to solder by watching and imitating a robot.

Large corporations are countering this trend by specially training employees in traditional skills. But smaller companies cannot afford this. Kiyoshi Mori, a section chief of manufacturing at the Haniuda Steel Works, where large-sized boilers and other equipment are made the old way—with skilled workers—has written extensively on robots in industry from the perspective of the small company and the man on the shop floor. He worries greatly about the need to preserve traditional skills. "People tend to downgrade them," he says, "but we need a balance between the old and the new. It is a problem that must be solved, and soon, or I fear that Japan may be ruined by high technology."[21]

Working in an automated environment can also cause increased stress. In more old-fashioned plants, work is often boring, labor-intensive, and physically demanding (not to mention dangerous), but amid the clatter of machinery a sense of solidarity often exists among workers. They are usually visible to each other, and there is time for winks, smiles, an occasional joke, and a little chatter—the basic glue of humanity. In the most automated manufacturing plants—the Fanucs or the Casios—there are fewer and fewer workers on the floor, with less physical work to do but more and more responsibility.

As part of a 1986 series on "technostress," the *Nikkei sangyo* newspaper ran an article on "The Isolation Syndrome of Automation." A state-of-the-art factory run by Star Micronics in Shizuoka Prefecture used automated NC tools and robotized machining centers that ran unmanned during the night—a source of great pride to the older workers. But several of the younger, new employees began to complain that they "felt like robots" as they operated and programmed the automated machinery during the day; one local parent complained that all his son did all day long was push a button.

As it turned out, there was a major perception gap between the old and new employees. The former, who had worked with the engineers to design the system, had a vested interest in it and a basic knowledge of its operation; they knew that pressing a specific button would operate the system in a specific way. But to the new employees, a button was merely a button to be pushed, and the total system was a technological black box that merely worked in unfathomable ways. The solution was easy—to rotate employees among different tasks and help them grasp the workings of the total system—but the problem was by no means limited to Star Micronics.[22]

———

While robots should also liberate humans from hazardous work, sometimes they themselves are the hazard. Robots only do as commanded by their programmers or operators, yet they are distinctly different from pre-computer-age industrial machines such as cranes or fork lift trucks that operate under direct human control. The robot's movements are set in advance. If equipped with sensors, a robot may begin moving through a programmed sequence or change its moves according to the information they feed it. But a malfunction due to component failure or electronic interference from other machines may make an industrial robot arm that seems at rest suddenly start moving, at a speed or in a direction never intended.

At the end of 1981, newspapers around the world widely reported what was billed as Japan and the world's first robot-induced fatality. Actually, the incident had occurred nearly six months earlier, and it may not even have been the first. At 5:10 A.M. on July 4, 1981, Kenji Urata of Kawasaki Heavy Industries noted that a finishing machine to which a Kawasaki-Unimate was supplying material had broken. Since the robot arm appeared stopped, he went to fix the machine, whereupon the robot suddenly went back to work, crushing him to death. Urata's death was reported immediately by the Japan Communist Party newspaper, *Akahata*, but ignored for half a year by Japan's mainstream press, presumably to avoid embarrassing the industrial establishment. According to Urata's fellow workers, one cause of the accident was worker fatigue; the plant had undergone drastic "rationalization" along with the introduction of robots, and each employee's workload had increased proportionately. Urata, killed in the wee hours of the morning, had been called to work on his day off.[23]

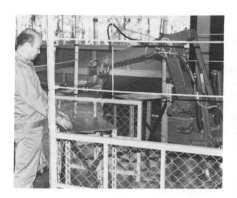
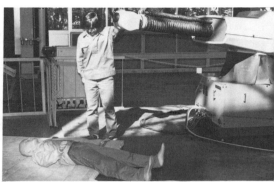

Urata's death became an issue in Japan's National Diet, and Japan eventually became a world leader in robot safety, with the robot industry, the government, and manufacturing concerns initiating a variety of safety measures. The Labor Safety and Health Law, for example, now mandates that plant operators enclose dangerous robots in a cage or fence or take similar safety measures. But as technology develops, and as more and more robots work on tracks or rails and (like AGV robot carts) are no longer fixed in place, static safety devices become more and more impractical. In addition to cages, optical sensors (laser and infrared beams) and tactile sensors for both robot arms and carts are widely used in Japan and the rest of the world today. If a person breaks a beam of light or steps on a special mat surrounding the robot arm, it will stop automatically; robot carts, likewise, will stop when their sensors detect a person in front of them, wait for a few seconds, and then proceed if the coast is clear. Still, unlike metal fences, it is hard to tell if a sensor is malfunctioning, and for many small manufacturers, any kind of safety device is a major expense. There have been over ten deaths due to Japanese-defined industrial robots to date in Japan. Since it is in the nature of humans to err, and machines to fail, in the future there will be many more.[24]

The correct way to work with a robot. At the Research Institute of Industrial Safety, the robot is caged, equipped with contact sensors, and surrounded by plastic tubes carrying light beams; if the light is interrupted, the robot shuts down.

The Institute's tests show a hydraulic robot can strike a worker with a lethal force of 90 Gs.

In addition to directly affecting individuals, robotization is also changing the traditional relationship between large and small companies. As noted earlier, giant corporations are at the apex of a pyramid of many primary, secondary, and tertiary subcontractors. The relationship among these companies is often expressed in parent-child-grandchild terms and governed by unspoken rules, ideally a variant of *giri-ninjo*, the social code of duty and compassion that many

Japanese feel has glued their culture together. In recent years, to cut costs, some parent companies have begun to use robots to do work in-house that was traditionally given to subcontractors. For work they still farm out, the large companies encourage cutthroat competition among their suppliers. The smaller companies who survive may then be rewarded with "affiliate" status; they will be told what type of assembly line to build and supplied with programs to run on its robots. At Yamasaki Seisakujo, the tiny subcontractor in a "grandchild" relationship with Tokyo Electric Power Company, one robot has welded parts for high-tension pylons for the last five years. "With our parent company automating and doing more and more work internally," says the president, "we are forced to become more technologically sophisticated just to stay afloat. . . . We're sandwiched, in competition with others in our group, and even with our parent. . . . Nowadays it's a free-for-all economy, and the old days of *giri-ninjo* are gone."[25]

When everyone uses robots, the terms of competition change. When parent companies push robotization on their subcontractors, or when subcontractors robotize to remain in the pyramid, company profits may decrease. Takumi Kojima of the Japan Small Business Corporation's Research Institute notes that human labor varies in cost, but if a robot at a subcontractor is of the same make and configuration as at the parent company, and uses the same program, the cost is fixed, and known in advance. One result is that there is little room to pad charges when manufacturing a product with a robot. Another way of looking at it is expressed by vocational researcher Kameyama. "There is hardly any room left for price cutting," he says. "The manufactured good is delivered at what we call *robotto tanka*, or the 'robot unit cost,' in which labor is not a factor. What the parent company looks for now is performance and the ability to meet shipping schedules."[26]

When economic times are truly difficult for the manufacturing sector, as they were during the exchange rate crisis of 1985–87, the large corporations at the top of the pyramid do more than encourage cannibalistic competition at the bottom—they may deliberately begin preying on members of the group. In the mid-1980s the Japanese media began focusing incessantly on the social problem of *ijime*, or "bullying," where school children torment classmates who for one reason or another do not fit the social norm, sometimes

ROBOTS AND SAFETY

Researchers at the Ministry of Labor's Research Institute of Industrial Safety are trying to develop new concepts of safety in robotics. Current thinking, claims chief researcher Noboru Sugimoto, is inadequate. To date, he says, designs have focused on a fail-safe approach that tries to insure against failure by using sensors to detect danger or malfunction, by building extreme reliability into the system, and by using redundant safety devices, each to cover the other in case one fails.

Operating under the assumption that machines will always fail and humans will always make errors, Sugimoto and his co-workers at the institute are advocating a new system design that detects not danger, but safe conditions. When such a system fails, the robot will stop. Sugimoto makes an analogy to a man hired to watch for fires. If his job is to yell "Fire!" only

when he sees one, there is always the possibility he may be asleep when the fire starts, and not see it. If, however, his job is to constantly yell "No Fire!" as long as he cannot see one, when no yell is heard one can safely assume that there is either a fire or the watchman is asleep, and proceed with caution.

Another approach to safety at the institute involves the design of robots that cause little or no injury when they do fail. Normal robots, made of heavy, inflexible steel can cause disaster on contact with human flesh—they are always rigid, even when not in operation. Working with Bridgestone and Hitachi, the institute is trying to develop robot arms with special inflatable rubber actuators that replicate the compliancy of human arms. These arms can be made rigid when necessary but are otherwise resilient and flexible to the touch.

---

beating them to death. *Ijime* also affects industry. On May 31,1986, for example, the *Daily Industrial News* reported on its first page that MITI and the Fair Trade Commission had decided to "warn" and give "guidance" to parent companies who were bullying their subcontractors by threatening to cancel business unless they accepted loans at unusually high interest rates.[27]

At the lower level of subcontractors, when times are bad, idled workers have no safety net under them and cannot be reassigned or shuffled off to subsidiaries. Despite lip service to lifetime employment and benevolent paternalism, when bankruptcies occur (as they did on a massive level during the exchange rate crisis), workers lose their jobs. Faced with bankruptcy, small Japanese companies and even big corporations lay off people.

How, then, does one reconcile the surface reality of the smooth man-machine interface with the other reality of sacrifices and problems? First, the structure of Japanese industry has contained any disruption that robots may have caused. Regular, unionized employees have generally benefited. Nonregular, nonunionized employees and employees of small companies who may have lost their jobs never had much voice anyway; the hierarchical, consensus-oriented nature of Japanese groups tends to quickly squash unorganized dissent. Second, since Japan has been a leader in the introduction of robots, it has been able to introduce them at its own pace (instead of as a competitive reaction) to areas where they would be most welcomed—that is, dirty, dangerous, and dull jobs. Finally, Japan has had the luxury of introducing robots in an expanding economy when its manufacturing sector was booming, as well as into brand-new industries where they caused little disruption.

But even the most enthusiastic boosters of robots in Japan admit the future may not be so easy. Japan's manufacturing sector is no longer growing at its old pace, and many of the workers who could be laid off easily have already been laid off. As robots are endowed with vision and other senses, and as the computers that control them become capable of making more and more sophisticated decisions, the range of human labor that they will replace will become ever greater. Not all the people displaced will be educated or flexible enough to get other jobs. A real social dislocation may occur when robots grow sophisticated enough to use in the service industries, because here they will begin to displace many of the same people they displaced earlier in manufacturing. And then where will the workers go?

Technological progress is almost impossible to stop, and it usually is a double-edged sword. For the moment at least, the voices of opposition to robots in Japan have been drowned—drowned in the avalanche of wealth and materialism that the robots helped create.

Robots and the Wealth of Nations

In 1985 the report of the United States President's Commission on Industrial Competitiveness, headed by John Young of Hewlett-Packard, noted that "Japanese productivity growth has been five times greater than our own. That country's productivity now exceeds that of the United States in steel; transportation equipment; and electrical, general, and precision machinery. American employees in those industries have experienced the competitive consequences of our lagging performance."[1] In other words, in economic terms, Japan was earning far more in output for the same units of investment in labor and capital; in plain English, it was getting more reward for the same amount of effort. The commission's report was widely ignored by the American media and the political establishment.

There are many reasons for the "productivity gap" between Japan and its competitors in the West, but it is more than coincidence that the fields in which Japan leads have a heavy concentration of robotics technologies. One way to increase productivity is to use tools that amplify labor. In the modern factory, industrial robots and flexible automation are state-of-the-art tools and, if properly mastered, can result not just in increased productivity in the sense of more widgets per hour for the same amount of work, but in a new synergy resulting in lower costs, greater diversity of products, and improved inventory control, process and product design, quality, and technological skills.

Polls taken of firms in Japan often show robots are introduced for the obvious reasons—to save labor and thus reduce costs. At Fanuc, as Joseph Engelberger often jokes, Dr. Inaba "can't reduce labor any more because there's just enough people to bow for him as he moves from factory to

Suzumo's sushi robot at a 1986 store automation show.

The sushi robot mechanism.

factory." But other companies have achieved equally impressive, less publicized labor-saving results on a smaller scale. In 1986 Knorr, best known for soup in Japan, announced it would introduce two Fanuc robots into the soup line of its Kawasaki factory and reduce employees on the line from fourteen to six; in its mayonnaise division it would install seven robots and reduce fifteen people to one.[2] The machines, of course, never ask for wages, overtime, or benefits.

But robots are not always cheap, and labor is not always expensive. In both Japan and American today, direct human labor costs often represent only a fraction of the total cost of manufacturing—between 5 and 10 percent.[3] So why replace cheap labor with expensive robots?

Many of the real benefits lie in other areas.

The Robotics Synergy

One advantage of robots can be illustrated by the sushi robot made by Suzumo Machinery Industries. Sushi is slices of raw fish resting on carefully molded patties of prepared rice. The sushi robot is a small contraption that makes the patties. With its limited degrees of freedom and its specialization, this robot may not fit all definitions of an industrial robot, but it is automatic and programmable, it uses optical sensors, it performs manipulation, and it is manufactured with the aid of "real" industrial robots. When rice is poured into a hole on top, the machine discharges it as loose lumps onto a tiny moving conveyor belt below. As the lumps move along the belt, two four-fingered "hands" descend from above and squeeze them into perfect patties, after which a special dispenser applies a dab of *wasabi*, or Japanese horseradish. The sliced raw fish must still be applied by humans.

COMPARING ASSEMBLY AND TESTING OF SMALL MOTORS BY PART-TIME WORKERS WITH ROBOTIC ASSEMBLY

"0" = superior "X" = inferior

Criteria	Robotic Assembly Score/Comments	Part-Timer Assembly Score/Comments
Flexibility		
Ability to handle short-lived products	X Line needs reworking	0 Easy when taught
Ability to handle changes in production volume	0 Easy, by running machines at night	X Requires personnel changes; once employees hired, hard to adjust to less volume
Quality	0 Superior, allowing for robot malfunction	X Difficult to manage careless mistakes
Cost		
Quality and number of personnel required	0 Requires small number of highly skilled workers who can do maintenance	X Requires large number of part-timers
Initial cost	X Requires large initial investment	0 Unnecessary
Future costs	0 Automatic assembly cost will decline in future	X Part-timer wages will increase (6% per annum)
Additional merit	0 Work can be done in-house	X More work tends to be commissioned to outside sources
Space requirements	0 Line can be implemented in small space if facilities designed properly	X Space needed for large number of part-timers to work in
Lead Time	0 Since a continuous line is used, when a product enters the line, it proceeds sequentially to end	X Depends on work structure, but tends toward batch production

It is easy to see why the Japanese media and public went wild over the sushi robot when it was first introduced in 1981. Rice is more than food in Japan; it is inextricably linked with two millennia of tradition and culture. Good sushi embodies this tradition and can be outrageously expensive, for reasons beyond the cost of the raw fish itself. Squeezing the rice patties properly is a performance art; an ideal patty requires an exact shape and exact mixtures of air and rice. A good sushi chef may spend ten years perfecting his craft. Yet in one hour only the best chef can make more than 400 patties. The Suzumo sushi robot can crank out 1,200 an hour.

Kisaku Suzuki, the president of Suzumo and a sushi zealot, had a twofold goal in developing the robot—to increase rice consumption in Japan (more and more young people prefer bread) and to make quality sushi more accessible to the masses. He also has his own perspective on robotization. "After the war," he expounds, "Japan was economically and materially destroyed. It's taken us forty years to rise to our current position, and this is largely due to our use of machines. If we look at the evolution of machines, we can divide them into four stages—of labor saving through automation; materials saving through multimodel, small batch production; energy saving, as in more efficient machinery; and finally, what I call skill-saving machinery, as in the case of the sushi robot."[4]

"Skill saving" is the flip side of "de-skilling." Sushi robots augment the work of a skilled chef or amplify the skills of an amateur—for take-out orders and quick snacks where time, rather than formality and tradition, is important and where the store can ill afford to hire another fully trained, highly paid chef. But skill saving is obviously not limited to the world of sushi. In traditional manufacturing industries, industrial robots combining both skill and labor saving can produce results that are even more dramatic. An example: In late 1985, Arakawa Buhin Seisakujo was making legs for folding tables and chairs, and instead of farming out welding work as it once did, it installed two Matsushita robots and began doing it in-house. The entire company, however, consisted of only the president and two employees, both part-timers, who were over seventy years old. Robots enabled the men to duplicate the skilled work of professional welders and the physical labor of much younger men, the former expensive and the latter in short supply in manufacturing.[5]

———

Better inventory control is a less obvious result of robotization. One of the most admired and imitated areas of Japanese manufacturing abroad is a system usually referred to in the West as "just-in-time," or JIT. A strong suit especially of Toyota, the car maker, JIT stresses the importance of being able to obtain only the quantity of parts needed (and no

WHY TRADE IMBALANCES OCCUR—ONE VIEW

According to Atsuyoshi Ouchi, the vice-chairman of NEC, one of Japan's largest computer and communications equipment firms, the roots of the trade imbalance between the United States and Japan lie in the division of labor that has developed.

"Japan handles all the high-volume, profitable items," he claims, "while the United States takes care of the inventions and discoveries—wonderful in their own right, but not as lucrative a business. From now on, in a macroeconomic sense, Japan must catch up in product innovation, and the U.S. must put more emphasis on process innovation."

---

more), only when needed. It thus reduces the costs associated with storage, record keeping, and waste. JIT is a system that Japan's industrial structure is especially suited to; parent companies are often located in the same area as their subcontractors, so it is therefore less critical to have a large stockpile of parts on hand—they can be ordered just by hollering to the fellow across the street.

The JIT system is not intrinsically dependent on robots, but robots can greatly assist it. Automating production lines makes it far easier to calculate how many units of a particular product will be produced in a particular time. Unlike human workers, who are subject to fatigue, boredom, and other idiosyncrasies, properly adjusted robots on an assembly line will perform their tasks in exactly the same amount of time, every time, and because of their precision they will create fewer defects. This allows people (and computers) to track materials with greater accuracy. Therefore fewer parts and spares are needed in reserve. On the most automated line at JVC's Yokohama plant, where video cassette recorders are made, the fact that each of the sixty-one robots performs its task in ten seconds makes it very easy for managers to calculate the time and estimate the number of parts needed to produce the day's quota. The JVC line produces 180,000 mechanical deck assemblies per month, but only one and a half days' worth of parts are kept on hand.[6]

Changes in the design process are an even greater hidden effect of robotization than skill saving or inventory control. In the fall of 1985, after the International Symposium on Industrial Robots, a group of experts from around the world visited a Ricoh plant at Atsugi, where copier machines are assembled. Copier machines are mechanically quite complex and may have between five hundred and two thousand parts, depending on their features and size. Before touring the factory floor, Koichi Endo, the general manager, as is his custom, showed guests a display of two models. The first model was older, rather large, bulky, and complex. The second, its successor, was designed specifically for automated assembly. Bending over in his white uniform, wearing an arm band that said, "Reach for the Twenty-First Century," Endo proceeded to take the new machine apart like a toy and, to the astonishment of the visitors, in a few seconds had it in pieces. By eliminating over eighty parts from the design and making it modular, with a vertical assembly, Ricoh had created a copier easier for robots to handle and for humans to assemble. "The old model used to require three man hours," said Endo, smiling, "but the new one only takes one and a half." As one of the Americans on the tour, Brian Carlisle, the president of Adept Technology, later noted, "One of the strengths of the Japanese is that they design both the product and the manufacturing process simultaneously. If you design a product, select the material, the configuration, assembly process, and so forth, you can influence up to 70 percent of the final product cost at the time of design."[7]

Designing for robotic assembly is fundamentally different from designing for human labor. Humans excel at interpreting fuzzy directions and, as in cooking or playing jazz, rather like to adjust things here and there to make them work. Most robots require that the objects they manipulate be precisely placed, that tolerances between parts being fitted together be exactly right, and that parts be inserted from directly above, rather than at an angle. They also require that each step and each movement in a task be taught them in painstaking detail. The result? Humans must reanalyze the simple tasks they normally perform so easily, break them down into key components and moves, reorganize them to suit the robot's requirements, and augment the robot's limitations with peripheral equipment and work-piece positioners. In doing so, a new understanding can take place, leading to more efficient designs of both the product and the manufacturing process.

It is no coincidence that most of the popular consumer goods from Japan today are modular and vertical in construction. At JVC's automated line that builds the video cassette recorder mechanical subassembly, the actual assembly contains screws on both top and bottom, but only one is actually inserted from below. To make it easier for the robots, the chassis itself is flipped four times as it goes down the line.

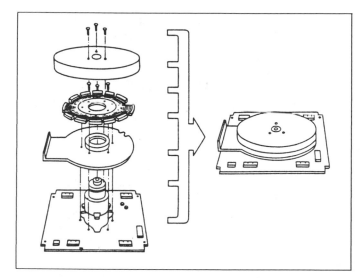

Vertical assembly of a DC brushless motor for a 5-inch floppy disk drive at a Yaskawa Electric automated assembly line. Total number of parts: 34.

At Toshiba, the company uses what it calls an Assembly Evaluation Index to rate the ease of assembly of a product— designers get good marks for vertical assembly and demerits if too many screws are used.

Increasingly, robot assembly is also linked with CAD (computer-aided design) and CAM (computer-aided manufacturing) that permit the product to be designed on a computer terminal and the robot movements required for assembly to be first simulated with computer graphics and then fed into the machine itself. This shortens the time required for both product and manufacturing-process design. Design speed is especially important in Japan because consumer product life cycles—the length of time before a design has to be changed—are becoming shorter and shorter. In 1985, for example, the life of a typical product model at Ricoh was one year, less than half of what it was three years earlier; at the end of 1986, the general manager of JVC's video plant in Yokohama, Katsuhiro Kawasaki, claimed the life cycle of products exported was one year, but only three months for those sold domestically. The fierce competition in consumer electronics in Japan, the fast pace of technological change, and the fickleness of consumers—conditioned by advertising and the economy to constantly expect something new, whether it be a new function or a design that matches the decor of their room—are all responsible for the need to constantly redesign and reconfigure product lines. "The managers in the stores," he lamented, "tell us our video equipment is like vegetables in a grocery—if it's not fresh the people won't buy it, and the price collapses."[8]

By far the greatest benefit of industrial robots, according to many in industry, is increased quality. But this may be the most misunderstood aspect of robotization—robots do not guarantee quality. It is true that robots can perform the same task as a human, over and over again with the same result and never get tired. It is also true that robots can increasingly work with a precision humans cannot hope to obtain—in electronics, garden-variety assembly robots can position their hands to within plus or minus 0.02 millimeters, over and over again; in arc welding, they can track and create seams accurate to less than a millimeter, all day long. But unless properly configured this capability is useless. In an unmanned factory, if all adjustments are not properly made, employees could conceivably come to work in the morning to find a mountain of parts, all assembled to the wrong specifications or welded in the wrong spots.

Rather than raise the level of quality, what the robot really does is stabilize it. Whereas human workers might perform well on Friday and poorly on Monday morning, the robot will be boringly consistent. And once the quality level of the work has been stabilized, it is then possible to raise it, by ironing out the bugs, by redesigning the product, by adjusting the peripheral equipment, and by perfecting the system. Says Hirokazu Shimatake of Nissan, who was involved in the early robotization of that company's car body spot-welding line, success "requires first mastering the manufacturing process itself. The robot doing the welding must be precise, and so must the peripheral equipment and transfer equipment that position the car and its parts for welding. They must be able to move and stop fast, with great accuracy. Door panels and other parts to be welded must be made exactly right or the system won't work. Precision results in good quality."[9]

In industry after industry, robots are used to augment existing techniques of quality control. Yamasaki Seisakujo, the subcontractor for Tokyo Electric Power Company, uses its single arc-welding robot to assemble foot pegs used on high-tension pylons. But proud president Kiyoshi Tawara carefully points out that, contrary to what people often think, robots are not always fast; the Hitachi Process robot he uses welds up to 700 foot pegs a day, the same amount as a skilled welder could theoretically do. What is the main advantage? "Using a robot," he says, "gives the worker time to inspect the product for quality as it is being made; before this wasn't possible." Kuwano Toso Kogyo, a firm of thirty employees, reported in 1985 that it had introduced a robot to paint its lacquerware bowls. Lacquerware production has traditionally been a craft and a cottage industry, and it takes nearly ten years to become truly expert at spraying the lacquer. The robot today paints around 4,000 bowls in an eight-hour day, approximately the same as the company used to turn out by hand. But as the president notes, "We used to need two workers—one to handle the bowls and one to handle the portable spray gun—but now we only need one. And before our defect rate was at least 1 percent, and sometimes as high as 10 percent—now it's almost zero." Toto Equipment, which makes nearly every toilet bowl in Japan, reports that using robots to paint them eliminates discrepancy in the finish. NSK-Warner, a U.S.-Japanese joint venture in Japan making seat-belt winder mechanisms, reports that with robots performing both assembly and inspection, defects have been reduced to near zero.[10]

At Nissan's Oppama plant, an inspection robot can scan the painted surface of a moving car body in 1.2 minutes and detect irregularities as small as 0.01 inches.

Japanese-style quality control has become world famous, but it is often assumed to be a system where products are simply inspected by experts for defects as they come off an assembly line. Nothing could be farther from the truth. In the ideal sense, and in the best factories, notes Hajime Karatsu (one of Japan's quality control gurus and a winner of the prestigious Deming Award), quality control really means the elimination of defects and "the ultimate deletion of the inspection process. Factories carrying out strict detailed inspection are considered to be inferior and something not to be proud of."[11]

Robots thus become a key element in total quality control within the entire factory. Their monotonous consistency helps stabilize the level of quality of the work they perform. Their moronic demands for precision force subcontractors and suppliers to improve the level of quality of their components (and often to robotize). Their technological immaturity forces workers to improve their own technical skills in order to make the machines work right. And finally, robots complement the still-important human work of quality control circles and inspectors. They can be equipped with tactile sensors or machine vision systems that allow them to do in-

At Daiwa House Industry, Kawasaki Puma arc-welding robots help make prefabricated house frames on an assembly line.

spection themselves. And they give workers a different perspective of the work being performed, which often leads to suggestions of ways to improve it. Says Shigeru Tabei, section head of JVC's automated video line, "Robots allow people to be more objective. Unlike manual assembly, where work can be fudged and passed on to the next person who may cover for you, robots can't be fooled. If there's a problem the whole line stops."[12]

Japanese Robots and World Industry

Robots do not guarantee a company's success, or that of a nation, and they are only one way of achieving manufacturing competitiveness. But the robotics synergy has given Japanese manufacturers such a powerful advantage that it has had a ripple effect on manufacturing in the rest of the world.

The huge trade imbalance that now plagues Japan and the United States (and Europe) is really an imbalance in the production and export of salable, sophisticated mechanisms and mechatronic devices, and of the high-tech components that go into them. One does not need to be an economist to know which nation's goods the world's consumers lust after —newspapers are filled with advertisements for Japanese mechanisms such as compact disks, VCRs, cameras, and cars. They have achieved this exalted status through scores of factors including government policy, and even luck, but also because of an advantage in quality, price, and technology— consumers around the world today *expect* Japanese goods to be "higher tech," of higher relative quality and lower relative

BUILDING HOUSES WITH ROBOTS

Robots make cars and electronic goods around the world, but Japan is surely the only nation where they make houses. Daiwa House Industry, like other large manufacturers of pre-fabricated houses in Japan, has to respond to the needs of finicky Japanese customers. It therefore puts out two to three new house models each year, and has installed a flexible manufacturing system to make them. Since employing its first robot—a painting robot that applied adhesive—in 1982, it has increased the number of robots at its factory in Ibaraki Prefecture to twenty, including eight arc-welding models that weld the steel frames in house panels. Whereas human welders work to an accuracy of 1 millimeter, the robots have a margin of error of only 0.1 millimeter.

The factory now has four hundred employees and mass produces five hundred houses per month.

price, without realizing what a very novel concept this is.

One way of looking at the trade imbalance is to relate it to the fact that by going through the learning curve with robots, Japan enjoyed the benefits of a robotics and quality control synergy, whereas by delaying, the United States did not. In the 1970s and early 1980s, the United States pursued a de facto industrial policy that was the mirror image of Japan's. Many manufacturers assumed that Japanese competitiveness stemmed from low wages; instead of automating, they began a quest for cheap labor, moving factories offshore to Taiwan, Singapore, Korea, China, Mexico, and even Japan. During this same period (1970– 84), Japanese manufacturing wages more than quadrupled. Some industries began manufacturing overseas, but usually reluctantly and as a means of avoiding protectionism and import restrictions. Only during the exchange rate crisis of 1985–87 was there a true rush to move Japanese production overseas. For the industries with products that robots could handle, the real battle against rising wages at home was fought by robotics and flexible automation.

Clearly, the American approach didn't work. Since U.S. manufacturers' offshore factories were now separated from the marketplace by thousands of miles, inventory lines became longer instead of shorter. Since designers and manufacturers were also separated, it became more difficult to design the manufacturing process and product together, and design changes became more cumbersome at a time when the product life cycles were becoming shorter. After acquiring manufacturing expertise, some subcontractor nations became competitors. Finally, some American manufacturers became so distant from the manufacturing process that they had to import experts from their Asian plants to teach their own technicians.[13]

Robots and flexible automation are not always the best solution to manufacturing problems, nor are they always necessary. But in more and more areas, as Hajime Karatsu notes, "human workers simply cannot compete with robots. However low wages may be, the advantage is offset by the impossibility of bringing manual work up to the uniformly high quality levels of robotized production."[14] In automobile assembly, the robotics synergy helped give Japan an early advantage over U.S. and European competitors. In assembly of electronics consumer goods it has done the same. Less well known, it has also given Japan an advantage in the fabrication of memory ICs, or integrated circuits, by enabling manufacturers to achieve greater volume, lower price, and higher quality as measured by "yield," the amount of usable chips in a batch made. The Japanese call IC chips the "rice" of our modern technological civilization because they are so critical to computers and other electronic products as well as to cars, ships, airplanes, and even guided missiles. To the embarrassment of U.S. manufacturers (who a short while ago dominated this field) and to the consternation of the Pentagon (which consumes vast quantities of ICs), Japan today monopolizes over 90 percent of the world market for many types of memory chips.

One of the most labor-intensive aspects of semiconductor manufacture has been the process of wiring the tiny integrated circuits to what is called the "lead frame." Most people who look at an integrated circuit see only the casing—a small square or rectangular black object with some wires poking out of it, like a many-legged insect. The actual integrated circuit, the IC chip, is a tiny sliver inside; it must be connected to the relatively huge wires in the lead frame, which protrude from the casing to the outside world and form the legs of the insect. This task requires great precision and care, and when done by long lines of women using microscopes has been a very costly operation. Both Japanese and American semiconductor firms initially did their wire bonding in Singapore and other nations, but Japan was able to bring much of this operation back on shore in the early 1980s with what are called "wire bonder robots."

Wire bonder robots, like sushi robots, have no mechanical arms protruding from them and thus may not fit the normal industry definition of "robots." But they are highly sophisticated, programmable, manipulating machines that use advanced robotic technology. With a television camera con-

ROBOTS IN THE SERVICE INDUSTRY

The most publicized "robots" in Japan's service industry today range from remote-controlled waiters in restaurants to small industrial robots rigged as coffee servers in coffee shops. Most of these are gimmicks. Yet if one broadens the definition of robots somewhat, Japan already has many automatons doing real work. In sushi restaurants, for example, in addition to thousands of sushi robots, conveyor-belt systems carry sushi from the chef to the client, and guests use specially wired pens on computer-linked tablets to order the item of their choice. On Japanese streets, a low vandalism rate permits the world's highest density of microprocessor-controlled vending machines, providing magazines, meals, drinks, condoms, and batteries twenty-four hours a day. In department stores the young women elevator operators who announce each floor and its wares are now often replaced by synchronized computerized voice systems. Similarly, where specially hired, uniformed "bus girls" used to assist drivers by announcing each bus stop and describing the stores in the area, now automated, synchronized tapes do the job. And small shop owners who once grew hoarse extending the mandatory formal greetings and farewells to their patrons can now purchase automatic systems to perform the same duty: when a patron enters a voice says, "Welcome"; when he leaves it says, "Thank you. Please come again." Labor is becoming extremely expensive in Japan, but the Japanese love of good service remains as strong as ever. Where affordable, the "human wave" approach to service is still used. But when the traditional approach is impractical, technology is needed to recreate it.

---

nected to a computer for artificial vision, they carefully position the unpackaged integrated circuit inside the lead frame and then under computer control solder the wires using a tiny pointed device in motions like those of a skilled seamstress, but working at a blinding 0.2 seconds or less per wire. To clearly see the entire process requires a magnifying lens—the points to be soldered on the chip must be positioned to within ten microns of accuracy, or ten-thousandths of a millimeter.

Wire bonder robots also demonstrate a new, unpleasant reality. Not only are robots more accurate than humans; they are cleaner. In the manufacture of semiconductors and other computer parts, humans are increasingly a liability because they are walking filth factories, constantly spewing out hair, particles of skin, and moisture wherever they move, thus contaminating the manufacturing process. Many operations in semiconductor manufacturing must be accurate to the submicron level, and as a result they require manufacturing in what are called "clean rooms"—specially designed rooms with high-powered air-conditioning systems that filter out dust.

A typical clean room with a designation of Class 10 usually means that there may only be 10 particles of 0.5 microns size in a cubic foot of air; by comparison, a speck of household dust is from 0.5 to 5 microns in size, and a typical office is class 100,000, with 100,000 0.5-micron particles in every cubic foot of air. Humans, therefore, enter clean rooms through air locks after putting on gloves, masks, and special full-body suits (called "bunny suits") to contain the dirt they normally shed. For ICs with greater and greater levels of integration, or density of circuitry (the one, four, sixteen, and eventually sixty-four megabit chips), and for the exotic biotechnologies, rooms cleaner than Class 10 will be required, making the use of robotics rather than humans imperative, regardless of labor costs.[15] It is thus the clean room that is one of the driving forces behind automation. Here, robot carts transport material about as robot arms load and unload cassettes filled with wafers of silicon into etching machines and test equipment. In the future, clean rooms will become the first truly "unmanned factories."

For the present, Japan's success with the robotics synergy is closely watched by both developing and advanced nations, who see an opportunity to advance opposing goals. To the former, robotics has become a potential tool in the quest for greater wealth and entry into the community of advanced nations. To the latter, robotics is increasingly seen as a tool to preserve industry and standards of living from the industrial encroachment of Japan and from poorer nations with lower wages.

For small, resource-poor nations, the phenomenal productivity of medium-sized companies like Fanuc and the sudden rise to great wealth of resource-starved Japan (not to mention the manufacturing prominence of tiny Sweden) holds out an exciting possibility. Like the imaginary giant warrior robots of Japanese comics and animation that amplify the strength of their ordinary human drivers, robots and flexible automation can amplify the power of nations. Robotics may offset a handicap in size, resources, the number of skilled or unskilled workers, or even the number of hours worked.

Japan's example of increased gains in productivity and quality with robots is one of the main forces behind robotization in the "little dragons" of Asia—the newly industrialized nations such as South Korea, Taiwan, Singapore, and Malaysia—where the cost of labor is still a fraction of that of the West and of Japan. Korean wage rates, for example, are only a sixth of Japan's, but even Korean industry is investing in

INDUSTRIAL ROBOTS AND PRODUCT CHANGES

In the consumer goods industry, robotization has helped factories keep up with the demands of their customers by making model design changes easier. But in doing so, it has also further stimulated consumer demands for change, resulting in an even shorter life of assembly lines. At JVC's automated video cassette recorder assembly line in Yokohama, for example, models of VCRs may have a lifespan of only three months; the design of their basic internal mechanisms will usually last a year and a half. The JVC line can produce ten different models without a redesign, but when the mechanism design reaches the end of its life, the robot end effectors, or hands, and the software have to be changed and the line reconfigured, a process managers say takes at least three months of planning and one month of construction.

Constant rebuilding of assembly lines is thus a way of life in Japanese consumer goods factories, and it is one reason many robots are now sold in modules that can be linked together in different patterns. For employees, however, shortened product life is rapidly becoming a curse. Managers must constantly plan ahead to make sure that facilities are not idled or wasted during changeovers, and technicians must constantly struggle to understand and implement the specifications for new products that pour out of the design department.

robotics. Conglomerate Daewoo manufactures many of its own robots and even markets them in the United States under the name Automaker. Tiny Singapore, while not making robots, has also begun to aggressively employ them. By 1985 Singapore had 6.5 industrial robots per 10,000 workers and was gaining on the United States. Japan has 80 percent of the market for robots in Singapore, and JAROL is the model for Singapore's Robot Leasing and Consultancy Company.[16]

Giants China and India, still struggling to emerge from poverty, also hope to duplicate Japan's robotics synergy. Norbert Wiener was perhaps the first to articulate the possibilities automation holds for such countries when in 1956 he wrote that "the future industrialization of India may bypass much of the drabness and misery of Manchester or Chicago through the early introduction of the automatic factory." Moreover, he foresaw that the "automatic factory" requires a relatively small number of highly qualified scientist-engineers and skilled trouble shooters and maintenance personnel, and that India was fully capable of supplying these in a short time, whereas providing a large base of skilled factory workers might take half a century.[17] Not surprisingly, India today has an agreement with Japan for robot technology transfer.

The People's Republic of China is also investing in its own robotics industry. In addition to importing robots from Japan, it is actively pursuing technology transfers from Japanese firms. As Wiener imagined for India, roboticist Hiroyuki

Yoshikawa, professor at the University of Tokyo's Mechanical Engineering Department, thinks one reason China is so interested in robotics, and especially in the training of software engineers for industry, is that a software engineer can be trained in three years, while it takes at least ten to train a skilled lathe operator.[18]

In the advanced, richer nations, robots have increasingly become a means of countering "deindustrialization," or what the Japanese call the "hollowing" of industry—the transformation of manufacturing concerns into marketing specialists who no longer make what they sell. According to Joseph Engelberger, Japan's success with robots is the real driving force behind their application in United States and European industry today. Prime Minister Margaret Thatcher of the United Kingdom has in the past heaped scorn on British manufacturers who fail to robotize, contrasting Japan's high number of robots and low unemployment with the opposite situation in Britain and noting that "the people who object to new technology will use their pay packets to buy the products of new technology from other countries."[19]

The advantages of using robotics are obvious, but why should the advanced nations even bother? Clearly, there are other ways besides manufacturing for nations to earn a living in the world community, whether through agriculture, finance, or the sale of resources. Why not accept the world trend of specialization and international division of labor and become, as many experts suggest, post-industrial societies based on software, design, and the service industries?

First, nations with strong manufacturing industries have historically dominated other areas as well. Process and product technology have become much more closely linked today, so that to remain technologically advanced an industry requires a mastery of manufacturing technology equal to or greater than its mastery of design technology. For the U.S., deindustrialization exposes a deep-rooted national schizophrenia—a political and military establishment fixated on the Soviet Union and committed to a defense policy that requires a maximum of industrial self-sufficiency, and an economic establishment increasingly dependent on Japanese and Asian manufacturing and technology.

Second, manufacturing is more than making money; it can be an expression of culture. Japan seems to have a better

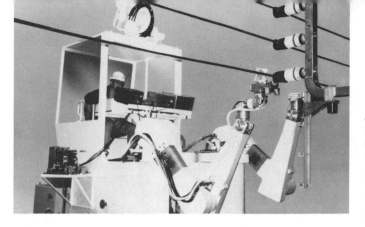

Although not a programmable robot, this joystick-operated aerial manipulator is being developed by Tokyo Electric Power Company for remote installation of power lines.

understanding of this than many advanced nations, and not simply because of the success of its postwar "make-it-yourself" industrial ideology. Gift giving is one of the most important and onerous rituals in Japan, and since ancient times Japanese travelers have been obliged to purchase local manufactures to take home to their friends and family. This tradition is supported throughout the Japanese countryside today by thousands of souvenir shops selling regional crafts and delicacies at railway stations and at gardens, temples, and other favored tourist destinations. Overseas, however, Japanese tourists have often found themselves in a quandary. Wishing to buy a local product to take back home with him, a Japanese may enter a souvenir shop in Los Angeles to find the shelves filled with goods made in Japan and Southeast Asia.

Even many people in the United States are nationalistic enough to want *some* mechanical goods they buy to be designed and made in their own country. This is reflected by the widespread grassroots support for Harley-Davidson, the last remaining domestically owned motorcycle maker in the United States. Tens of thousands of American riders of "Harleys" wear the manufacturer's logo tattooed on their arms and refuse to ride robot-produced Japanese replicas, despite the fact that the Japanese bikes are lower priced and technologically far more sophisticated. To them, a Harley is more than a motorcycle; it is a symbol of the American ethos. Even free-trade advocate Ronald Reagan seemed to acknowledge this when, in 1983, without obvious economic or military reasons, he authorized whopping tariffs to protect the Harley-Davidson company and its 1,400 employees.

Third, deindustrialization of the United States in particular has frightening implications both for the world economy and for Japan. Japanese labor unions have occasionally worried that their nation's robotization has aggravated unemployment overseas, but industrialists worry about deindustrialization, too. Hajime Karatsu in his 1985 article "Is U.S. Industry Going Down the Tubes?" wrote that "if present trends continue, U.S. industry will soon be in danger of complete collapse. World leaders must focus their attention on this impending crisis and consider what must be done to avert it."[20] In the postwar period, the tremendous purchasing power of the American consumer has fueled the economic growth of Europe and Asia, especially Japan. Economists rarely agree on anything, but many suggest that deindustrialization may result in a drop in the U.S. standard of living and thereby a drop in American consumers' purchasing power. Should this occur, Japan's robot-manufactured consumer goods will be hard pressed to find another market, particularly now that the U.S. and Japanese economies are so inextricably linked. It is at this point that the interests of Japan and the United States converge and demand that the latter's industries be modernized with increased use of robotics.

Many U.S. manufacturers, awakening to the need to become more competitive, have been busily installing robots. As in the case of General Motors, often the hardware they use is made in Japan. Consultant Gerald J. Michael of Arthur D. Little, in a 1986 *Forbes* magazine article entitled "Close the Door, They're Coming in the Windows," was quoted as predicting that in the coming years U.S. firms will invest $50 to $60 billion on automation equipment, "with at least half of that going to the Japanese."[21] But should U.S. companies fail to robotize because of their short-term profit orientation, the high cost of borrowing money to invest in machinery, or a continuing obsession with "cheap labor," Japanese companies will surely do it for them on the sites of auctioned-off U.S. factories, and the result will be the same: Japanese robots are going to play a major role in the reindustrialization of the United States.

When Japanese manufacturers move overseas, as they increasingly do, they often take the entire manufacturing process with them—the managerial system, their subcontractors, and robotics synergy. Japanese robots in America, running the same programs they do in Japan, create exactly the same products and do not argue over cultural differences or wages. Sales of Japanese robots soared in 1985, fueled by sales to new Japanese factories in the United States. Nissan uses Kawasaki-manufactured, Unimation-designed robots at

WITHOUT HARDWARE, THERE CAN BE NO SOFTWARE

Japan is often said to lag the U.S. in software development, but this may not necessarily be a handicap. A proper balance between hardware and software may be more important. Software and the programs computers run are part of the world of simulation and theory; in the real world, even computer-driven machine tools and robots must at some point physically interact with the things they shape, make, and handle. Perhaps with this in mind, many Japanese corporations today try to reinforce basic manufacturing skills, even as they pursue high technology. At Matsushita Electric Industrial, claims director Sukeji Ito, factory employees are instructed by older skilled workers, and compete in annual competitions where, for example, they might be assigned a problem on a lathe, required to find the best solution, and be checked on the precision of their work. Winners get a gold medal and a portable television. On a national level, special "skills Olympics" are also held in Japan. And at Waseda University, even robot scientist Ichiro Kato is careful to steer his students toward the real world. He makes them master the art of soldering before they go on to theory. As he wrote in his 1987 book *Dokuso wa dokuso nari* ("Creativity Means Going It Alone"), the success of Japan's industrial robot industry symbolizes the correctness of a balanced approach to hardware and software; the U.S. concentrated too much on software, and is currently in a state of "stagnation." "There is absolutely no need," Kato reassures his countrymen who worry about lagging behind the U.S. in software, "for Japan to imitate the United States in this area, and pursue such an uneven, warped type of development."

---

its Tennessee truck plant. NUMMI, the GM-Toyota joint venture in Fremont, California, uses Nachi-Fujikoshi robots. Seiko-Epson uses its own robots at its Oregon plant. And Mazda plans to use a hundred of its own robots at its plant in Flatrock, Michigan.[22]

Many of these Japanese firms moving factories overseas might appear to be following in the footsteps of their U.S. and European counterparts and thus furthering their own deindustrialization. There is some truth in this. Japan, after all, is subject to the same advanced-nation syndrome of rising wages and decreasing international competitiveness in labor-intensive industries, and there is at the same time considerable talk in the local media about the need for "internationalization" and a national shift to a more software/information/service–based economy. In fact, since the 1985 exchange rate crisis, some firms have been scrambling to relocate labor-intensive manufacturing overseas, particularly to Southeast Asia.

But there is a fundamental difference. For those Japanese firms that manufacture more sophisticated, value-added items, moving abroad is often motivated more by politics than by economics. In particular, when moving to the U.S. and Europe, although labor costs may still be lower than in Japan, the goal is to avoid protectionism in the markets for their products and to placate local politicians by generating jobs. To many Japanese executives, moving plants overseas for economic reasons is only a measure of last resort. They see the United States and Europe as civilizations in decline as a result of too much deindustrialization, and this strengthens their resolve not to let the same fate befall them, just when many believe Japan is about to inherit the twenty-first century.

Because of Japan's historical relationship with technology and manufacturing and the fragility of its resource-poor economy, the basic postwar formula for wealth generation—importing raw materials and manufacturing goods with added value for export—is very much ingrained in the Japanese national psyche. As Keinosuke Aida, president of Aida Engineering (one of the oldest Japanese robot manufacturers), said at the end of 1986, "Japanese take a great pleasure in making things, but even more important, they cling tightly to fields in which they are already established."[23]

In the future, then, for labor-intensive and inexpensive, simple mechanical components, Japan will increasingly depend on overseas labor and imports. For more sophisticated high-technology, value-added devices, manufacturers who can will milk robotics synergy for every drop of efficiency possible. Even when much of an industry has been relocated overseas, superefficient pilot "unmanned factories" will still be maintained in Japan.

Such widespread, aggressive use of robots by Japan and other nations in the future will likely require a reanalysis of manufacturing and the international division of labor. Traditionally, poorer nations have advanced themselves by developing manufacturing skills in labor-intensive industries (toys, textiles, shoe making, and light assembly operations) that advanced nations with higher standards of living no longer found profitable to pursue. This is how Japan itself modernized. But in the future, nations fearing deindustrialization may instead opt to use more robotics, thus relinquishing fewer of these industries.

Since robots are capital- or machine-intensive, they can impose a heavy financial burden on economies where labor is cheap and money is in short supply. Some developing nations may find that not only do they have fewer labor-

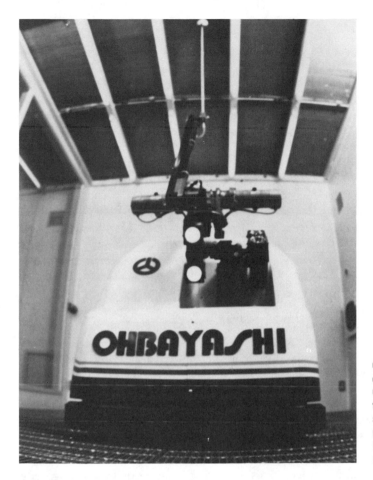

Obayashi Corporation's clean room robot, the CRIMRO, navigates around the clean room to check for air leaks. Its course can be programmed in advance or it can be operated by remote control.

intensive industries to inherit from their advanced neighbors, but also that the cost of equipping themselves with the tools they need to compete will be prohibitive. Just as robots have driven a wedge between large and small manufacturers in Japan, on an international level they may aggravate the existing technological and economic gap between rich countries and poor ones, making the need for international cooperation and aid even more acute than it is today.

Even in the richer nations, however, robots cannot be effectively used until managers used to thinking of human labor as a cheaper alternative to automation change their attitudes to labor and work. The large investment robots demand can only be recouped when they are put into widespread service. Joseph Engelberger describes his frustration trying to sell assembly robots in the United States:

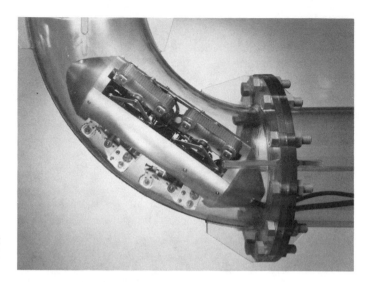

JGC's sensor-equipped inspection robot uses tracked feet to pull itself through pipes both straight and curved, horizontal and vertical.

They say "To hell with that. . . . All you need for assembly is a bench and some bins and some women who get paid next to nothing to pick up the parts and plug them in. We can't justify robots." Now the Japanese, on the other hand, immediately understood that the moment you put robots into assembly operations you've switched from a labor-intensive industry to a capital-intensive industry, and you've got to run the robots around the clock. You don't know what agony that's going to be to understand in the States.[24]

This suggests an interesting question. Is one of the reasons Japanese manufacturers seem to overproduce goods—and lay themselves open to accusations of dumping—partly that they are racing to depreciate their investment in robotics?

Expanding the Robotics Synergy

Japan's manufacturing industries are so successful that their growth can be sustained only if other nations can politically tolerate it. Japan's task in the immediate future is therefore to devise a means of applying robotics synergy to other industries. The great success stories of Japanese productivity are all in the field of mechanisms and mechatronics where current industrial robots excel, in cars, industrial machinery, Walkmans, video cassette recorders, autofocus cameras, and office automation equipment. The very success of these fields obscures the fact that in many other industries,

Kajima Corporation's concrete slab finishing robot operates either autonomously or by remote control and produces a quality finish equal to or better than that made by a skilled worker.

where robots are not used, Japanese productivity is rather dismal. Robots need to move out of the factory.

The race is already on around the world to develop robots for other industries. In Florida, researchers are developing robots with artificial vision to pick oranges. In the Netherlands, researchers are trying to develop a robot that can milk a cow. In Australia, researchers have spent years trying to develop a robot that can shear sheep. In France, robots are being developed for use in forestry. In Japan, too, researchers are developing robots for such diverse fields as agriculture, mining, and sewing, but their nation may be unique in that it has targeted robots for the construction industry.

The construction industry in Japan has extremely low productivity and a high accident rate, and it suffers increasingly from a lack of young workers who choose to enter it—in short, it is a perfect candidate for robotization. Aggressive research and development programs have now been under way for some years. In 1978, the JIRA began sponsoring design projects; since 1982, the System Science Institute of Waseda University has sponsored the WASCOR (WASeda COnstruction Robot) research project, working with eleven construction firms; and since 1983, the Ministry of Construction has sponsored several five-year projects on robotics. Most of the major construction firms and consortiums in Japan are also already developing or using robots.[25]

Kajima Corporation, for example, has a mobile robot for concrete slab finishing that can do the work of three plasterers with higher accuracy and quality. Kawasaki Heavy Industries has made prototypes of robots that paint the undersides of bridges. Takenaka, among other firms, has developed a robot that uses suction and tractor treads to climb walls on the outsides of buildings and inspect for a problem in Japan's cities—loose tiles that might fall and injure passersby. JGC has developed a little inspection robot that travels inside pipes. Finally, Obayashi Corporation developed a robot that inspects semiconductor plant clean rooms for potential leaks. All these robots share one thing in common: they move.

———

In a way, Japan, its economy, and its technology have become like a man on a bicycle in a race. The bicycle cannot stop or it will fall over. Close behind, and rapidly gaining, are the newly industrializing nations of Asia. Close alongside are stable three-wheelers, the United States and Europe. In front, if the racer can only pedal a little harder, is a window of opportunity, a technological future that will catapult Japan into a new world of security and wealth. The twenty-first century is talked about a great deal in Japan, and robots will help it get there.

PART FOUR

Beyond Industrial Robots

Poster advertising a
musical about robots
and children.

10
Religion and Robots

What is that indefinable something that lets Japanese embrace new technologies with such ease?

OMNI SPECIAL EDITION, "JAPAN 2000," JUNE 1985

Religion is often said to be one reason for the diffusion of robots in Japan. Henry Scott-Stokes, writing about "Japan's Love Affair with the Robot" in 1982 in the *New York Times Magazine*, notes that it "dates back several decades and, in the view of many authorities, is a unique, intensely personal reaction with roots in Buddhist values." Koichi Kawamura, in an article in the *Oriental Economist* in 1983, claims that religion led his countrymen to embrace robots, and solemnly pronounces them "mentally constituted to accept in place of the sword, for instance, the computer or the robot as one of their gods if they should come to believe that such things would protect them from external enemies or disasters."[1]

There are important areas where robots and religion intersect in Japan, but they are, unfortunately, often obscured by cultural dogma. One soon discovers that not everyone is talking about the same kind of robots or even the same kind of religion. Japan's religious landscape is dominated by Buddhism and Shinto, yet includes Confucianism, Christianity, folk religion, and scores of "new" religions. Many Japanese subscribe to several religions; they get married in Shinto ceremonies, are buried in Buddhist ones, and, as the saying goes, may attend Christian churches to practice their English. Fanuc's Dr. Inaba once joked to reporters that there were four gods at his high-tech complex—the sacred Mount Fuji, the two Chinese Buddhist deities of wealth and commerce whose stone statues guard its gates, and a local fox god. Inaba had a special Shinto shrine erected to placate the spirit of the fox, and he offered a reward to any employee who could photograph it.[2]

Points of Intersection

Most statements about religion and robots are inspired by Japan's tradition of animism. Animism is the belief that anything in the natural world—not just living things—can have a conscious life or soul. It exists in Buddhism but is especially strong in Shinto. Shinto is indigenous to Japan, and while over the millennia it has been overlaid with foreign deities, nationalism, and emperor worship, at its core is a form of nature worship and the belief that inanimate objects can be sacred. Mountains, trees, even rocks are worshiped for their *kami*, or indwelling "spirit," and samurai swords and carpenter's tools have "souls." Gods of local industries, such as rice growing, paper making, ceramics, and weaving, are also still worshiped today. Because of the way Shinto priests are regularly called upon to consecrate buildings and industrial machinery, Shinto itself has been called the "chaplain of much of the industrial and technological enterprise of modern Japan."[3]

When Joseph Engelberger once visited a rural Japanese factory, he witnessed a Shinto ritual consecration of two new Kawasaki-made Unimates. There were thirty-two employees, and as he recalls it, their

> suits are all cleaned and nice and crisp, and the two robots are standing in place, ready to go to work. In front of them is a Shinto altar, with the vegetables and the fruits and the fish twisted into shape. It's absolutely beautiful. Two Shinto priests are there, banging their sticks and moaning and groaning and making all kinds of different sounds, blessing the robots and blessing the general manager and blessing me, with garlands of flowers around the robots. The general manager then stands up and tells the people, "I want you to welcome your new fellow workers," and the two machines go to work and everybody in the place claps."[4]

Animism is present in nearly every society to some extent (Americans give names to hurricanes), but it does seem much closer to the surface in Japan, even outside of a Shinto context. In the introduction to a videotape on children's robot shows, a producer writes that "people not only make friends with each other, but with animals and plants, the wind, rain, mountains, rivers, the sun, and the moon. A doll [robot] in the shape of a human is therefore even more of a friend." The cover to a Japanese book on the *mecha* of *Mobile Suit Zeta Gundam* robots blares forth in English: "The warriors see in this strangely shaped machine a source of repose for their own sowls [*sic*]. It is a mirror which reflects what is in their hearts; it forms a strong axis supporting their lives."[5] In the real world, a Hitachi banner at a Tokyo science museum proclaims, "Let's Make Friends with Incredible Technologies!"

In the late 1970s and early 1980s, when countless foreign visitors traipsed through showcase automated factories in Japan, they often marveled over what seemed a striking example of animism at work: the practice of naming industrial robots. At Nissan's Zama plant, or at the early Fanuc plants in Hino, outside of Tokyo, employees often took the initiative and bestowed on industrial robots the names of popular singers, actors, and cartoon characters, and sometimes festooned them with photographs or drawings. It was a process widely imitated throughout Japan and later even the West as a means of "softening" the environment.

When writers began groping for reasons to explain Japan's early embrace of industrial robots, this mild example of animism on the shop floor became a convenient basis for some rather outrageous claims. Henry Scott-Stokes, in the article mentioned earlier, took Tokyo psychologist Seiichiro Akiyama's words at face value, quoting him as saying of robots, "We give them names. . . . We want to stroke them. We respond to them not as machines, but as close-to-human beings." Akiyama's words thereafter appeared widely in the Western media, giving the impression that the Japanese people had some sort of cosmic connection with industrial robots.[6]

On closer inspection, however, what seemed a spiritual connection may have been partly due to the newness and exotic nature of the machines. According to officials at Kawasaki, the ritual consecration of robots, once common, is now rare. Many of the plants that used to decorate robots with names and photos no longer do so—at the new Fanuc plants near Mount Fuji the robots are naked and nameless, and as a young plant manager says, "We have too many to name now." Furthermore, Japanese workers are no more likely to hug or stroke an industrial robot than American workers are to kiss the radiator of an overheated car engine—like any industrial equipment, robots are dangerous. Even Gensuke Okada, who helped shepherd Kawasaki and Japan into the robot age, declares that his company and others in the early 1970s were certainly not motivated by sentimentality, or even

School children cavort with a remote-control play robot made by inventor Jiro Aizawa. In 1910, when in fifth grade, Aizawa saw his first exhibition robot in London. Since 1925 he has made scores of entertaining robots, founded a "research institute" to produce and popularize them, and become something of a folk hero in his own right. In 1934 he unsuccessfully petitioned the government to recognize the word "robot" as his personal trademark.

religion or tradition. "Japanese industry," he sternly points out, "is very pragmatic; we just want to do the work faster and better, and if possible, have a little time for leisure."[7]

Religion is also invoked in another context with industrial robots. Even if Buddhism and Shinto contain nothing that intrinsically promotes robots, the argument goes, they also contain nothing to hinder them, whereas Judeo-Christianity does; ergo, since Japan is dominated by the former, it must have less resistance to robots. It is a line of thought that many intellectuals in the West might agree with; long before paying attention to Japan, they were complaining about attitudes to robots in their own religions.

Science fiction author Isaac Asimov, for example, periodically rails against what he calls the "Frankenstein Complex" in Western fiction, whereby "man creates robot; robot kills man." In an introduction to an anthology of robot science fiction, he once noted that "the creation of a robot, a pseudo-

ROBOTS AS SACRED TOOLS

Robots are tools, which may in part explain why the Japanese often seem to treat them rather special. The word *dogu*, meaning "tool," was originally a Buddhist term. In early religious literature, it was used for something that aided one in pursuing the path of Buddha's teachings and could refer to religious clothing or any articles used in religious rituals. Later, the word took on a more active meaning and was applied to tea-ceremony implements, weapons used by samurai, and tools for production.

The act of making things has always had a religious undertone in Japan. "When form and function were created through human labor," writes scholar Mitsukuni Yoshida, "that labor was a truly sacred act, and was determined by the degree to which man could understand and accommodate nature."

As Yoshida notes, the average peasant felt that by recognizing a magical quality in his tools, and sanctifying them, the results of his labor would be more fruitful. "When the New Year approached, every peasant would offer rice cakes to his washed and purified tools as an expression of thanks for working with him throughout the year and as a way of personifying and anthropomorphizing them. Praying for the restoration of the tool's magical powers once a year was a way of resurrecting its former existence solely as a religious tool in the sacred world."

---

human being, by a human inventor is . . . perceived as an imitation of the creation of humanity by God. . . . In societies where God is accepted as the SOLE creator, as in the Judeo-Christian West, any attempt to imitate him cannot help but be considered blasphemous." Even Norbert Wiener, who worried terribly in his later years about the misuse of technology, commented on this subject in a work aptly titled *God & Golem, Inc.: A Comment on Certain Points Where Cybernetics Impinges on Religion.* He noted that—like the legendary Rabbi Low of Prague, who created a living Golem-robot out of clay—in many minds the potential of cybernetics is equal to the sin of sorcery, and that had anyone created computers and autonomous machines several hundred years ago he would have incurred the wrath of the Inquisition.[8]

But do Westerners really associate today's one-armed industrial robots with the blasphemous humanoids of science fiction? Occasionally the media do seem to implicate industrial robots by association. In the climax scene of a 1984 Hollywood film called *The Terminator*, for example, a berserk metal humanoid monster symbolically meets his end next to two industrial robots (by coincidence, one made by Fanuc and the other by Yaskawa Electric). The issue is, at any rate, enough of a concern in America that in 1985, when the RIA produced a promotional film titled "Robotics: The Future Is Now," it still felt it necessary to specifically address such "robot-phobias."

Any real test of the Frankenstein Complex can only come

in the distant future when and if working robots assume a human form. It is reasonable to assume that the reaction to such robots will be more strongly negative in the West than in Japan. Christianity, after all, does assert the superiority of man over the rest of the natural and mechanical world, and Darwin's theories of evolution are still deliberately omitted in many textbooks in the United States. In Japan, antirational and antitechnological forces are usually variants of *seishinshugi*, or "spiritualism," of the sort that denied Japanese fighter pilots parachutes in World War II. Much of *seishinshugi* went down with the pilots. Unlike in the West, there has never been an organized, articulated attempt in Japan to assert the superiority of man over the rest of the natural and machine world; evolution has never been an issue.

For the present we can only speculate about the negative effects Judeo-Christianity has had on our collective unconscious. And there are some dissenters to the common generalizations. Walt Weisel, the president of Prab Robots and former head of the RIA, asserts that Christian compassion promotes robotics as a way of alleviating the suffering and hardship of fellow human workers. Yutaka Kanayama, a Japanese scientist in robotics, believes Americans create far more interesting research robots than Japan and even that they are more intellectually attracted to robots than Japanese—precisely because of their obsession with God, the Devil, and evil Frankenstein-type monsters.[9]

Focusing too closely on religious concepts may actually be missing the point, because it obscures the historical and social context of religion and robots in Japan. Beneath their romantic overlay, industrial robots—programmable mechanical arms—are mere machines, the descendants of a genre of tools brought to fruition in Europe during the industrial revolution in the late eighteenth century. In Europe, the industrial revolution occurred when class systems were rigidly entrenched. It caused enormous social disruption, unemployment, and suffering among the lower classes, who were in effect guinea pigs for new manufacturing technologies. In the extreme, it led to groups like the Luddites in England, who tried to smash the labor-saving weaving machines they blamed for their miseries.

Japan, on the other hand, escaped many of the negative aspects of the industrial revolution. Because it was isolated from the world during this period, machines were introduced later, as developed technologies, during the mid-nineteenth-century Meiji Restoration. This was a time of social ferment when the four-tiered caste system of warriors, farmers, craftsmen, and merchants was already in collapse. All the institutions of government, economy, and industry were in flux. "In the hundred or so years since then," says scientist Ichiro Kato, the former head of the Robotics Society of Japan, exaggerating only slightly, "we have had no history of people being victimized by machines; to most, machines have brought only good. In Japan today there is therefore absolutely no psychological resistance to them."[10]

The same social flexibility that Japan enjoyed in the nineteenth century—and that is so critical during the introduction of any new technology—continues today and may not be entirely unrelated to religion. Modern Japanese are not without their own fixed ways of thinking. Their love of formalities and hierarchy can make them positively hidebound by tradition. But in the last hundred years they have astounded foreign observers and themselves with their ready adaptability. From near-vegetarians to avid meat eaters, from wearers of swords to carriers of Walkmans, from rigid feudalists to eager believers in democracy, and from arrogant militarists to self-flagellating pacifists, probably no society in the world has undergone so many dramatic, radical changes in so short a time, with so little hesitation and introspection. Even Japan's language—the most basic element of culture—continues to absorb new words and expressions with breathtaking speed. To the unaccustomed, today's Japan is a schizophrenic, whirling mishmash of traditional and modern.

One reason for this may be Japan's racial and social identity, a core notion of what it means to be Japanese—so strong it usurps some of the socializing functions of "religion" in the Western sense and permits an external flexibility otherwise impossible. Another reason may be Japan's own brand of polytheism. Polytheism is not unique to Japan; it exists among Hindus in India and Buddhists in Thailand. But most Japanese are really pantheistic in that they pay lip service to more than one polytheistic creed at the same time. In the community of industrialized nations, where religion and reality are usually viewed only through the binoculars of a Judeo-Christian and Marxist-Leninist dualism, the flexible worldview of many Japanese people is truly unique.

What has all this to do with today's robots? First, the

flexible approach to religion—the anything-that-works-goes attitude—has an extremely pragmatic side to it. In a debate on technology and God compiled into a book titled *Robotto wa ningen o kaeruka* ("Will Robots Change Man?"), Chumaru Koyama, a professor of literature at Waseda University and an authority on religion, states that "in ancient times, Japanese religion was extremely 'this world' and 'gain'-oriented. Today we are said to be areligious, but I think we are actually substituting science for the old type of religion."[11] At times it seems nearly anything—whether it be one's own company, quality control, technology, or even robots—can be a pseudoreligion in Japan.

Second, Japan's lack of rigid religious dogma can permit a syncretic approach, that is, a borrowing from a wide variety of cultures and conflicting ideas and from them distilling something quite different. If one looks closely, beyond the surface familiarity of the borrowed ideas, it is sometimes possible to discern approaches to technological problems in Japan that are entirely unique to Japan.

In research robotics, in fact, two of the most famous Japanese scientists stand out because of their highly idiosyncratic work. Both men are outside the mainstream of research in the world and in Japan, but both have achieved considerable stature. Japan is a very tightly knit, hierarchical, and factional society where power can be measured by *jinmyaku*—chains of personal connections (often diagrammed in industrial newspapers) that are accumulated through years of work, study, socializing, and trading favors and obligations. If the number of robot researchers and technologists who have studied under these two men or come under their influence at one stage or another were counted, their *jinmyaku* would be vast.

Synalysis

Ichiro Kato, Japan's most famous roboticist, is a softspoken, bespectacled, graying man, and utterly conventional in appearance. Currently the dean of the Waseda University School of Science and Engineering in Tokyo, he has also served as chairman of the Robotics Society of Japan and of the Society of Biomechanisms, which he founded. Sometimes his colleagues jokingly refer to him as "Professor Ochanomizu"—the name of the surrogate father of Atom, the android hero in Osamu Tezuka's famous robot comic. Unlike

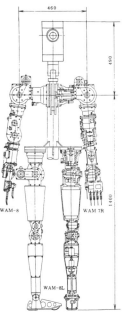

Ichiro Kato and pieces of his musician robot, the Wabot, in 1986.

An assembly diagram of Wabot. One day, it will walk up to the piano and sit down and play.

almost every other serious roboticist in the world, Kato is not trying to build a better industrial machine or conduct theoretical studies in locomotion or autonomy. Instead, in the tradition of some of the nineteenth-century European automata designers, his goal is to replicate man in metal.

An early researcher in robotics in Japan, Kato started with the human hand in 1963. "I had been working in automatic controls and servomechanisms," he says, "and I was interested in machines as an external extension of human abilities. The human motor system—arms and legs—is a type of servomechanism. I started studying hands because our use of hands is one of the main differences between us and other animals."[12]

From mechanical hands Kato (and his teams of students) graduated to arms, over ten walking robots, and even Wasubot, the organ-playing humanoid robot at Expo '85. None of these robots is practical in any sense of the word. Most of the bipedal robots are only truncated torsos that lurch forward for a few steps, still tethered to power supplies and computers. The musician robot, which Kato hopes will someday walk up to the organ, sit down, and play, must still be anchored to its seat.

But to foreign robotics researchers who are always strapped for finances, what Kato is doing is surely next to incredible. Not only is he pursuing a heretical line of research, but he receives steady funding (from sources he is reluctant to divulge), despite the fact that with today's limited technology his goal is clearly unattainable.

"My research is not just in function," says Kato, "but in shape. In thirty years, in the twenty-first century, I think that human form will be essential in robots. In factories, which are for work, robots can be of any shape, but the personal robot, or 'My Robot' as I call it, will have to exist in a regular human environment and be able to adjust to humans."[13]

Kato believes that machines can be divided into three categories or phases. The first emphasizes movement and power; most machines we see today, including what are referred to as industrial robots, fall into this category. The second category emphasizes information and includes computers. The third category, now on the verge of appearing, emphasizes information, intelligence, and power. The "My Robot," or personal robot, Kato says, will emerge as a machine of the third category to satisfy a long-standing desire of humans for a slavelike mechanical man. Far more advanced than the "personal robots" advertised by toy or hobby kit manufacturers today, it will be closer to the robots of science fiction. My Robot will take the form and size of a Japanese person, and one of the first places Kato foresees its use is in health and human services.

Kato believes in two important concepts. One is "biomechatronics," an attempt to replicate animal functions with mechanical systems. The second is "synalysis," a word he coined from "synthesis" and "analysis." In order to replicate a human function, for example, we have to analyze it, and in so doing come to understand it. "We are engineers, but we are also scientists," Kato says, "and like Socrates we are trying to understand humans. To do this we must study philosophy and physiology and practice synalysis. Synalysis is not something useful right away, but it will help us understand walking mechanisms and brain functions. In one sense it is extremely basic research."[14]

———

To date, Kato's approach has had almost no application to industry or industrial robots, but it is having some interest-

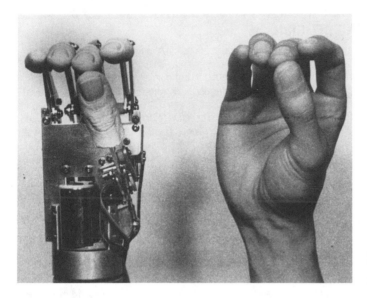

ing spin-offs. Kato has developed a multifingered robotic breast cancer detection device and many prostheses for the handicapped; he has already patented a lifelike mechanical hand for the disabled, called the Wime-hand, and developed motorized artificial legs. In the extreme, Kato's work on prostheses approaches robotics from an opposing angle— instead of creating robots to replicate men, he is augmenting men with robotics, making cyborgs, or cybernetic organisms. In the very distant future, he believes that we will have a pluralistic "cybot" society consisting of humans, robots, and cyborgs.

Kato's dream of replicating man has so inspired others that there are now teams at over twenty universities in Japan doing similar work on bipedal humanoid robots. At least one member of this group has taken deliberate aim at the factory floor. Professor Akira Sato of the Shibaura Institute of Technology, who in his laboratory has been developing a full-scale metal behemoth called Asshy, is also currently heading the project called the BORN System, described in chapter 1, to develop a bipedal robot for industry. Supported by the industrial robot firm Motoda Electronics, BORN incorporates the novel idea of supplying electrical power to the feet of the robot through a specially designed floor, thus eliminating a major problem with wires. But the concept of using a bipedal robot in factories is so alien to conventional thought and at this point so technologically preposterous that the project may be partly a publicity stunt.

MANUFACTURING AND RELIGION

Hajime Karatsu, one of Japan's quality control gurus, is currently a technical advisor to Matsushita Electric, nominally the largest robot manufacturer in Japan. In the spring of 1986, the Pentagon invited him to the United States to pick his brain for the "secrets" to Japan's technological success. Upon his return Karatsu talked about the development of industrial robots East and West almost as if he were comparing religions: "Engineers in the United States have a worldview colored by dualism, and they tend to see things in terms of 'black' or 'white,' 'yes' or 'no.' But industrial production is a battle with error; if a design differs from its specifications it won't work the way it should. On the floor, therefore, the 'gray area' is very important. There is no single truth, but many. . . . The U.S. relies heavily on specialists, who run the risk of being fired if they are wrong. Since they must be infallible, like God, the tendency is to rationalize mistakes and avoid blame. The U.S. always seems to be waiting for some 'superman' to solve its problems, but supermen only come along infrequently. In Japan we have an expression that if 'enough dust is collected, it will form a mountain.' We may not have very many spectacular individual engineers, but when their power is pooled, it is tremendous."

WABOT 1, 1973, was the first serious full-scale anthropomorphic robot in the world. With legs, hands, artificial vision, and speech synthesis, it was claimed to have the mental ability of a one-and-a-half-year-old human.

Kato believes that Japan's tradition of animism has strongly influenced its interest in robots. Yet he makes no connection between religion and his own work. He and his fellow humanoid researchers are clearly not losing any sleep over the fact that they are involved in work that might fit into the "blasphemous" category described by Asimov. Since they operate outside the pressures of Judeo-Christianity, why should they? But even Kato sees the danger in trying to usurp the functions of a higher being. In a recent interview/debate on "How Close Can Robots Come to Humans?" for example, he stated his opposition on ethical grounds to attempts to replicate life forms using organic materials. "The robots we are making," Kato notes, "are only lifeless machines. If anything goes wrong and we need to stop the robot, all we have to do is pull the plug.[15]

Becoming Robots

The other iconoclast of Japanese robotics is Masahiro Mori. Mori is much more overtly religious than Kato, and he is also more closely linked to industry. A contemporary of Kato's, he, too, specialized in automatic controls as a young man. In 1959 he began his involvement with robotics, starting with research into models of the human finger, then hands, walking mechanisms, robots for industry, and autonomous robots. After a long tenure teaching at the Tokyo Institute of Technology, Mori is currently chairman of the Robotics Society of Japan. Like Kato, his sphere of influence is vast; unlike him he is a flamboyant personality.

"Aah, 'robot' is indeed a word with unfortunate connotans," he says, smiling, discussing "robot-phobia" abroad, ut it's only a convenient label that doesn't reflect the sence of the object itself. A robot is neither good nor bad." With a series of charts and diagrams, Mori begins to explain a complicated Buddhist concept, but thinks twice, and, laughing, holds up a permanent-ink pen. "See?" he says. "To most people this may look like an ordinary magic marker, but watch . . ." Torching the tip with a lighter, the "pen" begins to burn steadily, and he gleefully exclaims, ". . . It's really a lamp!"[16] Mori, the eccentric elder of Japan's robotic research community, is a man with a mission: to spread the word about the relationship between man and robots and Buddhism.

"I always tended to become quite philosophical about my studies," he admits, "and in developing five-fingered manipulators I found a microcosm." Buddhism is a highly complex religion that developed in India and entered Japan in the sixth century A.D. It teaches that the buddha-nature is in all things (not just sentient beings) and that the parts of whole systems are simultaneously independent and connected; a universe and the source of all truth exists, for example, in the single petal of a flower. When studying the human finger, Mori found that he could not consider its functions independently, that he had to take into account their relation to the entire human body. This in turn helped him comprehend not only the human body but the universe in which it exists. Therein he saw the teachings of Buddha.

Ironically, like several other Japanese scientists, Mori was inspired to study the progressive field of automatic controls and robotics by the work of cyberneticist Norbert Wiener, who had once concluded that "Buddhism, with its hope for Nirvana and a release from the external wheel of Circumstance . . . is inexorably opposed to the idea of progress."[17] Mori, quite to the contrary, came to believe as a result of his studies that "to learn the Buddhist way is to perceive oneself as a robot." And conversely, as he later articulated in his book *The Buddha in the Robot: A Robot Engineer's Thoughts on Science and Religion*, he came to believe that "robots have the buddha-nature within them—that is, the potential for attaining buddhahood." According to Mori,

> man achieves dignity not by subjugating his mechanical inventions, but by recognizing in machines and robots the same buddha-nature that pervades his own inner self. When he does that, he acquires the ability to design good machines and to operate them for good and proper purposes.[18]

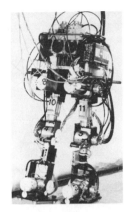

WL-10 RD, a dynamic walker, with a claimed speed of 1.3 seconds per step.

The WHL-11 (Waseda-Hitachi Leg) exhibited at Expo '85 had its computer and hydraulic power supply on board and was capable of static walking at 13 seconds per step.

Masahiro Mori holding a mechanical snake and a globe illustrating his favorite Buddhist principles of unity.

Most Japanese roboticists, including some of Mori's former disciples, feel ill at ease linking robots and Buddhism too closely. But Mori's goal is easy to misunderstand. Like Kato, Mori is a pioneer in the concept of biomechanisms, and in the practice of modeling mechanisms after life forms. Mori's use of religion is as a vehicle to rethink the relationship between man and robots and to develop new, creative approaches to robotics and automation. Mori in fact has long been critical of the humanoid approach, and many years ago advocated a theory called the "Uncanny Valley." To illustrate, he draws a curved graph that slopes upward, and then suddenly plummets for a brief period before rising again. On one axis is the level of familiarity humans feel when looking at robots; on the other is the level of similarity the robots have to humans. At the bottom of the curved line are industrial robots and other automated equipment, so clearly removed from the human form that they stir little emotional response in us.

MASAHIRO MORI ON HONDA MOTORS

Soichiro Honda, the founder of Honda Motors, is a "graduate" of the Mukta Institute, and Dr. Masahiro Mori considers his company a shining example of how to robotize. One of the hallmarks of Zen Buddhism is the acceptance and reconciliation of paradox. In many industries, concepts such as "robotization" and "humanization," or "hand-made production" and "automation" are considered contradictory. Honda, claims Mori, attempts to unify them with the following principles: (1) when automating or robotizing the factory, employees should not be laid off but transferred to other tasks; (2) employees should think of their plant as their own, not that of the "corporation"; (3) workers—not plant bosses or executives—should come up with the ideas for robots and peripheral devices; (4) employees should get their hands "dirty" by making their own automation devices; (5) employees themselves should be the ones to identify the work that is best suited for robots and least suited for humans.

Going up the curve, as robots become more identifiably lifelike, we feel closer to them, but just before the robot becomes a perfect replica of man, at the stage of wax dolls or android machines, the level of familiarity plunges and changes to a sense of the uncanny. Mori advocates that future roboticists be careful that their designs not fall into this "uncanny valley," because humans will always feel closer to a robot slightly different from man and a little more "robot"-like.

To help promote his ideas on religion and robots, in 1970 Mori founded the Jizai Kenkyujo, or the Mukta Institute as it is called in English. As a public employee in a national university Mori until 1987 could not hold office in the organization, but he has always been its guiding light, and through it he has been able to extend his influence to industry. *Jizai* is a Buddhist term sometimes translated as "free," but devoid of English connotations of individualism and libertinism; its real meaning is the spiritual freedom obtained through enlightenment, as expressed by the Sanskrit word *mukta*. Today the Mukta Institute has over thirty core members, most of whom are technologists, and it serves as a sort of think tank that provides consulting and educational services for corporations on production automation, robotization, and product development. Among its clients are Honda Motor Company and Omron Tateishi Electronics, both firms that manufacture and use robots and that have tried to incorporate the Mori philosophy.

Sueo Matsubara, the acting president of the Mukta Institute, exhibits the same enthusiasm as Mori when he explains

Sueo Matsubara and the Automax oil tank cleaning robot.

the organization's goal. "Japan has introduced technology from the West," he says, "and through improvements in quality, cost reduction, and manufacturing speed has achieved great success worldwide. But this is only in production, and we have reached a limit. Now we need true Japanese creativity and Japanese technology. . . . At Mukta we fuse Japanese spirit with technology, and we teach creative ways of thinking. . . . Mukta involves abandoning oneself and annihilating the ego to become 'free,' and allowing creativity to emerge. Technologies are shackled by the past and preconceptions, so we try to erase this and do something totally different."[19]

As part of this process, Mukta members regularly meet to recite Buddhist scriptures, meditate, and attempt to consider problems in new ways. On the wall of the room in which the meetings are held, along with Buddhist calligraphy, is an elaborate clock with no hands that tells no time; in the center is a yin-yang shaped table that can be split in half and reconfigured in a myriad of ways to encourage different methods of communication. Here the members imagine new robots, cars, and methods of automation, and, as Matsubara says with a chuckle, "occasionally sip some saké." Although Mukta membership is not strictly limited to any particular religion, the group has a core creed of Rinzai Zen—one of scores of Buddhist sects—which delights in shaking rigid human minds with riddles and paradoxes, thus allowing new truths to emerge.

"You really can't make a good robot without chanting the scriptures," says Matsubara, laughing and admitting that Buddhist ideas work well with robot design. He should know. He is also the chairman of Automax, a venture business in Tokyo that develops robots and automation equipment and serves as a laboratory in which to test the Mukta philosophy. Among its products are an undersea robot submarine with manipulators, a floor cleaning robot, an autonomous tracked robot with a manipulator, a cleaning robot for removing the sludge inside crude oil tanks, and a variety of computer-controlled robots for exhibitions and shows, including the popular Fuyo Robot Theater at Expo '85. The designs for all of them, Matsubara claims, are not imported from the U.S. or Europe but are entirely original.

The sludge cleaning robot for the inside of crude oil tanks is especially dear to his heart. Normally the sludge in such tanks is regarded as waste and is removed in an expensive

A ROBOTICIST WORRIES ABOUT THE FUTURE

Compared with their Western counterparts, sometimes Japanese technologists seem to worry very little about the future. Roboticist Ichiro Kato is different. He has two main concerns.

One, he often points out, is that the machine life cycle is becoming shorter and shorter. In his father's day, he recalls, men lived fifty years and the fundamental design of machines did not substantially change for that entire time. Today, however, people are living much longer while the lives of machines are becoming shorter. "When the machine life cycle becomes drastically shorter than our own," he warns, "the flexibility of humans will be outstripped, and it may result in a catastrophe." Kato's other concern is that there is a trend toward social autism, where humans relate less and less to each other and more and more to machines; with the advent of personal robots, he says, this could become a far more serious problem.

and hazardous process through a manhole in the tank. But Matsubara and his team instead first analyzed the nature of the sludge. After pondering the essential meaning of "clean" (by referring to Buddhist texts on purification) and the basic concept of "waste matter," they determined that sludge in and of itself is not functionless. It is merely unwanted. "We therefore saw the sludge as a resource," Matsubara says, "and designed the robot to descend into the tank, stir up the sludge at the bottom, and thus recycle as much as possible into usable crude oil again. The sludge itself, therefore, became an aid to the cleaning process. . . . We had to change our way of thinking."

"Many people like to think of robots as slaves," he says, discussing the Mori philosophy, "but from my experience this often causes them to break down and operators to become irritated and angry. Buddhism teaches us that all things have a soul. To comprehend the soul of a robot, and to understand its true potential and limitations, we must think of it as a friend. We must become a robot."[20]

What do the Ichiro Kato and Masahiro Mori factions have to do with the larger issue of robots and religion and Japan? Both men certainly raise some provocative questions, but neither directly demonstrates that religion has resulted in the diffusion of robots in Japan, industrial or otherwise. Despite the fact that Kato and Mori radically differ in personality and orientation, they do share one thing in common. Their approaches to robotics are utterly unique to Japan, and in that sense may provide a symbolic window onto what may be the nature of Japan's great strength in technology today.

In the debate on technology and God quoted earlier from

The Fuyo Robot Theater, designed by Automax.

the book *Will Robots Change Man?* a scientist named Kazuhiko Azumi expressed a view that sometimes surfaces in Japan. Instead of the Judeo-Christian dualism that characterizes the West, he argued, Japan is ruled by a "tri-ism," where reality is perceived, not as "black" and "white," but as "black," "white," and "gray," with all three supporting each other. Because robots are different from other machines and different from humans, he claims, they fit into the "gray" area. This recognition of the gray, or vague zone, he claims, is a "reason robots have developed so much in Japan, and also a driving force behind Japanese advanced technologies. . . . It's one of the reasons advanced technology has entered its Asian age."[21]

11

Six Legs, Four Legs, Two Legs, or None?

The technology for locomotion will have the biggest impact of all.

KANJI YONEMOTO,
DIRECTOR OF JIRA

The concept drawing for a new design of nuclear power plant robot created quite a stir when it was released in 1984. In the artist's rendering, the robot was part animal and part human in shape, with a four-legged torso like that of a horse, a pair of arms, four-fingered hands, and a "head" mounted on the front. A few days later, a cartoon in a national paper showed an angry archer in the heavens firing an arrow at a researcher on earth for daring to imitate him—the nuclear power plant robot looked uncannily like Sagittarius, the Centaur.[1]

The Centaur robot is part of a large-scale national research and development project called Advanced Robot Technology, or ART, which began in 1983 and is scheduled for completion in 1991. Three categories of robots are being developed: a robot (the Centaur) to perform maintenance and inspection work inside a nuclear power plant, along with a companion, smaller robot that can climb walls; a three-legged, crablike undersea robot to inspect and repair giant oil rigs at sea; and a six-legged "disaster prevention" robot that can be used to perform dangerous inspections and contain fires at refineries. The ART project is Japan's boldest national venture into advanced robot development, and a test of its management skills, technological resources, and creativity. Since at the 1982 Versailles Summit Japan was selected (along with France) to lead an international effort to further robotic technologies, considerable pride and prestige are also involved.

Unlike the specialized industrial robots Japan has mastered so well, which are mostly anchored to the ground, these new robots must be mobile, capable of a wide range of tasks, and at least partially autonomous. Ideally, they would be like science fiction robots, capable of functioning on their

Concept drawing for the ART nuclear power plant robot.

Concept drawing for the ART disaster robot.

Concept drawing for the ART undersea robot.

own in any situation. But this is impractical. Research on autonomous robots has been proceeding worldwide since around 1968, when a vision-equipped, wheeled robot named Shakey awkwardly navigated around the Stanford Research Institute. The problem, however, is always the same. Despite tremendous advances in computer power and software, autonomous robots are still inept at something even the lowly ant does with ease: sorting through the vast amount of information required to move and work in a random environment in real time. Like roboticists in the rest of the world, therefore, Japanese scientists are setting their sights on the possible.

One way to maximize a robot's performance is to limit the environment it must work in. Although the ART project was once introduced abroad as the Jupiter (JUvanescent PIoneer-ing TEchnology for Robots) project, in Japanese its name is "Kyokugen Sagyo Robotto," which means "Robots for Work in Hostile Environments." The nuclear power plant, the undersea oil rig, and the burning refinery are all environ-ments where humans are biologically unsuited because of radiation hazards, water pressure problems, and the intense heat and noxious gases from fires and leaks. Structurally, these environments are limited in area and static in physical shape, and can be mapped and simulated by computer in advance to help the robot navigate within them. Oil rigs have an additional advantage in that the sea around them is a medium with few obstacles.

Another way to compensate for the limitations of compu-ter technology is to create robots that are not totally indepen-dent, but hybrids between man and machine, to create something similar to the low-tech Iron Man No. 28, rather than the free-flying Mighty Atom. Led by Susumu Tachi, chief of robotics at the government's Mechanical Engineering Laboratory (MEL), a sophisticated form of remote control known variously as "teleoperation," "telepresence," and (in Japan) "tele-existence" has become the core technology be-hind all three of the project robots. Tele-existence involves an autonomous robot operating under its own power, capable of performing specialized tasks (such as simple navigating inside the reactor or tightening bolts), and a decision-making human operator who can intervene for complicated tasks while "driving" and operating the robot with joy sticks from a remote location. This division of labor allows humans to perform the most complex judgments and manipulations, and thereby augment the limited brain power of the robot. It also allows the robot to do autonomously what it does best—repetitive actions or actions that can be easily predicted and programmed in advance.

Tele-existence uses a "master-slave" system of manipula-tion. In the case of the nuclear power plant robot, the operator will probably wear a helmetlike device and mechanical "gloves" and look into three-dimensional color "TV glasses" or video screens in the safety of a central command post. With television cameras and tactile and force sensors, he or she will be electronically linked to the robot at another, remote location, with data sent back and forth in the air on laser beams (or via an optical fiber cable for the undersea robot). When the operator's head turns, the camera on the

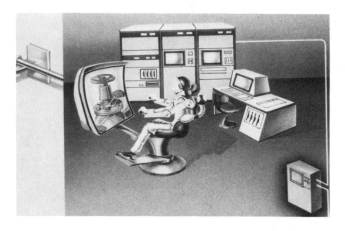

Operating the nuclear power plant robot remotely, with tele-existence.

Dr. Susumu Tachi, director of the robotics department at MEL, with an adaptation of his earlier "seeing-eye dog" robot, now used in tele-existence experiments. "We have a lot of fun driving this around remotely," he says.

robot turns in the same direction and angle and "shows" what it sees; when the operator (watching the scene on television monitors or "glasses") moves his hands (or hand), the robot hand moves identically in three dimensions; when the robot hand encounters an object, the operator "feels" it with feedback from force sensors; when he moves his fingers as if pretending to grasp the object represented on a TV monitor, the robot's fingers move identically and grab the real object.[2]

Selecting a limited environment and using tele-existence solves some problems at the same time it leaves others that are horrendously difficult. The nuclear power plant robot, for example, is theoretically required to move and to dismantle and inspect valves using tools with the "same speed and precision as man," an act that requires tremendous coordinated mechanical control of the four jointed legs, two jointed arms, and eight fingers. It is also supposed to work for three months without needing maintenance at 158 degrees Fahrenheit, 90 percent humidity, and 100 roentgens of radiation per hour. The undersea robot must do similar work but stabilize itself in three dimensions, despite tides that may be moving at 2 knots, and work 600 feet under the ocean with near-zero visibility. The disaster prevention robot must be able to work in scorching temperatures of 750 degrees for thirty minutes or 1,470 degrees for three minutes in air filled with toxic and corrosive chemicals.[3] To succeed, the project must do major work in fundamental technologies such as sensors, manipulation, locomotion, joint control, and systems support. The list of requirements—faster, more powerful computers; better three-dimensional artificial vision software; lighter,

INSPIRATION FROM THE PAST

For some areas of research, the past can be a source of creative inspiration. The Mukta Institute uses a religious tradition (Zen Buddhism) to stimulate new ways of thinking. Japan's rich crafts heritage is reflected in the push into "new materials" such as ceramics and the push into biotechnology (some of which draws on ancient fermentation skills). The June 24, 1981 *Daily Industrial News* reported that Hitachi's design team, when it developed Mr. AROS (one of the first microprocessor-controlled, sensor-equipped, arc-welding robots) in 1974, had been inspired by a traditional Japanese sword-making technique. Fusing layers of hard and soft steel, the Hitachi engineers were able to strengthen the moving column of the robot arm while at the same time making it lighter and smaller. Vibrations were also reduced.

---

stronger materials; and new mechanical controls—is endless. Robots are a form of systems engineering, and a fusion of all technologies. Therein lies the challenge for Japan.

Designing the Project

As a large-scale national project, ART is designed to enhance the national welfare and boost the national technological level. Like a parallel project in robotic sewing technologies, it is financed and controlled by the Agency of Industrial Science and Technology within the Ministry of International Trade and Industry (MITI) and requires a mobilization of business, government, and academic resources in pursuit of a single goal—a goal far too expensive for any individual organization to pursue on its own. An umbrella organization called the Advanced Robot Technology Research Association, or ARTRA, oversees a consortium of eighteen corporations and two organizations that work with the two major government laboratories, the Mechanical Engineering Laboratory (MEL) and the Electrotechnical Laboratory (ETL). ARTRA also receives the cooperation of researchers in universities throughout Japan.[4] The ART project is a massive Japanese technological juggernaut, with a design both elegant and flawed.

There has been fierce criticism of ART, from within and without the association, of the vast number of research themes that must be undertaken, of the lack of a clear goal, and of the small size of the budget. Actual work on prototypes did not begin until 1987, so the first years on the project were used to develop the concept of the robots and do feasibility tests on the basic technologies required. But what should the robots be asked to do? And what should they look like? If a robot operates only on smooth ground it only needs wheels, but if it has to straddle pipes or climb walls, ordinary wheels are clearly inadequate. And how much weight will it carry? Should the nuclear plant robot be built to work in high temperatures as well as high radiation? And should the refinery robot be able to extinguish fires as well as do inspections? Each decision affected the design, and each participant in the project had a different opinion. Indicative, perhaps, of the internal struggle that went on, concept drawings of the disaster prevention robot were not released until mid-1986, three years after the project began and two years later than its power plant cousin.

To accomplish the entire project, the government only allotted a budget of ¥20 billion (less than $100 million at the time), with hints that because of government fiscal difficulties the final amount would be even less. How Japan can hope to achieve such a lofty goal with so little money is a source of puzzlement to many inside Japan and out. While ART's budget is slightly larger than that for a similar advanced robotics project in France, it is tiny considering the over forty research themes involved and the amount of work to be done. The total ART budget, moreover, must be divided among the many participants. Even the prestigious government labs, where some of Japan's best robotics research is done, have their gripes. "I'm envious of researchers at Carnegie-Mellon or MIT," says Dr. Yoshiaki Shirai, director of the Automatic Control Division at the Electrotechnical Laboratory. "They get to plan projects and use the money quite freely. In our case 90 percent of the budget goes to the corporations. The remaining 10 percent is divided between us and MEL."[5]

But the government labs are flush compared to the universities—which get no funds at all. The Japanese media are fond of the word *sankangaku*, meaning cooperation among industry, government, and academia, yet in the ART project the universities' only role is indirect, and their professors, who have a wealth of experience, are restricted to working on advisory committees for the project. Why? To understand this requires knowledge of the Japanese research establishment.

Between MITI, which controls the budget for the ART project, and the Ministry of Education, which controls budgets for public university research, stands a towering bureaucratic wall. Since 1983 a joint research system has enabled university professors to work with their counterparts in industry and to obtain additional funding for proj-

ART PROJECT MEMBERS AND DIVISION OF LABOR

I. BASIC TECHNOLOGIES

A. Locomotion
- Mechanical Engineering Laboratory (MEL)
- Electrotechnical Laboratory (ETL)
- Fuji Electric Corporate Research and Development Ltd.
- Yaskawa Electric Manufacturing Co., Ltd.

B. Control
- MEL
- ETL

C. Systems Support
- ETL
- International Robotics and Factory Automation Center

II. NUCLEAR POWER PLANT ROBOT

A. High Reliability
- Mitsubishi Electric Corp.
- Mitsubishi Heavy Industries. Ltd.
- Japan Power Engineering and Inspection Corp.

B. Radiation Resistance
- Hitachi Ltd.
- Japan Power Engineering and Inspection Corp.

C. Locomotion
- Hitachi Ltd.
- JGC Corp.
- Toshiba Corp.
- Japan Power Engineering and Inspection Corp.

D. Manipulation
- Mitsubishi Heavy Industries Ltd.
- Fanuc Ltd.

- Japan Power Engineering and Inspection Corp.
- Fujitsu Ltd.
- Toshiba Corp.

E. Remote Control
- Mitsubishi Electric Corp.

III. UNDERSEA AND OIL PRODUCTION SUPPORT ROBOTS

A. Undersea Robot
1. Undersea Positioning and Navigation Control
   - Mitsui Engineering and Shipbuilding Co., Ltd.
   - Kawasaki Heavy Industries Ltd.
   - Sumitomo Electric Industries Ltd.
2. Undersea Vision
   - Oki Electric Industries Co., Ltd.
3. Undersea Manipulation
   - Kawasaki Heavy Industries Ltd.
   - Komatsu Ltd.
4. Supervisory Control
   - Oki Electric Industries Co., Ltd.
   - Mitsui Engineering and Shipbuilding Co., Ltd.

B. Disaster Prevention Robot
1. Duration
   - Ishikawajima-Harima Heavy Industries Co., Ltd.
2. Sensors
   - Matsushita Research Institute
   - NEC Corp.
3. Environmental Adaptation
   - Ishikawajima-Harima Heavy Industries Co., Ltd.
   - Kobe Steel Ltd.
   - International Robotics and Factory Automation Center

---

ects. Corporations, for their part, have long enjoyed the support of MITI. But MITI money and that of the Ministry of Education are rarely if ever mixed in projects, and while university researchers can act as consultants on MITI government projects, their labs receive no MITI money. "It's rather like the British constitution," says Yoji Umetani, roboticist at the Tokyo Institute of Technology. "It's an unwritten law."[6]

Historically, university robotics research in Japan has been

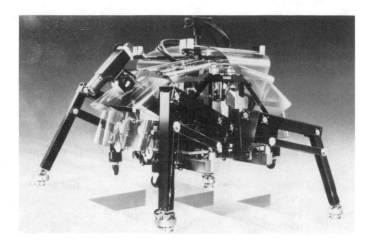

Sensors on the feet of the four-legged Titan IV enable it to find its way up and down stairs. From the Shigeo Hirose laboratory at the Tokyo Institute of Technology.

conducted in an ivory tower atmosphere, and a rather impoverished one at that. In a JIRA 1986 survey of 183 universities and colleges doing robotics research under the jurisdiction of the Ministry of Education, only 1.1 percent of laboratories had over ¥10 million ($66,000) in funding for the year, compared to 25 percent for 52 government-affiliated labs.[7] At the Tokyo Institute of Technology, the building walls are cracked and aging naked concrete, and professors' offices and labs are cramped and cold in the winter. At the private Waseda University, Ichiro Kato's office is quite modern looking, but despite his fame and the fact that his labs are probably some of the best funded in Japan, when his two-legged walking machines actually go for a stroll they must toe a narrow path among machine tools, generators, and industrial equipment in a building that the rest of the Mechanical Engineering Department shares.

One indirect result of the lack of money is that much of the robotics research done in universities in Japan tends to be rather quirky. With the exception of Dr. Makino's world-conquering SCARA assembly robot, most university research has little immediate industrial application, although it may have huge payoffs in the long run. "We often have a very free environment," notes Associate Professor Shigeo Hirose, also of the Tokyo Institute of Technology, "where we're left to pursue themes that are almost like personal hobbies."[8] This is what sustains Ichiro Kato and his faction of twenty or more universities engaged in humanoid research, the Buddhist robot-philosopher faction of Masahiro Mori, and the joint effort of Yoji Umetani and Shigeo Hirose, who are part of the

MASAHIRO MORI ON CREATIVITY

When Dr. Masahiro Mori assumed chairmanship of the Robotics Society of Japan at the beginning of 1987, the society journal published his Zen-Buddhist-flavored message to the readers. An excerpt:

"In Oriental philosophy we often use the famous phrase 'form does not differ from emptiness; emptiness does not differ from form.' Yet form is created from nothingness. . . . A robot has form . . . but it is also infinite. The robot's shape, the work it does, and the ways in which the robot is applied are all infinite; just as life itself is infinite. Our Oriental philosophy is suggesting to us that if we refine our insights and creativity we can create limitless robots that are both interesting and useful. In other words, robot research and production can become a far greater source of spiritual enjoyment."

Mori lineage but not Buddhist oriented. The Umetani-Hirose laboratory has concentrated on biomechanisms and on trying to replicate the means of locomotion of spiders and snakes in metal. Hirose, one of the best and brightest of university researchers, currently is working on a tiny robot snake to replace endoscopes, or stomach cameras, that will enter and explore a patient's digestive tract on its own.

For some younger researchers, this type of "freedom" is not enough, and the university environment is stifling. Yutaka Kanayama, for example, held a prestigious full professorship at Tsukuba University, where he led development of the little, wheeled Yamabiko 9 robot—one of the few truly autonomous robots in Japan, with its own power supply, sensors, and on-board computer for navigation. With a background in computers and artificial intelligence (and not, like most Japanese roboticists, mechanical engineering), Kanayama was a highly valued member of the Japanese robotics community. Yet in 1985 he gave up his professorship and moved to the United States, claiming that there is more interesting research being done in robotics and artificial intelligence in the U.S., that Japanese professors' salaries are too low, and that research budgets are too tightly controlled and too small—for his research he considers a U.S.-made Digital Equipment Corporation VAX computer and software tools essential. More than anything, Kanayama was frustrated by hierarchy and factionalism. As he later commented, "In the United States human relations are transparent and more fair. In Japan everything is organized by age. . . . It's hard to get funding."[9]

If interpersonal harmony and group cohesion are the strengths of Japanese society, in academic research the seniority system and factionalism are its curse. The seniority system denies researchers like Hirose full professorships until their superiors retire, and it frustrates the more ambitious researchers like Kanayama. Factionalism poisons not only relationships among researchers, but also among government bodies, academia, and industry, thus drastically increasing the odds that cooperative projects will fail. Often it even inhibits cooperation in the most logical areas. Kanayama, for example, claims that the people in the Fifth Generation Project, Japan's much-publicized project on artificial intelligence (also due to finish around 1990), "want to maintain a division between computer science and robotics, but one of the biggest problems in robotics is vision—how to see the world in three dimensions—and they are not very interested in it. They're mostly interested in Prolog, a dedicated programming language that is good for inference machines and not very suitable for robotics and vision."[10]

———

The real driving force behind the ART project will come from research and development done in the labs of the eighteen corporate members, where factionalism and budgets take on a different significance. In principle, work is consigned to the corporations on the basis of their ability and expressed interest in it. For the nuclear power plant robot, Hitachi is in charge of locomotion but works with Toshiba; Toshiba, Mitsubishi, Fujitsu, and Fanuc are handling various aspects of manipulation; and Kawasaki, which builds Japan's submarines, plays a central role in undersea manipulation and stabilizing technologies. These arch rivals can agree to work more or less unfettered in the beginning stage of research on fundamental technologies, but as the project continues communication becomes critical. Hitachi researchers in charge of the leg mechanism for the Centaur robot, for example, originally assumed the robot would carry only 100 kilograms (220 pounds) of weight, but the companies working on the vision system and the other equipment have kept adding requests, forcing changes in the design.

Exploiting the natural competitiveness of these corporations is nonetheless a brilliant strategy. At the end of the project all know-how and patents revert to the government. There are still big incentives for the corporate members, however. Any achievements they make will advance them in the industrial hierarchy, and they will also be able to use the technology for themselves commercially outside the project.

Furthermore, the corporations will make sure that the final budget for their projects will not be the same as the official one. "In the Japanese system," says a smiling Hiroaki Ando, the director of ARTRA's technical department, "corporations will invest their own money and own people. If the official budget is ¥20 billion, the real budget will probably be double that figure."[11]

Reliance on corporate members of the association also amplifies one of the great strengths of Japanese robotics research. Unlike the United States, where over 60 percent of all funding for robotics research may be defense-related (with much of it coming from DARPA, the Defense Advanced Research Projects Agency), Japan has had very little military-related research since the end of the war. The best and brightest of its engineers have been attracted to, and worked in, commercial manufacturing. Military-related research may have tremendous value at the basic research level, but it can easily funnel human and financial resources into a black box, where the end result is rarely seen or discussed. In contrast, despite the way Japanese corporations try to hide their process technology from each other, most of their technology eventually finds its way into commercial products and therefore is an open secret that can be bought and reverse-engineered—dissected and replicated. Corporate, civilian technology also speeds competition and improvements. It helps lower cost per unit if it is commercialized and mass produced. When publicized by the mass media, it becomes "accessible" to industry and the public and can attract even wider support.

At the Mechanical Engineering Lab, a researcher demonstrates MELSPIDER, a wall-climbing robot with sixteen motors and a suction force of 60 pounds.

The point here is that the ART robot is only as good as its components, which will be made by corporations that are world leaders in component technologies with vast, related resources at their disposal. Toshiba, for example, is a leading manufacturer of industrial robots, of computers, and of dynamic RAM LSI, or large scale integrated circuits (the computer memory chips that Japan monopolizes in the world market). When a Toshiba scientist working on a sophisticated vision system for a robot decides he needs a custom-made, state-of-the-art microchip, he need only pick up the phone and call his friend—who heads the design team for Toshiba's semiconductor plant across the street.

Smaller, more densely integrated circuitry means more

powerful computers. When coupled with the right software, this means smaller, more powerful robots. But unlike computers, robots must also interact with the real world. Dr. Eiji Nakano, the head of planning at MEL and one of the originators of the ART project, believes that major progress in robotics is contingent on improvements in hardware, especially in mechanisms that better approximate the muscles of animals in force-to-weight ratio, energy conversion efficiency, and controllability.[12]

Almost all roboticists would agree. The bipedal walker developed by Professor Kato and Hitachi for Expo '85, which took nearly five seconds per agonizing step, was only a pair of legs hooked up to outside power, yet it still weighed over 184 pounds. The Adaptive Suspension Vehicle, a five-mile-per-hour six-legged walking vehicle being developed at Ohio State University, can carry a driver and 500 pounds, but itself weighs 5,720 pounds. Shinnichi Yuta of Tsukuba University, currently developing Yamabiko 10 in the absence of Kanayama, is trying to attach a manipulator, or arm, to the little robot. "Until recently," he notes, "a 50-kilogram robot arm with the same reach as a man could only lift 1 kilogram; now a 20-kilogram arm can lift around 2 kilograms, and in the future, using newer materials, we might be able to build a 10-kilogram arm that could lift its own weight. But that still pales next to a man. A human arm and hand weighing only five kilograms can lift as much as 50 kilograms."[13] Unless major improvements are made, a humanoid robot built with today's technologies that incorporated all human functions would put a dent in the sidewalk.

Luckily, the miniaturization required for advanced autonomous robots dovetails with the current thrust of Japanese commercial manufacturing technology, called *keihakutansho*, or "light-thin-short-small." While this expression is sometimes used jokingly today to deride the intellectual and physical traits of others, it originally referred to the trend in industry of steadily making consumer goods smaller, lighter, and cheaper. In robotics, it helps fuel the race for more densely integrated circuitry, smaller actuators and motors, longer-lived batteries, and even stronger, lighter "new materials."

New materials in particular are the latest Japanese technological "religion" and may make a major contribution to future robots. They aptly illustrate the intertwining of commercial and research technologies in Japan. "Fine ceramics" are light, strong, and heat resistant and may have electronic and structural applications in robotics. Today they are used as packaging for semiconductors (one company, Kyocera, controls over 70 percent of the world market), in electronic sensors, in superconductive materials, and in scissors and the tips of ball point pens. Carbon-fiber-reinforced plastics (CFRP) are also light and strong and were used by Ichiro Kato in his piano player robot; they are now used in car bodies. Shape memory alloy (SMA) is a flexible metal alloy that "remembers" its previous shape on electrical impulse; when properly configured it has the potential of replacing some heavy motors and actuators in robots. Hitachi has received much publicity for its robot hand made with SMA. Shigeo Hirose's endoscope snake uses SMA, and the same material is now used in some Japanese brassieres.

Eiji Nakano, head of planning at MEL and one of the architects of the ART project, with an early prototype four-legged robot.

Given the above, one should expect a highly practical design of advanced robots to emerge from the ART project. Yet this might not happen. For the last hundred years, Japan has relied on basic technology imported from the West, which it has then improved, refined, and commercialized. This has required great innovation. But as symbolized by Ichiro Kato's bipedal walking robots, whose names have gradually changed over the last twenty years from WL-1 to WL-10RD, the approach in Japan has largely been one of progress by the increment. Improvements and refinements in existing technology may help develop the components for future robots. They may, however, be inadequate for the design of the total robot in the ART project.

When all the pieces of the robot are put together, will they really fit? Some people are skeptical. "I think the whole thing is a mess," says Shigeo Hirose of the nuclear power plant robot. "They're starting out without a long-range, completed vision, but with many corporations and a great deal of politics involved. The result, I fear, will be a very boring robot."[14]

Designing the Robot

The design of the nuclear plant robot, or the Centaur, is a classic illustration of the problem facing the robotics community and Japan itself. To succeed, to get all the pieces of the robot to work together, will require creative leaps of the imagination. For over a hundred years, however, the goal of Japanese industry and technology has mainly been to catch up to and surpass the West. Like the racer who finally pulls ahead of the pack, Japan must now decide, and agree, on which direction it wants to go. One of the goals of those involved in planning and designing the Centaur robot was to conduct an exercise in creativity that would at last produce something new, different, and uniquely Japanese.

Individual Japanese people are just as creative as anyone else, but Japan has strong forces working against the type of breakthrough ideas that can result from the open exchange and clash of opinions. As indicated by the Japanese adage "bang down the nail that sticks out," an intellectual totalitarianism exists in a rigid educational system, in office layouts (with all desks in one room, overseen by the section chief), and even in quality control circles in factories. At its best, this acts as a powerful motivator by shaming people into hard teamwork. At its worst it crams individual differences into cultural dogma, imitation, and fashion. An example: Robots and flexible manufacturing have encouraged a fragmentation of consumer tastes in Japan unparalleled in history, and cars can be purchased in several hundred different models and shades of color. But when "white" became a fashion color around 1986, so did the majority of passenger cars in Japan. At Toyota factories, 70 percent of the cars produced were white, with the figure climbing as high as 90 percent for some models.[15]

As a result, as Japan approaches the twenty-first century the fostering of original thinking has become a national obsession. The industrial media constantly analyze creativity. Corporations hold "idea" contests and festivals, and some contract with the Buddhist-flavored Mukta Institute. At Toshiba, researchers in the vision labs are allowed to use 10 percent of their time and 10 percent of their budget on any project of their own choosing. At tiny Motoda Electronics, engineers are all required to complete three research projects a year (for which they receive special bonuses). And many Japanese corporations now heavily subsidize research labs at United States universities such as MIT, where they regularly send their top researchers to soak up information and learn new ways of creative thinking that can be replicated in Japan.

But few Japanese labs yet have the free-wheeling interchange of ideas or the loose, almost anarchical style that exists in America. At Toshiba, researchers still punch time clocks, while in other corporate labs young people must still defer to hierarchy and the seniority system. In some com-

The Koryu-I, a recent snake-style robot designed by the Hirose laboratory to operate in nuclear power plants.

panies the atmosphere is almost militaristic. The pressure on researchers to perform today is so intense it may have contributed to a rash of suicides among them in recent years at the "technopolis" city of Tsukuba, site of a national university and the national research labs, including MEL and ETL.[16]

Designing mobile robots is an exercise in reconciling form with function. The Centaur—a four-legged robot with two-armed manipulators and two four-fingered hands—might seem an excellent design, but why should the robot look even vaguely human? Why not use another shape? The Mori-Mukta philosophy says that one must "become a robot" to understand its true potential and limitations. If this had been applied to the ART project, the nuclear power plant robot would certainly have been less human-looking. As it is, one well-known researcher calls its current design the result of a "lack of imagination." Yoji Umetani, while believing in the merits of modeling animal structures, suggests the project chose the wrong animal. Yutaka Kanayama, speaking in general of Japan's anthropomorphic trend, says, "A computer is totally unlike the form of a human, and an airplane is totally unlike a bird, which flaps its wings. In robotics we should be interested in moving, not in shape and size."[17]

It is in locomotion, especially, that design decisions become critical. The type of locomotion chosen can determine not only the robot's mobility, but its speed and even the loads it can carry. Robots using wheels, like cars, can move about at relatively high speeds and carry relatively heavy loads of equipment, but work best on flat, unobstructed ground. Caterpillar treads, while slower, are better equipped to go

The AMOOTY robot climbing stairs in a mock-up of a nuclear power plant.

ARI, Assembly Robot with Intelligence, a prototype third-generation assembly robot designed by the Toshiba Manufacturing Engineering center. Modeled after the human upper torso, with stereo vision and artificial intelligence, it can analyze a structure of blocks and then duplicate it.

over minor obstacles. To date, most mobile robots used in nuclear power plants around the world have been designed mainly to perform inspection in radioactive areas; most have therefore been remote-controlled vehicles equipped with a simple camera or a single manipulator arm and powered by wheels or tank-type crawlers. The ART nuclear power plant robot, however, must be able to navigate through narrow passageways of a typical nuclear plant and to go over pipes and climb stairways (not to mention turning valves, screws, and so forth). In short it must perform much of the same work as a normal human operator.

If cleverly designed, a robot on modified wheels or tank treads can still have considerable maneuverability. Separate from the ART project, three of the ARTRA members—Mitsubishi, Toshiba, and Hitachi—have been building their own mobile robots for nuclear power plants. Hitachi and Mitsubishi have in the past produced experimental models with modified tank treads that either bend in the middle or reconfigure themselves for stair climbing. Toshiba has created a wheel-based design.

Near Yokohama, inside a mockup of a nuclear reactor that contains stairs, valves, and ladders, Toshiba has experimented with traditional crawler-type robots and even a robot that does nothing but climb ladders. Its current pride and joy is AMOOTY, partly funded by MITI money. AMOOTY (an acronym based on the names of the six men at the University of Tokyo who designed it) is a semi-"intelligent" robot with a vision system enabling it to navigate—a TV camera allows it to recognize specially placed symbols in the reactor and a laser beam measures distance. Instead of a traditional industrial-robot-style manipulator, AMOOTY uses one that looks like an elephant trunk with nine degrees of freedom—two more than the human arm.

The most novel aspect of the AMOOTY robot is its means of locomotion. Inspired, perhaps, by the old stair-climbing carts used by Venetian porters, each "wheel" is in the shape of a clover, with each "petal" of the clover containing a smaller, independent wheel. On flat ground the clovers do not turn—only the smaller wheels do. To climb a staircase, or cross over an obstacle, however, the larger clovers themselves are rotated. AMOOTY still has many problems. Its power is supplied by a cable, its speed is too slow, and it is too heavy and large. But it is a stable design. When engineers in a remote command room (watching through television cameras, with robot positions in the reactor displayed on computer screens as both outline and three-dimensional shapes) put AMOOTY through its paces, the "wheeled" robot lurches right up the stairs.

Professor Hiroyuki Yoshikawa of the University of Tokyo Mechanical Engineering Department led the team that worked with Toshiba to design AMOOTY. "In Japan we tend to neglect research on the basic purpose of our design," he says. "My specialty is design theory, and I consider design to be the science of function. For AMOOTY, for example, we used functional analysis to research the concept of maintenance in nuclear reactors, and came up with a system of locomotion and an arm that does not exist in nature."[18]

Because of control problems, robots with legs are only just now becoming technologically feasible. The most common number of legs they are given is six. Ohio State University's Adaptive Suspension Vehicle (a "robot" with a driver), uses six legs, as does one of the most unusual designs of mobile robots currently in operation—the Odex 2. Manufactured by the Anaheim, California, firm of Odetics, this robot is teleoperated and equipped with a manipulator, but its legs are in a circle, not unlike a spider's. By configuring the legs in different patterns, the Odex can climb thirty-degree slopes and stairs, step over obstacles, and change its height and stance to fit through narrow doorways. At only one mile per hour it is slow, but as one of the designers jokes, "If it has to get somewhere fast, we could have it climb into a pickup truck."[19] Significantly, even ARTRA has chosen a six-legged design for its disaster prevention robot, with an innovation; since the robot must be able to cross pipes and obstacles and also get to its destination in a hurry, it has been designed with wheels on each of its six feet.

Six legs are favored in robotics because six is the smallest number that guarantees a stable triad of support, even when two or three other legs are lifted. Six legs have "static stability" as opposed to "dynamic stability." When a robot or animal is "statically stable," its center of weight is always directly over its legs; it will not normally fall over. When "dynamically stable," however, it is balancing, and may fall over unless it keeps moving. Most of the insect world is statically stable; most mammals, when walking fast or running, are dynamically stable. When humans run, for example, our legs leave the ground temporarily, and we are constantly recovering from a state of falling, a type of "ballistic trajectory."

Some day, robots may have animal-like dynamic stability. Marc Raibert, Associate Professor of Computer Science and Robotics at Carnegie-Mellon University, has done some of the world's most advanced work in this area, starting with a one-legged hopping model, and then creating a two-legged hopping "chicken" and, finally, a four-legged, running robot. Shigeo Hirose of the Tokyo Institute of Technology produced a four-legged, dynamically stable "spider" robot that was displayed at Expo '85. And Ichiro Kato has developed "quasi-dynamically stable" bipedal robots (which maintain their center of weight over their legs except for a brief moment when stepping forward), as well as a stripped-down model with true dynamic stability. The engineering, however, still presents a tremendous challenge in control.

Will the Centaur be statically or dynamically stable? To move at the speed of a human, as is required, and to ascend and descend stairs, it would likely need at least a limited form of dynamic stability. "I wouldn't put a dynamically stable robot in a nuclear power plant at the present stage of technology," says Kenneth J. Waldron, Professor of Mechanical Engineering at Ohio State University, where the six-legged Adaptive Suspension Vehicle is being developed. "If

THE THRILL OF MAKING ROBOTS

Shigeo Hirose, associate professor at the Tokyo Institute of Technology, is the creator and designer of many of Japan's most unusual robots, including a four-legged spider robot equipped with sensors on its feet that allow it to navigate stairs. About its development he says, "It's almost impossible to describe the sensation when the robot first moves. Recently, when our four-legged walking machine was completed, we wanted to take some still photographs of it with a flash, so we turned out the light in the room and started it up. Sure enough, it began to climb the steps, creaking as it went. Now in daylight this wouldn't have seemed unusual at all, but hearing it slowly search its way up the stairs in the darkness made it seem truly alive."

---

the damn thing falls over, what do you do then?" But if the Centaur were to operate solely at a statically stable gait, lifting one leg at a time, it would be very slow. And it might still have other problems. Even Hirose, whose four-legged spider robot reportedly influenced the ART project design, has his doubts. "It's almost impossible to use a four-legged robot in a nuclear reactor," he says. "The passageways are too narrow, and it's supposed to carry a huge load of equipment. I don't think it's practical, and I keep telling the people in charge that they should use a snake design, which no one else has used. . . . We need a form that is more functional."[20]

So why were four legs chosen for the nuclear power plant robot? Engineers from Hitachi applied for, and were selected to develop, the four-legged mechanism. They are convinced of the correctness of their design. According to Hideo Maki, who heads the Hitachi effort, and Yoshiyuki Nakano, the chief researcher, they did consider other ideas, and they are aware of the problems involved with four legs. "Two legs are obviously not stable," says Nakano, "as they must always be balancing. Three legs are stable, but the moment you lift one, the other two become unstable. Any number over four is obviously stable and better, but then you have more joints involved. The controls become more difficult, the robot becomes heavier, and the size increases. We felt, therefore, that four legs is the best solution in terms of both stability and size."[21]

On close analysis, the Centaur design can actually be seen as a victory for the Ichiro Kato humanoid faction in Japan. Nakano claims that one reason for Hitachi's interest in the project is precisely its difficulty. Unlike factory robots, the ART robots are designed for maintenance, not mass production. The work is therefore random, not fixed, and cannot be described in advance. "To build a robot to work in this environment," he notes, "is both a challenge, and a dream for roboticists—to make the machines do what humans have been able to do."[22]

But the project is influenced by more than a desire to replicate human functions. The Hitachi team is also thinking, indirectly, about human shape. Maki and the Hitachi team worked with Professor Kato on WHL-11 (Waseda-Hitachi Legs-11), the slowly shuffling two-legged torso robot displayed at Expo '85. Maki claims the experience gave him the confidence to create a four-legged robot. "I think two legs is the ideal, and I would like to try to develop such a robot," he says, "but technologically, that's ten to fifteen years in the future, so we're settling for four. Professor Kato says that man used to walk on all fours, but that when he stood up and freed two of his limbs, a whole new world opened up for him. Our robot has four legs, and two arms, and we think it will yield the same results."[23]

The Spin-offs

If the ART project robots are successful, they will first be employed in the fields for which they are designed, taking over the hazardous work currently performed by humans at nuclear power plants, undersea oil rigs, and refineries. Demand in these specific areas is of course limited, but with modest modifications similar robots could be used in many other places. Using tele-existence and the strategy of limiting the robot's environment, robots could be put to work inside the boiler rooms of large ships, in other kinds of power plants, and in Japan's emerging space program. Robots could also be used in remote maintenance of automatic factories—one person could operate several factories from a central command post, even when the factories are separated by continents.

There is no guarantee the ART project robots will all work exactly as planned. That may not be important. Like other national projects, one of ART's purposes is to boost Japan's technological level. Robots are a form of systems engineering, and while the total robot may not be a success, the individual components and technologies will certainly be improved. This alone may have a profound effect on other areas of research in Japan. Most of the earth's land surfaces are currently inaccessible to wheeled or tracked vehicles.

RESEARCH AND DEVELOPMENT SCHEDULE FOR THE ART PROJECT

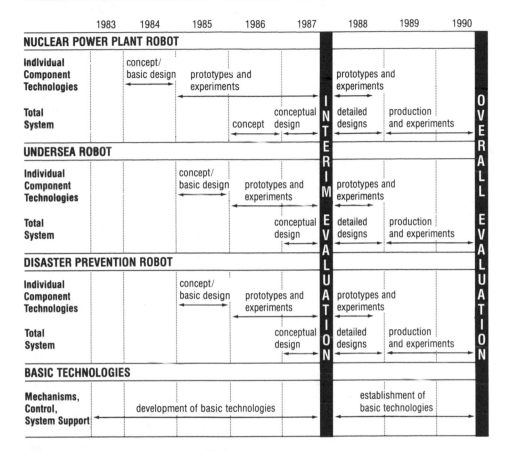

	1983	1984	1985	1986	1987		1988	1989	1990	
NUCLEAR POWER PLANT ROBOT										
Individual Component Technologies		concept/ basic design ←→	prototypes and experiments			**I N T E R I M**	prototypes and experiments ←			**O V E R**
Total System				concept	conceptual design ←→		detailed designs ←	production and experiments		
UNDERSEA ROBOT						**E**				**R A L L**
Individual Component Technologies			concept/ basic design ←→	prototypes and experiments		**M E V**	prototypes and experiments ←			
Total System					conceptual design ←→	**A**	detailed designs ←	production and experiments		**E V A**
DISASTER PREVENTION ROBOT						**L U**				**L U**
Individual Component Technologies			concept/ basic design ←→	prototypes and experiments		**A T I**	prototypes and experiments ←			**A T I**
Total System					conceptual design ←→	**O N**	detailed designs ←	production and experiments		**O N**
BASIC TECHNOLOGIES										
Mechanisms, Control, System Support	←	development of basic technologies			→		establishment of basic technologies ←		→	

"The technology for locomotion," writes Kanji Yonemoto of JIRA, "will have the biggest impact of all. It will spur the advance of robots into construction, agriculture, forestry, and even the welfare and service industry."[24]

One big application of advanced robot technology is certain to be maintenance, robots. Hiroyuki Yoshikawa, who helped develop the AMOOTY robot, has pointed out that Japan spends nearly 5 percent of its gross national product on maintenance, keeping up machines in factories, buildings, and roads. In Europe the figure is nearly 10 percent. In Yoshikawa's view, all manufacturing nations must eventually make a transition to a new level of technology if they are to survive. England, for example, switched from manufacturing but preserved and exploited its base of knowledge by dominating the world of insurance and finance. America is currently doing the same thing with software. Dominating maintenance technology, Yoshikawa believes, would be a way for Japan to maintain its position in the future. To accomplish this would require huge increases in productivity in the maintenance sector of the economy (which at present depends entirely on human labor). The logical tool for this is an advanced maintenance robot capable of a variety of tasks.[25]

The largest beneficiary of the new advanced robot technology, however, may be the faction of researchers doing work on humanoid designs. Should the Centaur, the four-legged nuclear power plant robot, be even a modest success, it will vastly speed up the development of truly functional bipedal robots. What will they be used for? The Robot Kingdom, with all its many facets—with its technological and economic power, its tea-carrying doll, its robots of the imagination and of industry and the laboratory, and its robot ideology—is a logical incubator for a single emerging entity, a variant of the My Robot, the personal robot envisioned by Ichiro Kato.

The My Robot is still a long way off, but we can imagine what it will look like. It may not be perfect. It will probably be small, and, in the tradition of Japan's cuddly machines in comics and toys, it will probably be cute and emotive. It will be used for simple types of housework and office work. It will take care of the old and the sick, and it will watch the house while the owners are away.

Most important, it will be designed as a consumer product, first for the domestic market and then for export. Many of Japan's largest consumer electronics manufacturers have always been very aggressive about industrial robots, both as a means of automating their own production and as an object to sell. But industrial robots have a limited market. If affordable personal robots can be developed for the home, and mass produced on an affordable level, the market for them will likely be bigger than that for the automobile. Japan will be able to take advantage of all its flexible manufacturing technologies and will have no serious competitors.

The robots will come in a wide variety of styles and colors with various optional attachments. They will become fashionable.

And everyone will want one.

ARTIFICIAL INTELLIGENCE AND ROBOTS: SOME PROBLEMS

AI, or "artificial intelligence," is often spoken of in glowing terms today, but in its present form it may have limited application for mobile robots. The first problem is that like "robot," the term "AI" has been horribly abused, and expectations far exceed reality. AI means replicating human intelligence, but it also is used for state-of-the-art software that is still in a developmental stage—once AI programs enter wide use, they are often no longer called AI and become merely a part of the growing body of sophisticated software the world enjoys. Second, AI nowadays generally refers to "expert systems," which are essentially "intelligent" data bases, vast computerized libraries of information to which sets of general rules are applied to gain answers to queries about the information in them. While expert systems certainly have many applications for industrial robots, and even research models, they are specialized, they only replicate a limited area of animal intelligence, and they are inadequate for the task of moving in an unstructured, real world. It might be possible to program autonomous, vision-equipped robots to operate in a limited environment by feeding the computer all known knowledge about that environment, and then giving it a set of rules with which to make decisions. But outside of a room or a building, the volume of information required for this becomes horrendous—there are simply too many variables. Since most computers process information in a step-by-step fashion, imagine a vision-equipped robot searching for a specific man in a crowd. After recording height, hair color, facial features, and other details, and checking these against a data base profile, it might be able to identify him. But what if the man sits down, turns sideways, or in other ways alters his shape, size, or appearance? For an autonomous, mobile robot that must simultaneously identify scores of objects in its environment and make split-second decisions on how to react to them, this is a truly inefficient and time-consuming mode of thinking. Scientists therefore are racing to develop faster computers running AI programs that can process information in a parallel rather than purely sequential fashion and that can be more "human-like" in the ways they identify and analyze images. The real problem is that no one yet knows exactly how animals really think. Future robots will likely require not only brains that think logically and sequentially, but brains that have "common sense"; that can think in a "fuzzy" fashion; that can glean new rules or truths from a limited set of experiences; and that can prioritize or even forget information no longer needed.

Conclusion: The Robot As Metaphor

The robots are coming, and they are Japanese. In the larger sense, however, the story of the robot is but a metaphor for the relationship between the Japanese people and their technology. Japanese technology has now reached critical mass. Having adjusted to Japan's "overnight" economic miracle, the rest of the world must now come to terms with the emerging Japanese technological superstate. The robot metaphor may help.

There has been a tendency among Westerners to focus on the "form" or 'style' of Japanese economic and industrial culture. To lap up the cultural dogma proffered as explanation by Japanese and Western media. To focus on management. But all too often, one suspects, this serves to create an aura of invincibility about Japan and to obscure the real formula behind its postwar success. This formula has two basic strategies: (1) manufacture increasingly sophisticated, value-added products for sale on the world market and (2) continually and incrementally refine the manufacturing process and its technology. As we have seen, a unique set of historical factors has arisen to stimulate and reinforce the former, while the industrial robot symbolizes the apex of the latter.

Ultimately, it is the relationship between humans and technology that determines how technology will be used. As the robot—in all its forms—demonstrates, among the great strengths of Japanese technology are its accessibility and its broad public acceptance. This does not mean that everyone in Japan has mastered or understands technology, but that it is widely perceived as something useful, immediate, practical, personal, and friendly. The key point here is that postwar Japan has largely managed to avoid—until now—the corrupting attitudes to technology engendered by militarism, large-scale technological disasters, and overt misuse. And the industrial establishment has been very careful to insure that these do not emerge. It is no coincidence that simplification and humanization of technology are important topics in Japan today and that corporate slogans—the "Sociotech" of Mitsubishi, the "Humanication" of Hitachi, and the "Human Electronics" of Matsushita—are designed to soften the harder edges of a high-tech society.

The story of the robot also shows how technology in Japan is far more than a means of making money or enhancing military strength. In the postwar period, technology has been a tool to build and to peacefully advance Japan in the hierarchy of nations. The perceived success of this strategy has meant that in Japan today, technology is intrinsically linked to a sense of national (and implicitly in Japan's case, racial) power, and even to a sort of technological manifest destiny. There is nothing sinister about this; most nations try to advance their own interests, and often in far less peaceful ways. But it does mean that Japan's competitors will surely have a hard time of it if they believe that Japan, its corporations, and its people are motivated solely by quantifiable, economic rationales.

Lastly, the robot metaphor demonstrates how the future is indeed something that does not yet exist. The future is waiting to be created, by those who have the vision, the drive, and the resources.

Notes

References that appear in full in the Bibliography appear here in shortened forms.

Chapter 1: The Robot Kingdom

Epigraph from Ichiro Kato, *Dokuso wa dokuso nari*, p. 9.

1. Reikichi Shirane, "Tsukuba kagakuhaku to Nihon no kagaku gijutsu" [Nature of Japanese Science and Technology Represented in Tsukuba Expo '85], *Journal of the Robotics Society of Japan*, vol. 4, no. 4 (August 1985), p. 42.

2. Japan Industrial Robot Association (JIRA) survey, 1987.

3. U.S. Department of Commerce, *A Competitive Assessment of the U.S. Robotics Industry*, p. 55.

4. Interview with Joseph Engelberger, 30 January 1986.

5. Interview with Victor Sheinman, 12 January 1987.

6. JIRA, *Sangyoyo robotto ni kansuru kigyo jittai chosa: hokokusho*, p. 46.

7. Interview with Tatsuya Nakamine, 18 March 1986.

8. *Ibid.*

9. "Robots 11," *Robotics World* (June 1987), p. 42; *Nikkan kogyo shinbun*, 9 September 1985, p. 2.

Chapter 2: What Is a Robot?

Epigraph from Niwa and Ozaki, *Daisan sedai robotto no shogeki*, p. 28.

1. *Webster's Ninth New Collegiate Dictionary*, s.v. "Robot."

2. *Kojien*, 3rd ed., s.v. "Robotto."

3. Devol, "U.S. Patent No. 2,988,237: Programmed Article Transfer," pp. 1–20.

4. Wiener, *Human Use of Human Beings*, p. 69.

5. Interview with Engelberger.

6. "Brainier Robots for Brawny Jobs," *Business Week*, 28 January 1961, pp. 81–82.

7. Alfred B. Bortz, "Joseph Engelberger: The Father of Industrial Robots Reflects on His Progeny," *Robotics Age*, April 1985, p. 15.

8. *RIA Robotics Glossary*, p. 28.

9. Toshio Kaneko, "Robotto ni kansuru teigi to yogo (ISO/TC 184/SC2WG1)" [Robot-Related Definitions and Terminology (ISO/TC 184/SC2WG1)], *Journal of the Robotics Society of Japan*, vol. 4, no. 1 (February 1986), pp. 28–32.

10. Interview with Kanji Yonemoto, 31 March 1986.

11. "Report on Revised JIS B 0134 (Glossary of Terms for Industrial Robots)," *Robot*, no. 53 (August 1986), p. 4.

12. Interview with Yonemoto.

13. Jean Chabrol, "Industrial Robot Standardization at ISO," (paper read at 15th International Symposium on Industrial Robots, Tokyo, 11–13 September 1985), p. 1.

14. *Ibid*.

15. Tachi, *Mekatoronikusu no hanashi*, p. 1.

16. Wiener, *Human Use of Human Beings*, p. 181.

17. Nakano, *Robotto kogaku nyumon*, p. 238.

Sidebar "Mechatronics." From *Kikai sangyo no shisaku ni kansuru chosa kenkyu 8, mekatoronikusu* [Report on Policies in the Machinery Industry, No. 8, Mechatronics], in Tachi, *Mekatoronikusu no hanashi*.

Sidebar "The Real Meaning of *R.U.R.*" From Karel Capek, "The Meaning of *R.U.R.*," *Saturday Review* (London), vol. 136, no. 3534 (21 July 1923), p. 79.

Chapter 3: The First Japanese Robot

Epigraph from Wiener, *Human Use of Human Beings*, p. 166.

1. Norbert Wiener, *Cybernetics, Or Control and Communication in the Animal and the Machine* (Cambridge, Mass.: Technology Press of MIT, 1949), p. 39.

2. Tatsukawa, *Karakuri*, p. 18.

3. Wiener, *Human Use of Human Beings*, pp. 164–66.

4. *Karakuri*, p. 4.

5. *Ibid*., pp. 27, 139.

6. *Ibid*., p. 213.

7. Interview with Shobe-e Tamaya, 13 April 1986.

8. Ichiro Kato, "Karakuri ningyo no nagare" [Automata Throughout History], *Nihon kikai gakkaishi*, vol. 85, no. 766 (September 1982), p. 43.

9. Interview with Shoji Tatsukawa, 15 April 1986.

10. Alcock, *Capital of the Tycoon*, vol. 2, p. 225.

11. Ernest Satow, *Diplomat in Japan* (London: Seely, Service, and Co., 1921), p. 278.

12. Imazu, *Kindai gijutsu no senkusha*, pp. 17–37; interview with Tatsukawa.

13. Imazu, *Kindai gijutsu no senkusha*, pp. 40–81.

14. Alcock, *Capital of the Tycoon*, vol. 1, p. 95.

15. Kato, "Karakuri ningyo no nagare," p. 43, quoting Kigure's *Futari no karakurishi* [Two Automata Artists] (Tokyo: Kin no Hoshisha, 1977), p. 21.

16. Imazu, *Kindai gijutsu no senkusha*, pp. 53–54.

Sidebar "Early Robot Legends." From Ishihara, *SF Robottogaku nyumon*; Tatsukawa, *Karakuri*.

Sidebar "A Modern Automata Artist." Interview with Shunji Mizuno, November 1986.

Sidebar "Yorinao Hosokawa." From Tatsukawa, *Karakuri*.

Chapter 4: Robots of the Imagination

Epigraph from Nakano, *Robotto kagaku nyumon*, p. 4

1. "Robotto ga dotto!!" [A Flood of Robots!], *New Type*, May 1986, p. 76.

2. Masaki Sakamoto, *Tanku Tankuro* (Tokyo: Kodansha, 1976), p. 216.

3. Yokota, *SF Daijiten*, p. 85; interview with Osamu Tezuka, 16 April 1986.

4. "Tetsuwan Atomu no sekai to robotto gijutsu" [Mighty Atom and Robot Technology], *Journal of the Robotics Society of Japan*, vol. 4, no. 3 (June 1986), p. 103.

5. Interview with Tezuka.

6. Takemochi Ishii, *Tekunorando Nippon no gijutsu ga saiko ni omoshiroi* [Technoland Japan's Technology Is By Far the Most Interesting] (Tokyo: President-sha, 1983), pp. 44–46.

7. "Emperor's Letter from War End Disclosed," *Japan Times*, 16 April 1986, p. 1; interview with Tezuka.

8. Mitsuteru Yokoyama and Fujio Ishihara, "Tetsujin 28go o kaitai suru!" [Dismantling Iron Man No. 28!], *Robotopia*, no. 1 (20 July 1982), pp. 4–5.

9. *TV animeshi: robotto animehen*, p. 135.

10. Schodt, *Manga! Manga!* p. 14.

11. *Ibid.*, p. 140.

12. *TV animeshi*, p. 135.

13. Schodt, *Manga! Manga!* p. 79; interview with Go Nagai, 11 April 1986.

14. Interview with Nagai.

15. *Ibid.*

16. *Ibid.*

17. Yoshiyuki Tomino, *Dakara Boku wa . . .* [That's Why I . . .] (Tokyo: Animeju Bunko, 1983), p. 303.

18. Interviews with Yoshiyuki Tomino, Takeyuki Kanda, Ryosuke Takahashi, and Eiji Yamaura, 22 March 1986.

19. *Ibid.*

20. "Italian Kid-Vid 'UFO Robot' Is a Bonanza," *Japanese Fantasy Film Journal*, no. 13 (1981), p. 4.

21. Interview with Yamaura.

Sidebar "Laws of Robots and Robotics." From Isaac Asimov. *I, Robot* (New York: Ballantine Books, 1950); *Mushi Production Data File 1962–73* (Tokyo, 1977).

Sidebar "Theme Song of the *Mighty Atom* Series." From *Mushi Production Data File 1962–73*.

Sidebar "Researchers Talk about Atom." From "Nisoku hoko robotto kenkyu no genjo" [Status of Research on Bipedal Robots], *Journal of the Robotics Society of Japan*, vol. 1, no. 3 (October 1983), p. 45; "Tetsuwan Atomu no sekai to robotto gijutsu," p. 100.

Chapter 5: The Toy Robot Kingdom

Epigraph from Kamata, *Robotto zetsubo koji*, p. 84; John Naisbitt, *Megatrends: Ten New Directions Transforming Our Lives* (New York: Warner Books, 1982), p. 20

1. Saito, *Omocha to gangu*, pp. 155–64.

2. *Ibid.*, p. 157.

3. Kitahara, *Wonderland of Toys*, p. 110.

4. *Heibonsha sekai dai hyakka jiten* [Heibonsha's World Encyclopedia], 1975 ed., s.v. "jisu" [JIS]; "Omocha no Machi: Guide to Toy Town" (Yushutsu Gangu Kojo Danchi Kyodo Kumiai, 1981).

5. *Omocha ichidai*, pp. 190–93, 283–84.

6. *Ibid.*, pp. 270–71, 285.

7. Interview with Satoru Matsumoto, 27 March 1986.

8. Interview with Hideaki Yoke, 18 March 1986.

9. Schodt, "Invasion of the Robots," pp. 30–35.

10. Interview with Tetsuro Sugawara, 4 March 1986.

11. Takaichi Ushiyama, "Omocha seisan kaigai shifuto kasoku" [Toy Production Overseas Accelerates], *Nikkei sangyo shinbun*, 22 January 1987, p. 20; Susumu Arakawa, "Kore ga 1 doru 150 en e no 'hissaku' da" [The 'Secret Plan' When One Dollar Is Only 150 Yen], *President*, July 1986, pp. 193–94.

12. Interview with Akira Murakami, 27 March 1986; interview with Yoke.

13. Interview with Yoshiro Yamazaki, 5 March 1986.

14. "Kigyo senraku: shohin kaihatsu—Tomi Kogyo no hai teku gangu ga odoru" [Corporate Strategy: Product Development—Tomy Corporation's High-Tech Toys Take Off], *Nikkei Business*, 28 October 1985, pp. 36–40.

15. Interview with Yamazaki and Yoshiyuki Matsumoto, 5 March 1986.

16. *Ibid.*

17. Interview with Hideki Konishi, 3 March 1986.

Sidebar "Riots over Robots." From Yutaka Sasayama, "Follow the Plastic Warrior!" *Japan Quarterly*, April–June 1982, pp. 252–56.

Chapter 6: Japan Manufactures the Industrial Robot

Epigraph from Marlene Zimmerman, "The Robot Master," *Datamation*, vol. 28, no. 4 (April 1982), p. 194.

1. Society of Manufacturing Engineers, "Robots 6: Tomorrow's Technology on Display" (videotape), 1982; interview with Engelberger.

2. Interview with Gensuke Okada, 4 March 1986.

3. *Ibid.*

4. Yukio Hasegawa, "Sangyoyo robotto wa naze Nippon de hiroku mochiirareteiru-ka," [Why Industrial Robots Are Widely Used in Japan], *Nippon kikai gakkaishi*, vol. 85, no. 766 (September 1982), p. 46; interview with Engelberger.

5. Interview with Naohide Kumagai, 20 March 1986.

6. *Ibid.*

7. *Ibid.*

8. Interview with Kosei Minami, 8 April 1986.

9. Interview with Engelberger.

10. Interview with Minami.

11. *Ibid.*

12. *Ibid.*

13. Ichiro Kato, ed., *Mujinka kojo e no chosen*, pp. 20, 94.

14. JIRA, *Sangyoyo robotto hando bukku*, p. 13.

15. JIRA, *Teikan* [Charter], October 1972.

16. Interview with Yukio Hasegawa, 18 November 1986.

17. JIRA, "JIRA Membership Information and Application."

18. Interview with Engelberger.

19. Interview with Takumi Kojima, 5 April 1986.

20. Interview with Seiji Furihata, 5 April 1986.

21. Interview with Victor Sheinman, 12 January 1987.

22. Mita Shuppankai, ed.,"'Byobu' kara kangaetsuita 'Skara-gata' kanirobotto" [A Crab-style SCARA Robot Inspired by a Folding Screen], in *Kagaku gijutsu no saizensen*, vol. 2, pp. 172–81.

Sidebar "Mr. Aros." From Fumio Fukuchi and Hiroshi Awane, "Recent Trends and the Future of Hitachi Robots," *Hitachi Review*, vol. 34, no. 1 (February 1985), pp. 1–6.

Sidebar "Comparing Japan and the U.S." From Sugimura, *Nihon no robottokai o irodoru*, p. 93.

Chapter 7: An Empire of Yellow Robots

Epigraph from former GMF employee's conversation with author, April 1987.

1. Joseph Engelberger during panel discussion at RIA Annual Meeting, Scottsdale, Arizona, 31 January 1986; Roger Eglin, "Iron Lady Riveted by Robots," *Sunday Times*, 1 May 1983, p. 53a.

2. "Fanuc: Far From Bananas," *Economist*, 29 June 1985, pp. 70–72.

3. Inaba, *Robotto jidai o hiraku*, pp. 57–58.

4. Interview with Seiuemon Inaba, 12 March 1986; Inaba, *Robotto jidai o hiraku*, pp. 149–53.

5. "Deta ni miru Nichi-Bei kigyo hikaku: Bei ga Nippon no hobo nibai" [Comparing Data on U.S. and Japanese Corporations: U.S. Nearly Double That of Japan], *Nikkei sangyo shinbun*, 11 September 1986, p. 22.

6. "Tsuyosa no kenkyu: Fanuc" [Analyzing Strength: Fanuc], *Nikkei Business*, 26 October 1985, p. 12.

7. "Tsuyosa no kenkyu: Fanuc," p. 7

8. Interview with Inaba.

9. *Ibid.*

10. Inaba, *Robotto jidai o hiraku*, p. 154; "Tsuyosa no kenkyu: Fanuc," p. 8; Ken Nukui, *Kiiroi robotto*, p. 155.

11. Interview with Inaba; conversation with Shinpei Kato, 12 March 1986; "Tsuyosa no kenkyu: Fanuc," p. 11; "Shacho no 24 jikan: Inaba Seiuemon" [24 Hours with the President: Seiuemon Inaba], *Shukan Diamond*, no. 26 (July 1986), p. 11.

12. *Bijinesuman kiki toppa heihozenshu* [Military Techniques For Businessmen to Overcome Crises] (Tokyo: Gakushu Kenkyusha, 1984), p. 61.

13. Inaba, *Robotto jidai o hiraku*, p. 108.

14. Interview with Eric Mittelstadt, 30 January 1986.

15. Interview with Walt Weisel, 31 January 1986.

16. Interview with Mittelstadt.

17. "Kigyo senryaku: kyosha rengo. Fanuc—GM to robotto kyodo kaihatsu. Mazu Bei shijo o seiha, Nippon e gyakujoriku" [Corporate Strategies: An Alliance of the Mighty. Fanuc to Develop Robots with GM, Conquer U.S. Market, Then Land in Japan], *Nikkei Business*, 3 February 1986, p. 31.

18. "GE, sangyoyo robo tettai: FA senryaku o kodoka" [GE Withdraws from IR: Will Develop FA Strategy], *Nikkei sangyo shinbun*, 30 January 1987, p. 11; "Fanuc shudo iro koku—GE to no FA goben" [GE-Fanuc FA Joint Venture: Fanuc Appears Leader], *Nikkei sangyo shinbun*, 17 January 1987, p. 11.

19. Interview with Inaba.

20. Conversation with Shinpei Kato.

Sidebar "My Dream." From Inaba, *Robotto jidai o hiraku*, pp. 151–52.

Sidebar "Inaba on Mechatronics." From Yasuhiko Ota, "Haiteku no yukue kiku: Inaba Seiuemon Fanuc shacho," *Nikkei sangyo shinbun*, 16 January 1986, p. 21.

Chapter 8: The Man-Machine Interface

Epigraph from Capek, *R.U.R. and the Insect Play*, p. 21.

1. "Revolt of the Robots," *New York Times*, 7 March 1972, p. 38.

2. Hasegawa, *Robotto to shakai*, p. 68.

3. Interview with Mittelstadt.

4. Hiroshi Takeuchi, ed., et al., *Encyclopedia of Japanese National Strength: International Comparison* (Tokyo: Kodansha, 1984), p. 335.

5. Norihiko Shimizu, "Nichi-Bei toppu bijinesuman no nenshu" [Annual Pay of Top Businessmen in Japan and U.S.], *Will*, June 1986, pp. 145–49; interview with Michael Caine, 3 April 1986.

6. Brian Kuttner, "Factories Need a Communications Link," *Robotics World*, September 1986, p. 32.

7. Interview with Kiyoshi Tawara, 11 April 1986; Inaba, *Robotto jidai*, p. 185.

8. "The Memorandum of Understanding Concerning the Introduction of New Technologies," Nissan Motor Company.

9. Interview with Naoki Kumagai, 20 March 1986; Hasegawa, *Robotto to shakai*, p. 68.

10. Wiener, *Human Use of Human Beings*, p. 189; interview with Naoyuki Kameyama, 31 March 1986.

11. Interview with Kameyama.

12. Nano, *Robotto shitsugyo*, p. 9.

13. Hisabumi Kato, *Ima, robotto kojo ni haittara ikigai wa aruka*, p. 134.

14. Kamata, *Robotto jidai no genba*, p. 143.

15. "Kokuden zenmen stoppu: shutoken 480mannin no ashi ubau" [National Railways Totally Stopped: 4.8 Million Paralyzed in Capital], *Nihon keizai shinbun*, evening ed., 29 November 1985, pp. 1, 19.

16. "Kokutetsu shokuin no mana shinan" [Teaching JNR Employees Manners], *Nikkei sangyo shinbun*, 3 March 1986, p. 16; "Kokutetsu shokuin aitsugu jisatsu; shusho chosa o shiji" [More and More JNR Employee Suicides: Prime Minister Orders Survey], *Nihon keizai shinbun*, evening ed., 29 September 1986; union fliers passed out on streets in November 1986.

17. Kai Funado, "Zosen shokuba ni okeru robotto donyu no jittai" [The True Situation When Robots Enter Shipyards], *Kaiho*, 8 September 1986, p. 5.

18. Kazuhisa Hirata, "Denki kumitate shokuba e no robotto donyu" [Introducing Robots into Electronics Assembly], *The Communist*, 3 March 1986, pp. 102–7.

19. Interview with Kameyama.

20. Interview with Katsuhiro Kawasaki, 26 November 1986.

21. Interview with Kiyoshi Mori, 7 November 1986.

22. "Technostress: jidoka no 'sogai shokogun'" [Technostress: The Isolation Syndrome of Automation], *Nikkei sangyo shinbun*, 22 January 1986, p. 1.

23. Okamura, *Robotto wa ningen ni kigai o kuwaete wa naranai*, pp. 29–65.

24. Interviews with Noboru Sugimoto and Soichi Kumekawa, 22 November 1986.

25. Interview with Tawara.

26. Interview with Takumi Kojima, 11 April 1986; interview with Kameyama.

27. "Oyakigyo no kokinrika, ukeijime keikoku e. Tsusansho ga chosa e" [Parent Firms Using High Interest Rates, Warned Against Bullying Subcontractors. MITI to Conduct Survey], *Nikkan kogyo shinbun*, 31 May 1986, p. 1.

Sidebar "Hasegawa's New Laws of Robotics." From Hasegawa, *Robotto to shakai*, p. 145.

Chapter 9: Robots and the Wealth of Nations

Epigraph from Adam Smith, *The Wealth of Nations: Books I–III* (Harmondsworth, England: Penguin Classics, 1986), p. 383.

1. *Global Competition: The New Reality*, 1985, p. 11.

2. In a 1982 poll, 75.9 percent of 521 firms in Aichi Prefecture introduced robots to reduce labor; 68.9 percent reported success. Eiji Ogawa, "Robottoka to sangyo kozo" [Robotization and the Structure of Industry], *Journal of the Robotics Society of Japan*, vol. 3, no. 1 (February 1985), p. 35; Engelberger's opening speech at the RIA Joseph F. Engelberger Awards ceremony, 28 April 1987; "Robotto daidonyu" [Major Introduction of Robots], *Nikkei sangyo shinbun*, 28 June 1986, p. 1.

3. Donald Zook, "President's Message: Avoiding the Service Economy," *Manufacturing Engineering*, April 1987, p. 7.

4. Interview with Kisaku Suzuki, April 4, 1986.

5. "Robotto genba kara no hokoku: Arakawa Buhin Seisakujo—70sai no pato tsukau, seisan fuyashi, yosetsu sagyo raku ni" [Report from Robot Users: Arakawa Buhin Seisakujo—70-Year-Old Part Timers, Increased Productivity, and Easier Welding], *Nikkei sangyo shinbun*, 30 October 1985, p. 10.

6. Interview with Kawasaki and Yoshiaki Maeda, 26 November 1986.

7. Tour of Ricoh Atsugi plant, 19 September 1985; interview with Brian Carlisle, 20 February 1986.

8. Interview with Kawasaki.

9. Interview with Hirokazu Shimatake, 12 November 1986.

10. Interview with Tawara; "Robotto genba kara no hokoku: Kuwano Toso Kogyo—owan urushi nuri ni donyu, furyohin wa hobo zero ni" [Report from Robot Users: Kuwano Toso Kogyo—Introduced to Paint Lacquer Bowls, Defects Nearly Zero], *Nikkei sangyo shinbun*, 18 September 1985, p. 9; "Robotto genba kara no hokoku: Toto Kiki—benki no shisai o jidoka, kinitsu toso de hinshitsu mura kaisho" [Report from Robot Users: Toto Ltd.—Automates Toilet Bowl Materials, Uniform Painting Solves Variations in Quality], *Nikkei sangyo shinbun*, 1 May 1985, p. 9; "Robotto genba kara no hokoku: NSK Warner—furyohin zero kiroku koshin, kumitate, kensa o ittaika" [Report from Robot Users: NSK Warner—Zero Defects Record Broken, Assembly and Inspection Combined], *Nikkei sangyo shinbun*, 5 June 1985, p. 9.

11. Hajime Karatsu, "Quality Control, QC Circle and Productivity," unpublished ms., n.d.

12. Interview with Shigeru Tabei, 26 November 1986.

13. I am indebted to Brian Carlisle of Adept Technology for many of these points; see also "Special Report: The Hollow Corporation," *Business Week*, 3 March 1986, p. 62.

14. Hajime Karatsu, "The Deindustrialization of America: A Tragedy for the World," *Keizai Koho Center Brief*, no. 31 (October 1985), p. 3.

15. Craig L. Stevens, "The Design of a Clean Room Robot for Wafer Handling," Proceedings of "Robots 11, 17th International Symposium on Industrial Robots," pp. 4/59, 90; Tom Papanek, "Design and Test of a Robot for Class 10 Clean Rooms," Proceedings of "Robots 11, 17th International Symposium on Industrial Robots," pp. 101, 113.

16. M. H. Pang, "Robotization of Singapore," Proceedings of "15th International Symposium on Industrial Robots," p. 19.

17. Norbert Wiener, *I Am a Mathematician* (New York: Doubleday, 1956), p. 335.

18. Interview with Hiroyuki Yoshikawa, 25 November 1986.

19. Joseph Engelberger, "The Ultimate Worker," in *Robotics*, ed. Marvin Minsky (New York: Anchor Press/Doubleday, 1985), p. 200; Bill Johnstone, "Mrs. Thatcher Sides with the Robots," *The Times*, 19 May 1981, p. 19.

20. Hajime Karatsu, "Is U.S. Industry Going Down the Tubes?" *PHP Intersect*, January 1986, p. 27.

21. Marc Beauchamp, "Close the Door, They're Coming in the Windows," *Forbes*, 27 January 1986, p. 84.

22. "Mekatoronikusu: sangyoyo robotto 87nen ko ugoku—tanomi wa jidosha muke" [Mechatronics: Industrial Robots in 1987—Shipments to Auto Manufacturers Look Good], *Nikkei sangyo shinbun*, 16 January 1987, p. 10; "Matsuda no honsha kojo: 87dai donyu de koka wa oo(kii), Beikoku kojo ni mo 100dai keikaku" [Mazda Main Plant: Major Benefits from 87 IR, to Use 100 in U.S. Plant], *Nikkan kogyo shinbun*, 23 June 1986, p. 11.

23. "Danwashitsu: Bei hodo kudoka sezu" [Parlor Talk: Not As Much Hollowing to Occur in Japan as the U.S.], *Nikkei sangyo shinbun*, 10 December 1986, p. 10.

24. Interview with Engelberger.

25. Kenji Kobayashi, "Development of Advanced System for Construction Technologies with Proper Use of Electronics," Proceedings of "15th International Symposium on Industrial Robots," pp. 79–88; Yukio Hasegawa, "Robotization of Reinforced Concrete Building Construction in Japan," paper presented in 1986.

Sidebar "Comparing Assembly and Testing of Small Motors." From Shunji Rikumaru, "Assembly and Test Line of Small Motors," *Robot*, no. 52 (June 1986), pp. 106–12.

Sidebar "Why Trade Imbalances Occur." From Seiichiro Saito, "Nichibei 'keizai senso' no shinario" [Scenario for U.S.–Japan "Economic War"], *Voice*, June 1987, p. 96.

Sidebar "Building Houses with Robots." From [Shigesaburo] Kabe, "Robotto genba kara no hokoku: Daiwa House Kogyo" [Report from Robot Users: Daiwa House Industry], *Nikkei sangyo shinbun*, 3 June 1987, p. 8.

Chapter 10: Religion and Robots

Epigraph from a caption in "Japan 2000," *Omni Special Edition*, June 1985, p. 34.

1. Henry Scott-Stokes, "Japan's Love Affair with the Robot," *New York Times Magazine*, 10 January 1982, p. 26; Koichi Kawamura, "Industrial Robots in Japan," *Oriental Economist*, August 1983, p. 28.

2. "Shacho no 24 jikan," p. 11.

3. H. Neill McFarland, *The Rush Hour of the Gods: A Study of New Religious Movements in Japan* (New York: Macmillan, 1967), p. 26.

4. Interview with Engelberger.

5. Toru Hirayama, in introduction to *Toei kaijin kaiju daihyakka, robotto hen* [Toei Encyclopedia of Monsters and Demons: The Robot Edition], Toei Video; Cover to *Z GUNDAM Mechanical Edition*, vol. 1 (1985), Kadokawa Shoten.

6. Scott-Stokes, "Japan's Love Affair," p. 26.

7. Interview with Okada.

8. Asimov, Warrick, and Greenberg, *Machines That Think*, pp. 1–11; Wiener, *God & Golem, Inc.*, pp. 49–55.

9. Interviews with Weisel and Kanayama.

10. Interview with Ichiro Kato, 26 March 1986.

11. Ichiro Kato, *Robotto wa ningen o kaeruka*, pp. 66–67.

12. Interview with Kato.

13. *Ibid*.

14. *Ibid*.

15. "Robotto wa doko made ningen ni sekkin dekiruka" [How Close Can Robots Come to Humans?], *Nikkei Business*, 6 January 1986, p. 117.

16. Interview with Masahiro Mori, 17 March 1986.

17. Wiener, *Human Use of Human Beings*, pp. 28–29.

18. Mori, *The Buddha in the Robot*, pp. 13–22, 179–80.

19. Interview with Sueo Matsubara, 27 February 1986.

20. *Ibid.*

21. Ichiro Kato, *Robotto wa ningen o kaeruka*, p. 84.

Sidebar "Robots As Sacred Tools." From Yoshida, *Kikai*, pp. 196, 199, 209.

Sidebar "Manufacturing and Religion." From interview with Karatsu, 3 April 1986.

Sidebar "Masahiro Mori on Honda Motors." From interview with Mori.

Sidebar "A Roboticist Worries about the Future." From interview with Kato.

Chapter 11: Six Legs, Four Legs, Two Legs, or None?

Epigraph from Kanji Yonemoto, quoted in *Holonic Innovation*, no. 136.

1. Sanpei Sato, "Fuji Santaro," *Asahi shinbun*, 26 June 1984, p. 23.

2. Interviews with Susumu Tachi, 14 March and 27 November 1986.

3. Proceedings of "Kogyo Gijutsuin ogata purojecto."

4. *Ibid.*

5. "Holonic Innovation: mito kakushin gijutsu e no chosen 139—kyokugen sagyo robotto, ido gijutsu ni kakukai ga chumoku" [Holonic Innovation: The Challenge of New, Innovative Technologies, no. 139—All Sectors Interested in Locomotion Technologies for ART Robots], *Nikkan kogyo shinbun*, 22 May 1986, p. 32; also no. 138, "Kyokugen sangyo robotto, kenkyu kaihatsu wa juncho ni susumu" [Research and Development Proceeding Smoothly for ART Project Robots], *Nikkan kogyo shinbun*, 21 May 1986, p. 24; interview with Yoshiaki Shirai, March 14, 1986.

6. Interview with Yoji Umetani, 27 April 1987.

7. JIRA, *Sangyoyo robotto ni kansuru daigaku*.

8. Interview with Shigeo Hirose, 3 March 1986.

9. Interview with Yutaka Kanayama, 20 December 1985.

10. *Ibid.*

11. Interview with Hiroaki Ando, 26 March 1986.

12. Eiji Nakano, "Kagaku gijutsu no nyu furontia to naruka? Ugokidasu HFSF keikaku" [The HFSF Project Starts to Move: Will It Become the New Frontier for Science and Technology?], *Robotist*, Fall 1986, p. 2.

13. Interview with Shinnichi Yuta, 4 March 1986.

14. Interview with Hirose.

15. Takashi Ota, "Nihonsha dezain shinjidai: tomaranai 'shiro' ninki" [New Age of Japanese Car Designs: Relentless Popularity of 'White,'" *Nihon keizai shinbun*, 26 June 1986, p. 17.

16. Hiroshi Magami, "Kokusai zuno toshi—Tsukuba—10nin no jisatsusha" [Tsukuba, the International Brain City—Ten Suicides], *Bungei shunju*, June 1986, pp. 198–209.

17. Interviews with Umetani and Kanayama.

18. Interview with Hiroyuki Yoshikawa, 25 November 1986.

19. Conversation with Steven J. Bartholet, 27 April 1986; Proceedings of "Kogyo Gijutsuin ogata purojecto."

20. Interview with Kenneth J. Waldron, 12 January 1987; interview with Hirose.

21. Interview with Yoshiyuki Nakano and Hideo Maki, 4 November 1986.

22. *Ibid.*

23. *Ibid.*

24. "Holonic Innovation," no. 139.

25. Yoshikawa, *Robotto to ningen* [Man and Robots] (Tokyo: NHK Books, 1985), pp. 12–24.

Sidebar "Inspiration from the Past." From [Makoto] Tsuchihashi, "Rekishi o hiraita hitobito 3: judai seihinsho ni miru—yushikaku robotto 'Nihonto no gijutsu' o saiyo" [Pioneers of History, Vol. 3: A Look at the Top Ten Product Awards—Vision-equipped Robot Uses Japanese Sword Technology], *Nikkan kogyo shinbun*, 21 June 1984, p. 28.

Sidebar "ART Project Members." From Proceedings of "Kogyo Gijutsuin ogata purojecto."

Sidebar "Masahiro Mori on Creativity." From "Kaicho shunin no goaisatsu" [Words from the New Chairman], *Journal of the Robotics Society of Japan*, 2 February 1987, p. 3.

Sidebar "The Thrill of Making Robots." From "Tetsuwan Atomu no sekai to robotto gijutsu," p. 105.

Sidebar "Research and Development Schedule for the ART Project." From Proceedings of "Kogyo Gijutsuin ogata purojecto."

Bibliography

In the abbreviated list of references below, Japanese sources that are primarily visual are marked with an asterisk.

*Akiba, Yoshinori. "Bandai: Yuniiku hasso de kodomo shijo o sekken suru" [Bandai: Conquering the Children's Market with Unique Ideas]. *Common Sense*, vol. 2, no. 10 (October 1985), pp. 132–53.

Alcock, Sir Rutherford. *The Capital of the Tycoon: A Narrative of a Three Years' Residence in Japan*. 2 vols. New York: Harper and Brothers, 1863.

Aron, Paul. *The Robot Scene in Japan: The Second Update*. Paul Aron Report, no. 28. 15 April 1985.

Asimov, Isaac; Patricia Warrick; Martin H.Greenburg, eds. *Machines That Think: The Best Science Fiction Stories about Robots and Computers*. New York: Holt, Rinehart and Winston, 1984.

Asimov, Isaac, and Karen A. Frenkel. *Robots: Machines in Man's Image*. New York: Harmony Books, 1985.

Capek, Karel. *R.U.R. and the Insect Play*. London: Oxford University Press, 1961.

Chapuis, Alfred, and Edmond Droz. *Automata: An Historical and Technological Study*. Translated by Alex Reid. New York: Central Book Co., 1958.

Colligan, Douglas. "Robotic Soul." *Omni Magazine*, June 1985, pp. 67–70, 118–22.

Development of Waseda Robot: The Study of Biomechanisms at the Kato Laboratory. 2nd ed. Tokyo: Ichiro Kato Laboratory, 1987.

Devol, George C. "U.S. Patent No. 2,988,237: Programmed Article Transfer." U.S. Patent Office. 13 June 1961.

Engelberger, Joseph F. *Robotics in Practice: Management and Applications of Industrial Robots*. New York: Amacom, 1980.

Global Competition: The New Reality. Report of the President's Commission on Industrial Competitiveness. 2 vols. 1985.

Hasegawa, Yukio. *Robotto to shakai* [Robots and Society]. Tokyo: New Science Age, 1983.

———, ed. *Tahinshu shoryo seisan shisutemu* [Diversified Production Systems]. Tokyo: Nikkan Kogyo Shinbunsha, 1984.

Hayashi, Masami. *Sangyo no kamigami* [The Gods of Industry]. Tokyo: Tokyo Shoseki, 1981.

Hirose, Shigeo; Yutaka Kanayama; and Susumu Tachi. "Form and Function in Robotics Research: A Trialogue." Translated by J. S. Harp. *Flux*, vol. 2, no. 3 (Fall 1985), pp. 4–8.

*Hosokawa Hanzo, Yorinao. *Karakurizui* [A Manual of Karakuri]. 3 vols. Kyoto: 1796.

Imazu, Kenji. *Kindai gijutsu no senkusha: Toshiba soritsusha Tanaka Hisashige no shogai* [A Modern Technology Pioneer: The Life of Hisashige Tanaka, Founder of Toshiba]. Tokyo: Kadokawa Shoten, 1964.

Inaba, Seiuemon. *Robotto jidai o hiraku: kiiroi shiro kara no chosen* [Pioneering the Robot Age: The Challenge from the Yellow Castle]. Tokyo: PHP, 1982.

Inagaki, Soji. *Sangyoyo robotto nyumon* [An Introduction to Industrial Robots]. Tokyo: Taiga Shuppan, 1985.

Ishihara, Fujio. *SF robottogaku nyumon* [An Introduction to SF Robotics]. Tokyo: Haya-kawa Shobo, 1981.

Iwai, Masakazu. *Hitachi, Toshiba, Matsushita FA no saizensen: "shijo taiyogata" seisan genba o yuku* [On the Front Lines of Factory Automation at Hitachi, Toshiba, and Matsu-shita: On the Site of Market-Oriented Production]. Tokyo: Diamond-sha, 1986.

Japan Industrial Robot Association (JIRA), ed. *Sangyoyo robotto hando bukku* [Industrial Robot Handbook]. 1985 ed. Tokyo: Japan Industrial Robot Association, 1985.

———. *Sangyoyo robotto ni kansuru daigaku—kokuritsu kenkyu kikan nado no kenkyu kaihatsu doko chosa hokokusho* [Survey of Trends in Industrial Robot Research and Development at University and National Laboratories]. Tokyo: Japan Industrial Robot Association, 1986.

———. *Sangyoyo robotto ni kansuru kigyo jittai chosa: hokokusho* [Survey of Corporate Conditions Relating to Industrial Robots]. Tokyo: Japan Industrial Robot Associa-tion, September 1986.

Kamata, Satoshi. *Robotto jidai no genba: kyokugen no gorika kojo* [On the Shop Floor in the Robot Age: Factories Rationalized to the Extreme]. Tokyo: Mii Shobo, 1982.

———. *Robotto zetsubo kojo* [Robot Factory of Despair]. Tokyo: Gendai Shuppankai, 1983.

Kameyama, Naoyuki, ed. *Gijutsu kakushinka no chusho kigyo: atarashii keieishazo* [Small and Medium Businesses and Technological Change: Portraits of New Managers]. Tokyo: Nihon Rodo Kyokai, 1985.

Kato, Hisabumi. *Ima, robotto kojo ni haittara ikigai wa aruka* [Is Life Worth Living in a Robot Factory Today?]. Tokyo: Management-sha, 1983.

Kato, Ichiro, and Kuni Sadamoto, eds. *Mechanical Hands Illustrated*. Tokyo: Survey Japan, 1982.

Kato, Ichiro, ed. *Mujinka kojo e no chosen: kogyoyo robotto no hanashi* [The Challenge of the Unmanned Factory: A Discussion of Industrial Robots]. Tokyo: Kogyo Chosakai, 1973.

———, ed. *Robotto wa ningen o kaeruka: robotto, seimei, ningen no yukue* [Will Robots Change Man? Robots, Life, and the Future of Man]. Tokyo: Kodansha, 1983.

———. *Sekai hajimete no nisoku hoko robotto: baiomekatoronikusu no saizensen* [The World's First Bipedal Robots: On the Front Lines of Biomechatronics]. Tokyo: Asahi Shup-pansha, 1983.

———. *Dokuso wa dokuso nari.* [Creativity Means Going It Alone]. Tokyo: Kodansha, 1987.

Kigami, Susumu. *Robotto wa nani o motarasuka: ningen, robotto jidai no makuake* [What Will Robots Bring? The Curtain Rises on the Age of Man and Robots]. Tokyo: Nikkan Kogyo Shinbunsha, 1983.

Kitahara, Teruhisa. *Wonderland of Toys: Tin Toy Robots*. Tokyo: Synco Music, 1983.

Koestler, Arthur. *The Lotus and the Robot*. New York: Harper and Row, 1960.

Makino, Hiroshi. *Uragaeshi no menyu: jidoka koborebanashi* [The Reversed Menu: Ruminations on Automation]. Tokyo: Gijutsu Chosakai, 1984.

———. *Shiibas Riigaru robotto: jidoka koborebanashi 2* [The Chivas Regal Robot: Ruminations on Automation 2]. Tokyo: Gijutsu Chosakai, 1987.

Minsky, Marvin, ed. *Robotics*. New York: Anchor Press/Doubleday, 1985.

Mita Shuppankai, ed. *Kagaku gijutsu no saizensen: "Nihon no zuno" o genba ni ou* [On the Front Lines of Technology: On-Site Interviews with Japan's Best Minds]. 4 vols. Tokyo: Diamond-sha, 1984.

Mori, Kiyoshi. *Machi koba no robotto kakumei* [A Robot Revolution among Neighborhood Factories]. Tokyo: Diamond-sha, 1982.

———. *Robotization*. Tokyo: Gijutsu to Ningen, 1984.

Mori, Masahiro. *The Buddha in the Robot: A Robot Engineer's Thoughts on Science and Religion*. Translated by Charles S. Terry. Tokyo: Kosei, 1974.

———. *Himajime no susume* [In Favor of Playfulness]. Tokyo: Kodansha, 1984.

Nakae, Katsumi. *Omocha sengo bunkashi: jidai no shogensha tachi* [A Postwar Cultural History of Toys: Witnesses to the Age]. Tokyo: Tairyusha, 1983.

Nakano, Eiji. *Robotto kogaku nyumon* [An Introduction to Robot Engineering]. Tokyo: Omusha, 1983.

Nakayama, Shigeru, ed. *Nihon no gijutsuryoku: sengoshi to tenbo* [Japanese Technological Strength: Postwar History and Future Prospects]. Tokyo: Asahi Shinbunsha, 1986.

Nano, Biko. *Robotto shitsugyo* [Robot Unemployment]. Tokyo: Tairiku Shobo, 1982.

———. *Chino robotto no kyoi: kyokugen ni idomu "idogata" saizensen* [The Surprise of Intelligent Robots: State-of-the-Art "Mobile" Robots Challenge the Limits]. Tokyo: Nihon Keizai Shinbunsha, 1985.

Nevins, J. L. "Mechatronics." Paper prepared for the "Symposium on U.S.-Japan Science and Technology Exchange Experience: Patterns of Interdependence," Washington, D.C., 17 November 1986.

Nihon kogyo shinbun Special ME Staff. *Suchiiru kara no kyoi: robotto jidai no atarashii nami* [Steel Collar Threat: A New Wave in the Robot Age]. Tokyo: Nihon Kogyo Shinbunsha, 1984.

Nikkan kogyo shinbun Special Staff. *Robotto sangyo chizu* [A Map of the Robot Industry]. Tokyo: Nikkan Kogyo Shinbunsha, 1982.

Nikkei Sangyo Shinbunsha, ed. *Kensetsugyo no haiteku senryaku* [The High-Tech Strategy of the Construction Industry]. Tokyo: Seibunsha, 1986.

Niwa, Koichi, and Shotaro Ozaki. *Daisan sedai robotto no shogeki: jinko chino jidai no makuaki jidai* [The Third Generation Robot Shock: The Curtain Rises on Artificial Intelligence]. Tokyo: Keirin Shobo, 1985.

Noble, David F. *Forces of Production: A Social History of Industrial Automation*. New York: Alfred A. Knopf, 1984.

*Nomura, Shohei, and Shobe-e Tamaya. *Karakuri ningyo no sekai* [The World of Automata Dolls]. Nagoya: Chunichi Shinbunsha, 1976.

Nukui, Ken. *Kiiroi robotto: Fujitsu Fanuc no kiseki* [Yellow Robots: The Miracle of Fujitsu Fanuc]. Tokyo: Yomiuri Shinbunsha, 1982.

Ohashi, Tsutomu; Susumu Oda; ToshitakaHidaka; and Yoichiro Murakami. *Jocho robotto no sekai* [The World of Emotive Robots]. Tokyo: Kodansha, 1985.

Okamura, Chikanobu. *Robotto wa ningen ni kigai o kuwaete wa naranai* [Robots Must Never Harm Humans]. Tokyo: Rodo Kijun Chosakai, 1985.

Omocha ichidai: Tomiyama Eiichiro-den [A Life of Toys: A Biography of Eiichiro Tomiyama]. Tokyo: Tomy Corporation, 1980.

Raibert, Marc. *Legged Robots That Balance.*Cambridge, Mass.: MIT Press, 1986.

Reichardt, Jasia. *Robots: Fact, Fiction, and Prediction.* Great Britain: Penguin Books, 1978.

RIA Robotics Glossary. Dearborn, Mich.: Robot Institute of America, 1984.

*Robotto daizukan [The Great Pictorial of Robots]. Special edition of *Taiyo*, no. 220 (June 1981).

*Robotto no subete [Everything About Robots]. Special edition of *Newton*, 20 February 1984.

*Roman Album Special: Yoshiyuki Takani Anime Illustrations. Tokyo: Tokuma Shoten, 1983.

Sadamoto, Kuni, ed. *Robots in the Japanese Economy: Facts about Robots and Their Significance.* Tokyo: Survey Japan, 1981.

*Saishinban hiiro robotto daihyakka [Latest Encyclopedia of Robot Heroes]. Tokyo: Keibunsha, 1983.

Saito, Masahiko, ed. *Robotto shakai to ningen* [Man and Robot Society]. Tokyo: Tokyo Daigaku Shuppankai, 1985.

Saito, Ryosuke. *Omocha to gangu* [Toys and Playthings]. Tokyo: Miraisha, 1965.

Sangyoyo robotto donyu katsuyo gaido: kumitate robotto hen [Guide to the Introduction and Use of Industrial Robots: Assembly Robots]. Special edition of *Shoryoku to jidoka*. Tokyo: Omusha, March 1986.

Schodt, Frederik L. *Manga! Manga! The World of Japanese Comics.* Tokyo: Kodansha International, 1983.

———. "Invasion of the Robots." *PHP Intersect*, December 1985, pp. 30–35.

**Sorayama, Hajime. *Sexy Robot.* Tokyo: Genkosha, 1983.

Sugimoto, Masayoshi, and David Swain. *Science and Culture in Traditional Japan: 600 A.D.–1854.* Cambridge, Mass.: MIT Press, 1978.

Sugimoto, Noboru. *Sanrobo o umaku tsukau: sangyoyo robotto no anzen kanri chekku pointo.* [Using Industrial Robots Properly: Safety Check Points for Industrial Robots]. Anzen Eisei Jissen Series, no. 8. Tokyo: Japan Industrial Safety and Health Association, 1986.

Sugimura, Jiro. *Nihon no robottokai o irodoru: 100nin no robotist* [One Hundred Robotists: Creating Japan's Robotics Landscape]. Tokyo: Kogyo Chosakai, 1987.

Tachi, Susumu. *Mekatoronikusu no hanashi* [Speaking of Mechatronics]. Science and Technology. Tokyo: Nikkan Kogyo Shinbunsha, 1984.

Tachibana, Takashi, and Hiroyuki Yoshikawa. *Robotto ga machi o aruku hi* [When Robots Walk in the Streets]. Soft Technology Series. Tokyo: Mita Shuppankai, 1987.

**Tagaya, Kanchusen. *Karakuri kimmo kagamigusa* [Instructions on Automata]. 3 vols. 1742. Reprint. Tokyo: Yoneyamado, 1929.

Tatsukawa, Shoji. *Karakuri: mono to ningen no bunkashi* [Automata: A Cultural History of Man and Things]. Vol. 3. Tokyo: Hosei Daigaku Shuppankyoku, 1969.

Todd, D. J. *Walking Machines: An Introduction To Legged Robots.* New York: Chapman and Hall, 1985.

**"Tokushu: Tomy—Asobi o dezain suru" [Special Edition: Tomy—Designing Play]. *Designer's Workshop*, vol. 1, no. 4 (October, 1984).

Tomino, Yoshiyuki. *Kido senshi Gundam* [Mobile Suit Gundam]. 3 vols. Tokyo: Asahi Sonorama, 1980.

TV animeshi: robotto animehen [A History of TV Animation: The Robot Animation Edition]. Anime Bunko, no. 1. Tokyo: Asahi Sonorama, 1981.

Unger, J. Marshall. *The Fifth Generation Fallacy: Why Japan Is Betting Its Future on Artificial Intelligence.* New York: Oxford University Press, 1987.

U.S. Department of Commerce, International Trade Administration. *A Competitive Assessment of the U.S. Robotics Industry.* GPO, March 1987.

Usher, Abbot Payson. *A History of Mechanical Inventions.* Boston: Beacon Press, 1929, 1954.

Wiener, Norbert. *The Human Use of Human Beings: Cybernetics and Society.* Boston: Houghton Mifflin, 1950.

———. *God & Golem, Inc.: A Comment on Certain Points Where Cybernetics Impinges on Religion.* Cambridge, Mass.: MIT Press, 1964.

Yokota, Junya. *SF daijiten* [Dictionary of SF].Tokyo: Kadokawa Shoten, 1986.

Yonemoto, Kanji. "General View and Future Outlook of Industrial Robots in FA." Japan Industrial Robot Association, September 1985.

———. "Robotization in Japan: Socio-economic Impacts by Industrial Robots." Japan Industrial Robot Association, September 1986.

Yoshida, Mitsukuni. *Kikai: mono to ningen nobunkashi* [Machines: A Cultural History of Man and Things]. Vol. 13. Tokyo: Hosei Daigaku Shuppankyoku, 1974.

Yoshikawa, Hiroyuki. *Robotto to ningen* [Man and Robots]. Tokyo: NHK Books, 1985.

Yoshimura, Shoichiro. *Robotto no hanashi* [A Discussion of Robots]. Tokyo: C & C Bunko, 1985.

Symposium Papers

Proceedings of "'85 International Conference on Advanced Robotics." Tokyo: September 1985.

Proceedings of "15th International Symposium on Industrial Robots." Tokyo: September 1985.

Proceedings of "Robots 10." Chicago: April 1986.

Proceedings of "Daijukkai robotto oyobi oyo shisutemu shinpojiumu" [10th Symposium on Robots and Systems Applications]. JIRA. Tokyo: November 1986.

Proceedings of "Kogyo Gijutsuin ogata purojecto: Kyokugen sagyo robotto kenkyu kaihatsu seika happyokai yokoshu" [Agency of Industrial Science and Technology's Large-Scale National Project: Preliminary Papers on Advanced Robot Technology Research and Development]. Kyokugen Sagyo Robotto Gijutsu Kenkyu Kumiai. Tokyo: November 1986.

Proceedings of "Robots 11–17 International Symposium on Industrial Robots." Chicago: April 1987.

Proceedings of "Symposium for International Cooperation on Industrial Robots '87." Tokyo: September 1987.

Useful Periodicals

The Industrial Robot. International quarterly. IFS Ltd., Kempston, Bedford, England [contains articles by correspondent John Hartley on Japanese robots].

Journal of the Robotics Society of Japan. Bimonthly. Robotics Society of Japan, Tokyo, Japan.

Nikkan kogyo shinbun [Daily Industrial News]. Nikkan Kogyo Shinbunsha, Tokyo, Japan.

Nikkei sangyo shinbun. Daily. Nihon Keizai Shinbunsha, Tokyo, Japan.

Robot. Bimonthly. Japan Industrial Robot Association (JIRA), Tokyo, Japan.

Robotist. Quarterly. R & D Community, Miura, Kanagawa, Japan.

Index

transformation, 84–85, 87, 96–98
Transformers, 98, 101, 108
"Treatise on Pneumatics," 55–56
Tsuda, Tsukezaiemon, 63
Tsukuba, 22, 224, 227
twenty-first century, 13, 23, 174, 191, 204

Umetani, Yoji, 219–20, 227
"Uncanny Valley," Masahiro Mori's theory of, 208–9
Unimate, 113, 116–17, 128–30, 161; description of first model, 34
Unimation Inc., 34, 111–13, 126–28, 130
unions, 151–52, 155–56, 158–60, 167; All Japan Federation of Electric Machine Workers Union, 156; All Nissan Motor Workers Union, 155; Federation of Japan Automobile Workers' Unions, 158
United States President's Commission on Industrial Competitiveness, 169
United States Robots, 127
universities, research environment, 218–22
"unmanned factories," 45–46, 159, 188
Unno, Juza, 75
Urata, Kenji, 164
U.S. robot manufacturers' dependence on Japan, 127–28, 145

VAL, 161
Vaucanson, Jacques de, 56, 65
Versatran, 111–12, 114

vision, 36, 47–48, 51, 119, 129, 149, 177, 216, 222

Wabot, 203, 206. *See also* Wasubot
wages, 95, 101, 118–20, 153, 182
wakon-yosai ("Japanese spirit—Western learning"), 69
Waldron, Kenneth J., 230
WASCOR (WAseda COnstruction Robot), 191
Wasubot, 13, 203
Weisel, Walt, 43, 144, 200
welding robots, 17, 116–17, 119
Wiener, Norbert, 31, 48, 55, 58, 156, 183, 199, 207
wire bonder robots, 180–81
women: promoting technology, 26; in workforce, 100–101, 158
word processors, 41
workforce: feeling of equity, 153–54; high wages of, 119; need for flexibility, 151–52; shortage in, 119–20

Yamabiko, 221, 224
Yamasaki Seisakujo, 20–21, 154, 166, 176
Yamaura, Eiji, 90
Yaskawa Electric, 114, 149, 175
Yoke, Hideaki, 98, 101
Yokoyama, Mitsuteru, 78
Yonemoto, Kanji, 38–39, 122, 213, 233
Yoshikawa, Hiroyuki, 229, 233
Yuta, Shinnichi, 43, 224

Credits

The following individuals and organizations graciously allowed reproduction of photographs and illustrations in their possession. All other photographs are by the author: page 12 (*top*), Ichiro Kato; page 18, Nissan Motor Co., Ltd.; page 19, Kanematsu-Gosho (U.S.A.) Inc. and Seiko Epson; page 20 (*bottom*), Komatsu Ltd.; page 22, Seibu Department Stores; page 25, R & D Community; page 30, Waseda University Drama Department; page 31, U.S. Patent Office; page 32, Joseph Engelberger; page 34, National Museum of American History, Science, Technology and Culture, Smithsonian Institute; page 35, Canon, Inc.; page 41, Marol Co., Ltd.; page 44, Motoda Electronics Co., Ltd.; page 47, Casio Computer Co., Ltd.; page 51, Shinko Electric Co., Ltd.; page 54, University of California, Berkeley, Mitsui Collection; page 56, Fuyo Information Center; pages 58 and 59, University of California, Berkeley, Mitsui Collection; page 60, doll from Nagoya Municipal Science Museum, photo from Kodansha archives; page 64, Kodansha archives; page 68, Toshiba Science Institute; pages 104 and 105, Tomy Corporation; page 110 (*top*), Fanuc Ltd.; page 112, Kawasaki Heavy Industries Ltd.; page 127 (*left*), Sankyo Seiki Manufacturing Co., Ltd.; pages 132, 133, 134, and 138, Fanuc Ltd.; page 149, Robotics Industries Association; page 153 (*left*), Victor Company of Japan Ltd.; page 175, Shunji Rikimaru of Yaskawa Electric Manufacturing Co., Ltd.; page 177, Nissan Motor Co., Ltd.; page 178, Daiwa House Industry Inc.; page 185, Tokyo Electric Power Co.; page 189, Obayashi Corporation; page 190, JGC Corporation; page 191, Kajima Corporation; page 198, Kodansha archives; pages 203 (*right*), 205, 206, 207 (*top*), Ichiro Kato; pages 214 and 216 (*left*), Advanced Robotics Technology Research Association; pages 220 and 227, Shigeo Hirose; page 228, Toshiba Corporation.

定価3,200円
in Japan